SHAKESPEARIAN DIMENSIONS

By the Same Author

On Shakespeare

The Wheel of Fire (Tragedies)
The Imperial Theme (Tragedies)
The Crown of Life (Final Plays)
The Shakespearian Tempest (Symbolism)
The Sovereign Flower (Royalism, General Index)
The Mutual Flame (Sonnets and 'The Phoenix and the Turtle')
Shakespearian Production
Shakespeare and Religion
Shakespeare's Dramatic Challenge

On Other Writers

Poets of Action (Spenser, Milton, Swift, Byron)
The Starlit Dome (Wordsworth, Coleridge, Shelley, Keats)
Laureate of Peace (reissued as *The Poetry of Pope*)
Lord Byron: Christian Virtues
Lord Byron's Marriage
Byron and Shakespeare
The Golden Labyrinth (on British drama)
Ibsen
The Saturnian Quest (John Cowper Powys)
Neglected Powers (Powys, and other modern literature)
Powys to Knight (Letters, ed. Robert Blackmore). Contributions by G.W.K.
Symbol of Man (Stage poses)

On Poetry and Religion

The Christian Renaissance (The New Testament, Dante, Goethe)
Christ and Nietzsche (Christian dogma, Germanic philosophy and *Thus Spake Zarathustra*)
Hiroshima (Literature and the Atomic Bomb)

General

Atlantic Crossing
The Dynasty of Stowe

Drama

The Last of the Incas

Biography

Jackson Knight: a Biography

Poetry

Gold-Dust

Tapes

Sound

BBC
Jeffrey Norton, New York

Video

(monochrome) – Simon Mauger, Yeovil College
(colour) – Keith Keating, Nassau Community College, State University of New York

SHAKESPEARIAN DIMENSIONS

G. WILSON KNIGHT
Emeritus Professor of English
University of Leeds

A spirit I am indeed;
But am in that dimension grossly clad
Which from the womb I did participate.
(*Twelfth Night*, V i. 246)

In literature a too exact attention to the facts of occult science
may be less potent than an entwining of them with
earth-plane apprehensions and experiences.
('The Seraphic Intuition', *The Christian Renaissance*, 1962)

THE HARVESTER PRESS · SUSSEX

BARNES & NOBLE BOOKS · NEW JERSEY

First published in Great Britain in 1984 by
THE HARVESTER PRESS LIMITED
Publisher: John Spiers
16 Ship Street, Brighton, Sussex

and in the USA by
BARNES & NOBLE BOOKS
81 Adams Drive, Totowa, New Jersey 07512

© G.R. Wilson Knight, 1984

British Library Cataloguing in Publication data

Knight, G. Wilson
   Shakespearian dimensions.
   1. Shakespeare, William – Criticism and
interpretation
   I. Title
   822.3'3   PR2976

   ISBN 0–7108–0652–3

Library of Congress Cataloging in Publication Data

Knight, George Wilson, 1897–
   Shakespearian dimensions.

   1. Shakespeare, William, 1564–1616 – Criticism and
interpretation – Addresses, essays, lectures. 2. English
drama – 17th century – History and criticism – Addresses,
essays, lectures. I. Title.
PR2976.K625   1984   822.3'3   83–27265
ISBN 0–389–20458–7

Photoset in 11 point Bembo by Thomson Press (India) Ltd., New Delhi.
and printed and bound in Great Britain by
Butler & Tanner Ltd., Frome, Somerset

To
The Interdiscipline Society (New York)
With gratitude for the honour of their regard

Contents

Preface

In presenting this collection of Shakespeare essays I would record my obligations to Mr John D. Christie for advice as to which essays to include; for checking my references; for observing and listing many textual errors; and for compiling my indexes. His general editorial advice and sympathetic insight have been throughout, as so often before, my safeguards.

I would also record my gratitude to Mr Hugh Stubbs and Miss Theo Brown for putting forward my lectures on Shakespearian folklore in, respectively, Exeter and London; to Major A.A. Anderson and Mrs. Olivia Anderson, and to Mr. Gordon Lothian and his wife Elizabeth, for secretarial and other help; to Mrs. B. Fulford for typing my untidy scripts; to Professor R.J. Clark for a vital reference, and to the Harvester Press for their valuable support.

To the University of Exeter, the Devonshire Association and other cultural centres or academic journals, as duly recorded below, which were responsible for the first appearances of certain essays, presented here with the occasional slight revision or addition, I offer my gratitude for their permission and for the original stimulus of their collaboration. I thank Professor Gordon P. Jones for permission to use in my Introduction a substantial extract from his review of Shakespeare Studies in *The University of Toronto Quarterly,* and to Mr J.I.M. Stewart for my report of his sensitive discussion of *Shakespeare's Dramatic Challenge.*

For some years Mr Simon Mauger of Yeovil College, Somerset has devoted continual care to the creation and marketing of my Shakespearian Videotapes. Across the Atlantic, Professor Keith Keating of Nassau Community

College, Garden City, New York has worked assiduously in organising both publications and colour tapes, and generally furthering my work's advance, in America; where also both Mr Fred Cannan's bibliography and Professor John E. Van Domelen's biography are nearing completion. Professors R.L. Blackmore and David Toor have been generous in support; as also in England has Professor John Jones, whose Oxford lecture concentrating on my labours was a notable honour.

I hope soon to see more of Professor John Harcourt's acute discussion of *Cymbeline*.

I would here draw attention to the papers of Mr Norman Yendell lodged in The Research Library, The Shakespeare Birthplace Trust, The Shakespeare Centre, Stratford-on-Avon. Though concerned with deeply esoteric readings, and often drawing on relevances beyond my own field of knowledge, I find them so frequently highlighting Shakespearian elements hitherto unstudied that I assume them to be pursuing trails and touching dimensions which should challenge our response.

Much also, though of a different sort, is demanded by Professor F.W. Clayton's Jackson Knight Memorial Lecture, *The Hole in the Wall,* designated as 'a new look at Shakespeare's Latin base for *A Midsummer Night's Dream*' (published by the University of Exeter, 1979); wherein a wide range of Latin, and even astrological, learning is forcibly presented. The lecture has been reviewed in *Pegasus* (University of Exeter Classical Society, June 1983).

I would record also Professor Antony Landon's lecture '*Macbeth* and the Folktale *The Fisher and his Wife*', given at the Second Nordic Conference for English Studies (Hanasaari, Finland; 19 May 1983).

In the following pages I give references throughout to the Oxford Shakespeare. The sources of other references are given where they occur. Page numbers appear without the letter 'p', except for those referring to my own, present volume, which alone bear the prefix.

G.W.K.
Exeter, 1983

Introduction

I here offer as introduction a blend of personal apology, in the sense of defence, and personal manifesto. I look back on nearly sixty years of my life's work, and see it, from my early unpublished three dramatic novels and *Myth and Miracle,* my booklet on Shakespeare, as composed on behalf of a new spirituality, either direct or through the medium of poetic drama. Another, as yet unpublished, book, *Behind the Veil* written in 1951–2 after the death of my mother, recorded my first involvement in Spiritualism, and was followed in 1975 by the biography of my brother, with its account of communication following his death. These came later, but my first novel, *Klinton Top* (1927), bears witness to the presence from the first of an other-dimensional intuition.

Here I am concerned mainly with Shakespeare. In a recent review of Shakespeare studies in the *University of Toronto Quarterly* Professor Gordon P. Jones attributes to my Shakespearian contribution a strikingly high status in this century's unfurling response:

The last giant of Romantic Shakespeare interpretation, and one of the most influential shapers of the modern vision of the Shakespearian play as dramatic poem, George Wilson Knight, is out of fashion at present. From generation to generation our *amour propre* requires that we dismiss our giants once we have possessed ourselves of their wisdom. But Wilson Knight is a rather tough giant, whose massive vitality drives him still to lecture platform and printing house in the Shakespeare cause.

Knight's achievement is the centrepiece of S. Viswanathan's *The Shakespeare Play as Poem,* which chronicles the rise of the poetic school of Shakespeare interpretation. A chapter is devoted to the moral and political 'thematics' of L.C. Knights. Another appraises sympathetically the image studies of Caroline Spurgeon. It is Wilson Knight, however, who receives most of Viswanathan's attention, for it is Knight who has been largely responsible for crystallizing the modern apprehension of the Shakespeare play as an integrated expression of 'the logic of the imagination'. It was Wilson Knight who insisted that, while the spectator's experience of the play is sequential, the creative vision and the critical effort are not limited to that sequentiality. Grasping the plays whole and simultaneously, extending in space 'like a map or unrolled tapestry', his prime achievement, in the view of Viswanathan, 'is to have used the spatial mode of approach to show how the "latent" content of drama, comprising imagery, symbols, and thematic suggestions, reinforces or modifies the "manifest" content of plot, character and situation.'

As well as precipitating new critical procedures Knight also formulated influential readings. He offered new insights into the major tragedies; he helped rehabilitate undervalued plays such as *Troilus and Cressida, Coriolanus, Measure for Measure,* and *Timon of Athens;* he expanded our awareness of the importance of the romances.

The play-as-poem vision is currently out of critical favour; but there is a further reason why Knight is not more highly regarded nowadays. His very success has militated against recognition. His insights have been so fully assimilated into the common stock of received ideas that they have lost their individual identity. Just as we are all the heirs of Bradley, who is now coming back into fashion, so we are all the inheritors of Wilson Knight, who has passed out of fashion for the time being. It would be idle to pretend that Knight's vision is unflawed. Contemporary scholarship has grumbled about his inattention to historical research, his impressionism, his idealism, his ideological hobbyhorses, his neglect of qualitative discriminations within the canon, and so on. Such caveats qualify, but they do not invalidate, the vision which has stamped itself indelibly on the critical sensibility of the twentieth century.

After reviewing a number of other books, he concludes:

So we return to the crisis of confidence that plagues contemporary Shakespearean scholars, who yearn to say something about the subject on which they are experts, but who fear that their utterances will express only a subjective reality or a partial truth. If we are not visionaries and prophets, like Wilson Knight, we can still achieve our own limited illuminations from time to time, small victories in private raids on the inarticulate.

I am indeed honoured by the high rating here accorded my work.

The implied criticisms call for a reply. They are, in the main, just. Historical research I have avoided, being quite unqualified and also, as my Appendix A to the enlarged *Wheel of Fire* indicates, being aware of its possible deceptions. For 'impressionism', meaning imaginative subjectivity, I must plead guilty; I try to keep my eyes always on the object, but may, on occasion, have wavered; 'ideological hobbyhorses' may refer to my emphasis (as on pp. 22, 37 below) on Shakespeare's royalism; but it should be recognised that my contention was never limited to a patriotic nationalism, but was intended to be widely expansive (*The Sovereign Flower,* I, 90–1; App. C, 275–9). 'Idealism' is true enough: this book is saturated in it, and my claim is that Shakespeare was too, as a comparison of the different ends, the one realistic and the other idealistic, of Marlowe's *Edward II* with Shakespeare's *Richard II,* abundantly illustrates; this example being, as I show throughout *Shakespeare's Dramatic Challenge,* entirely typical.

'Neglect of qualitative discriminations': guilty. This has been forced by my engagement throughout in interpretation rather than criticism. Criticism I would never have regarded as my natural pursuit, which drives towards what is positive, eschewing negations. Besides, criticism and value judgements from me would never have been well received: my high rating of *Timon of Athens* and *Henry VIII* would have been rejected, and so I remained content with revealing their patterns without discussing their merits.

Literary criticism I would never discount: indeed, I admire it when convincingly advanced. After reading the articles published in *The Times Literary Supplement* I am again and again staggered by the subtlety, range of knowledge, and critical sensibility shown today by reviewer after reviewer. These are abilities well outside my limited domain; they wield implements that I could never match. This is not false modesty, but plain truth.

A natural critique of my work might concentrate on its apparent lack of interest in scholarly mechanics. It is true that I have for the most part left this to the specialists, who have always had my unbounded respect. Without their labours, I should have had no adequate texts among which to adventure. Nevertheless I strongly repudiate the suggestion – it has been asserted – that I, in 1931, came to take up my position at Trinity College, Toronto as a kind of wild Caliban ignorant of the rudiments of scholarly disquisition. Fortunately I can point to my lengthy review of E.K. Chambers' *William Shakespeare* in the New York periodical *Symposium* in April of that year, written before I started for

Canada. It is reprinted in my *Shakespeare and Religion* (App.
13, 337–42), and serves as a complete rebuttal of such
rumours.

A more important criticism might complain of my
engaging in philosophic and poetic propensities while
ignoring the stage. Stage matters were for many years
confined to my book on *Production,* which comparatively few
people read. I did more about them in my book on my
dramatic recital, *Shakespeare's Dramatic Challenge,* and in
reviewing it J.I.M. Stewart, himself author of a fine
Shakespearian study, outlines the problem neatly. He recalls
that he had originally tended to underrate my interpretations
as limited to poetic readings and philosophic inquiry, but he
now found that this new book showed that I had been from
the start equally interested in production and acting. He
writes (*Encounter,* July 1977):

All the more interest, then, attaches to the fact that Wilson Knight has
from the beginning been closely implicated with Shakespearian acting and
production. *Shakespeare's Dramatic Challenge* is largely about acting – but
about something that he calls 'poetic acting'.

> This means that the actor should act not the character alone, but the
> poetry; and especially towards the close, the poetry more than the
> character.... Hamlet as a 'character' may be confused but his poetry is
> not; he is less a 'character' than a poetic voice, speaking from a height
> overlooking his problems.

Shakespeare's dark tragedies invariably celebrate in their conclusion 'a
poetic rise rather than any fall.' But this rise, since it is in fact the
attainment of a new state of being, involves, as it were, the shedding of the
carapace of character, so that the voice we ultimately hear from the hero is
no longer merely his but poetry's also – and this complexity the actor must
convey. As cognate with his own thought here Professor Wilson Knight
cites Granville-Barker's maintaining that

> people in poetic drama have to express both what is known to them
> and also truths about themselves they do not know; all of which
> things, diverse and sometimes contradictory, must be expressed at
> one and the same time and in one and the same fashion.

Professor Wilson Knight has given much thought to 'poetic acting',
bringing his own stage experience to bear on the conception, and patiently
perfecting a technique of what he calls 'dramatic recital' which he now

expounds at considerable length. The play most relied upon here is *Timon of Athens,* which he has always held in high regard as being, with all its imperfections, 'the culmination to which all else moved' in the development of Shakespearian tragedy. He prints *in extenso* the script of that part of a recent recital which is based on the play. It consists of a dramatic monologue on Timon's part, variously built up from the text, delivered with action and in costume (or an absence of costume), variously lit, and accompanied by a linking and explanatory commentary spoken by another voice.

If 'another voice' means my own voice as commentator, that is correct; but no other voice but mine formed part of the performance. Voices off were used in my *This Sceptred Isle* at the Westminster Theatre (London) in 1941, but I have used only non-vocal sound effects in my performance of 'Shakespeare's Dramatic Challenge'.

It is clear that my devotion to the stage has been wholehearted; I have never, in allotting my time, put commentary before performance. The trouble is, those who know only my books have seldom been aware of this. It is not my fault that my stage work has not been better known; on each occasion I did what I could to further publicity. Even of late I have tried to get a London presentation of my one-man performance 'Shakespeare's Dramatic Challenge' at the National Theatre and again at the Mermaid but, though at first the suggestion was warmly accepted, the expectation gradually faded. Stratford, too, I have tried, but without success; and television. Performances have been limited to the Northcott Theatre, Exeter and various cultural centres, mainly universities and schools, in England, with five University tours in Canada and the United States.

I recently composed a full account of my problems and experiences for over fifty years as an actor, and thought of including it in the present collection; but it seemed, though its emphasis was similarly on spirituality – it was called 'Spiritualised Acting' – not to blend easily with the other essays presented here. To be convincing certain rather vivid adulatory reviews would have had to be included, and to do this might have appeared presumptuous and unmannerly. I accordingly withhold it; possibly I shall have some copies printed for private circulation. It is a little strange that, though the academic world regularly pays lip-service to Shakespeare as a stage dramatist, yet if someone who has earned his living as an academic and is therefore quite wrongly supposed to be academically constricted, thrusts himself forward in print as an actor (a producer might not matter) the response is likely to be cold. This does not apply to actual performances, for which the acclaim, academic and otherwise, has been on each occasion vigorous and enthusiastic. Tapes are available, some in colour, lodged at the Brotherton Collection, University of Leeds, and in the USA.

Acting and commentary have been for me joint endeavours. They may roughly be allowed to correspond to 'body' and 'soul', and are covered by my book, *Symbol of Man* (London, Regency Press; USA, University Press of America, Washington; reviewed in *The Times Literary Supplement* by Peter Redgrove, 30 July 1982, in *Psychic News* by W.H. Mackintosh, 24 November 1979, and in *The Exeter University Club Bulletin* by O. Mordue Anderson, Autumn 1980; and also by John E. Van Domelen, *The Texas Review,* Spring 1982). This composite analysis of body and soul in mutual interaction is illustrated by physical photographs and has implications both metaphysical and histrionic. I offer two example showing the kind of development, involving categories spiritual and extrasensory, with which these various activities are entwined.

For the first, I draw on *Timon of Athens,* describing his life – death transition as performed in my dramatic recital. The concept 'transition' deserves attention. I refer anyone interested to Rudolf Steiner's *Eurhythmy as Visible Speech,* on transitions *between* sounds (VIII, 98; XI, 149; XV, 197); to the life – death transitions described in John Cowper Powys's *Rodmoor* (XXVII, 456–8) and *After my Fashion* (X, 145–7), and his discussion of the half-life of the inanimate in *The Art of Happiness* (1935; I, 42–3); and to the plays of Wole Soyinka, dramatising people in transition to death, or half-dead (discussed in my essay 'The Transitional Enigma' in a volume of essays on Soyinka, OUP, New York). We have here a new centre, a nucleus, round which swirl energies of many kinds, blending with twilight and all marginal states, such as marsh and fog. I have an essay on the matter, but it cannot be here presented.

Timon has scorned man and the whole created scheme; nowadays I see 'scorn' rather than 'hate' as his motivating spur. It is usual to show him as submerged and degraded, as on a recent BBC production, grovelling on earth. I show him as *above* his tragedy, not *below* it; and to meet the conception he wears a gold cord round his loin-cloth and a gold-brown wig, a figure of health and even glamour, in tune with his new, god-given, nuggets of gold. This suits his all-important speech:

> My long sickness
> Of health and living now begins to mend
> And nothing brings me all things.
> (V. i. 191–3)

Beyond 'health' he is advancing; 'begins' for the transition; 'all things', for the positive purpose; the lines spoken rapturously, with eyes up. Then the transition, fading beyond our senses, described on pp. 89–90 below. At this transitional moment we watch Timon under illumination as both earth-body and spirit-body, at the heart of existence, of life-death, at the very hyphen, as covered by Hamlet's inclusively bifurcating words: 'To be or not to be...'. Being and not-being; 'both and neither; the mystery is enacted before us.

I take this to be as important a stage action, depending on correct lighting and sound-effects and Timon's pose, as has ever been devised. This I have attempted to perform during the last eight years.

My second example is as follows. In the essays collected here, I say little of *Antony and Cleopatra*. I now quote from my review in *Books and Bookmen* (XVI, 5; February 1971) of H. A. Mason's fascinating *Shakespeare's Tragedies of Love*, in which he advances certain intriguing criticisms:

The case against *Antony and Cleopatra* is more easily defined. Mr Mason argues that the almost superhuman status accorded Antony by the poetry has no dramatic basis in what we see him do: we are asked to believe far more than we are shown. This is undoubtedly true.

Even so, is not the attempt somehow justified by its result? We cannot but admire the temerity with which Mr Mason offers clusters of the most mind-ravishing quotations as a logical part of his indictment. What has happened?

Antony and Cleopatra is not only a play about 'infatuation'; it is actually written as from a consciousness of infatuation. We are continually, though not always, being invited to see the lovers as they see each other. The drama is conceived, and the poetry written, from this centre; and from this centre must it be understood. Romantic 'love' is an abnormal state. I am referring to 'love' as infatuation, as a magical transfiguration, not to 'love' as a deep and lasting comradeship; the difference is pretty well ultimate. We may in some moods agree with Rosalind in *As You Like It* (III. ii. 426), when she tells us that love is 'merely a madness', but she does not really mean it, nor expect us to. In love-magic there is a sudden transmutation, as in mystic vision. In his sonnet, *Love*, Rupert Brooke was peculiarly aware of this, and of its gradual shrinking back to normality when 'astonishment is no more in hand or shoulder'. That such experience may be, however ephemeral, an insight into reality – Eliot's 'the one veritable transitory power' in *Ash-Wednesday* – was also once suggested by Brooke in his poem *In Examination,* where the 'scribbling fools' become suddenly transfigured and are seen as a company of flame-haired angels. Whatever our metaphysical beliefs, this is anyway what *Antony and Cleopatra* is about. Antony is no superman, he is a very ordinary leader with, like Othello, a notable soldier's record, but with a number of human failings also. This man we watch as, to adapt Cleopatra's phrase, 'gilded' with love's 'tinct' (I. v. 37). He is a normal man glorified.

That granted, we could still complain that all this may be poetic vision, but scarcely drama. We could – except for the one shattering rejoinder that, given a sensitive producer and an Antony with a golden voice, the oscillating sequences of Act IV are as compelling on the stage as anything Shakespeare ever composed. I am thinking of Edward Roberts' Antony in my production of *Antony and Cleopatra* at Toronto in 1937.

My argument throughout depends on our acceptance of categories beyond normal artistry.

At Antony's dying we have an interesting transitional speech. Thinking Cleopatra has died, he now casts off his armour:

> Off, pluck off!
> The sevenfold shield of Ajax cannot keep [contain]
> The battery [coming] from my heart. O, cleave, my sides!
> Heart, once be stronger than thy continent,
> Crack thy frail case!
>   (IV. xii. 37–41).

His disarming is part of the transition, corresponding to Timon's stripping-off of his garments.

The 'heart', or emotion, is felt as shattering his body to

emerge as a chicken from a cracked egg-shell. Though we cannot see it, we have to assume some other, invisible, body emerging intact, its new 'strength' having mastered all old 'force' (IV. xii. 48–9) to end with

> Where souls do couch on flowers, we'll hand in hand,
> And with our sprightly port make the ghosts gaze.
>   (IV. xii. 51)

'Sprightly port' compactly means 'proud bearing as spirits'. The speech enacts verbally the transition. At Cleopatra's death we attend a more fully embodied transition accompanied by other-worldly intimations.

Cleopatra's words

> I am marble constant, now the fleeting moon
> No planet is of mine
>   (V. ii. 239)

signify her entry into an eternal dimension (compare 'moon' with a similar contrast at *King Lear*, V. iii. 16–19); the words link the tragic sequence to Hermione's statue in *The Winter's Tale* (pp. 100–9 below).

In both *Timon of Athens* and *Antony and Cleopatra* we have transitions that form a link between tragic death and the mystery. We have, in both commentary and performance, to accept poetic intangibles to assure our comprehension and save us from unnecessary complexities and ambiguities. In *Symbol of Man* and my own acting nudity has functioned, under artistic treatment, as a true accompaniment to the spiritual. We may call the contrast between my attempts and what is normal a contrast of great simplicities with intellectual abstractions. Objections may arise: one has to accept imponderables, to believe, with Margot Davies, that

> The man who truly lives is he
> Who sees invisibility.

I quote from poem No. XI in *Calling Newfoundland* (Memorial University, St. John's, Newfoundland and The Warren House Press, North Walsham, Norfolk). The author once let fall to me a good comment on life and death: 'They're really the same thing, aren't they?' (Introduction, xi): a paradox bearing on much that I have said of transition. We feel an invisible dimension. It works again and again through John Cowper Powys's *Dostoievsky,* wherein he senses another 'dimension' through the author's seemingly confused exteriors. My present title, in tune with Shakespeare's use of the term, has authority.

A recognition of such further dimensions through Coleridge's 'willing suspension of disbelief' is needed for the following essays. I hope I may be forgiven for sometimes seeming to expand the poetry, as when I read Caliban's 'music' lines as a poetic universal, whereas they are, in their context, inspired by Ariel's music and might be said to refer only to the island. I claim, however, that they cry out for my interpretation whatever the first context, and harmonise exactly with my reading of Caliban, which will not be disputed, as a primitive being.

Perhaps, lest I be accused of allowing my own philosophic or religious authorities to intrude into what should be a dispassionate inquiry, it may be as well to say briefly what are these authorities. I would say that I am not a Jewish prophet, nor a Buddhist, nor a primitive Red Indian, though each of these are in the following essays brought in for discussion. I am, by upbringing, a Christian and though my observance is neither doctrinal nor devotional, my imaginative reading of the New Testament in *The Christian Renaissance* was vivid, and I retract nothing of it. The New Testament still has my trust, supplemented naturally by the great Spirit guides. To these I should add Nietzsche's *Thus Spake Zarathustra* developing power to love, as those others love to power.

I think my own, more intimately personal religious views should be stated. They were given in a BBC talk on 27 May 1974, entitled 'Is God Dead?'. I asked whether a God of Love was acceptable. The greatest authorities say so: Christ in the New Testament, a succession of spirit guides speaking through trance-mediumship, among them 'Imperator' in the last century, through Stainton Moses (*Spirit Teachings,* 1949, 1962 ed., XIX. 153), and a number of mystics and poets. For

the rest, we must face the facts, as indeed the Christian
Church has, with the Cross central to its system. Terrors, as
described by Llewelyn Powys in a number of poignant
vignettes (as in *Damnable Opinions,* 'Africa's Wisdom'), exist
throughout nature. I concluded that, while our intelligence
must take due note of the worst horrors, in nature as well as
in human society, yet the more one can accept God as Love,
the more creatively we shall live. So that God = Love is
intellectually questionable but creatively true. I rate creation
high and so accept a God of Love.

The New Testament statement that God is Love comes
from John's Epistle; John, the beloved disciple of Christ. I
myself regard what I term the 'seraphic' ideal, as handled in
my *Gold-Dust* and studied in the Epilogue to the second
edition of *The Christian Renaissance,* as a star. Shakespeare, in
Sonnets 113 and 114 feels this ideal as expanding, so that he
sees his loved youth in all created beings, whether noble or
corrupt. These two sonnets are accordingly autobiographical
explanations, the only ones we have, of what lies behind
Shakespeare's artistry and inspires his positive and idealistic
reading of human kind. My emphasis on them has, I fear, not
received the attention I expected; nor has my explanatory
paraphrase of the Sonnets' dedication to 'Master W.H.'
(*Times Literary Supplement,* 26 Dec. 1963; reprinted in my
Shakespeare and Religion, App. A, 329).

So much for my personal beliefs. I must not think of more:
these are quite enough for my readers to digest at – to borrow
a strange modern cliché which seems for once apposite – this
point in time.

The essays here collected have been independently written,
each stands on its own, but when grouped together they
make a unity, as designated by the book's title. I have added
essays on Lyly, Webster and Ford, which will be found to
cohere naturally with the rest.

PART ONE

I Soul and Body in Shakespeare

I

I offer some suggestions on the reason and nature of Shakespeare's use of poetry in his dramas and then develop the argument to wider considerations. My essay at first may seem to draw attention to the obvious; but, as so often happens, the obvious, though all-important, is in danger of neglect.

As a start, I draw attention to two recent articles in *The Times Literary Supplement*, which appear to me peculiarly significant as pointing to the probable future of literary discussion. They are Professor John Carey's 'Viewpoint' (22 February 1980) and Professor L.C. Knights' 'Poetry and "things hard for thought"' (29 February 1980). The first argues that the formulation of exact standards of literary excellence is futile, and the second concentrates on the tendency of poetry to express what cannot be, in the usual sense of the word, *thought*. Poetic thinking has spatial qualities of metre, rhyme and stanza, and also, as Knights emphasises, the use of silence. What it says cannot be exactly paraphrased, but it may be experienced. Both essays assume what may be called the 'imponderables'. Critical judgements are, beyond a certain point, inept; what we can legitimately criticise is the technique of expression, as when we complain, for example, that a work is too obscure. For the rest, the poetry – and prose too – invites collaboration and some degree, no doubt, of explication.

What we need is a new vocabulary, or a new recognition of past usage. For some years literary exegesis has been

3

hampered by our reluctance to use such terms as 'soul' and
'spirit'. Even in poetic composition, where they should only
be relied on with care if not suspicion, I have suggested, in
the Preface to my own poems *Gold-Dust* (Routledge, 1968;
xxvi), 'If fear of them becomes inhibitory the result may
be a complex of obscurities – one sees it happening – far less
precise than an honest use of the time-honoured term.' Since
they exist to denote the indefinable, they cannot, of course,
be defined with any exactitude. We may here adduce an
example where the term is taken for granted: Andrew
Marvell's *A Dialogue between the Soul and Body*. The Soul is
imagined as complaining of the strictures it endures from the
body and its senses:

> Here blinded with an Eye; and there
> Deaf with the drumming of an Ear.

Marvell would have been surprised if anyone were to doubt
the very existence of the soul; he relied on an immediate
understanding.

There is no reason why our response today should not also
be immediate. Obviously much is meant that we all
recognise. A good modern discussion is presented in Edward
Carpenter's fine book *The Drama of Love and Death* (1912).
Carpenter, grouping soul with mind, regards soul-mind as
a ruling power in and over the physical body, forming and
controlling it, consciously or unconsciously, and on occasion
miraculously aware of, and handling, complexities beyond
our understanding. He adduces strange abilities revealed by
hypnosis, the extraordinary power of youthful prodigies,
spiritualistic phenomena of various kinds, and possibilities of
reincarnation. Powers are observed, subconscious or subliminal, for which we have no easy definition and which
outspace our understanding. These are, of course, extreme
and off-centre examples, but they serve as pointers. Carpenter's discussion is throughout cautious; he writes as an
enquirer, envisaging possibilities. As a result, soul and
super-mind are seen to expand beyond analysis. They
outspace an individual's life; they touch, or include, other
lives and perhaps some mass soul of humanity. It is all part of

an ultimate and inclusive mystery which cannot be handled by reason alone. We know so little. All good poets may have been inspired. The ancients recognised the 'Muse'. Of the inadequacies of reason Pope's *Essay on Man* is the classic statement: 'In Pride, in reasoning Pride, our error lies' (I. 123). It has for long been my contention that the conflict of what has been called 'the two cultures' will only be resolved by recognition of the occult. See my letter in the correspondence ' "Literarism" versus "Scientism" ' [not my title], *Times Literary Supplement*, 14 May 1970.

All this is covered by mind and soul; up to a point, mind may be understandable, but where the deeper mysteries are in evidence, we need to fall back on 'soul' or 'spirit', terms which I use for my present purpose without distinguishing them, in order to clear the field for my application of them to literature. Literature, especially poetic literature, might be called the language of the soul. In Shakespeare the people do not talk normally; they for the most part talk poetically. From now on I lay my primary emphasis on Shakespeare.

II

Shakespeare's own use of the word 'soul' is conventional; it may hold religious connotations, or be extended into colloquial phraseology meaning little, or it may mean a great deal, fitting the mysteries of love, as in Romeo's 'It is my soul that calls upon my name' (*Romeo and Juliet*, II, ii. 164) or Olivia's

> Make me a willow cabin at your gate
> And call upon my soul within the house.
> (*Twelfth Night*, V. i. 245–8)

Sebastian has an interesting comment:

> *Viola*:   If spirits can assume both form and suit
>   You come to fright us.
> *Sebastian*:   A spirit I am indeed;
>   But am in that dimension grossly clad
>   Which from the womb I did participate.
>   (*Twelfth Night*, V. i. 245–8)

The personality is defined exactly as a Spiritualist would today define it. The terms used may vary; 'heart' is an obvious synonym. In *A Midsummer Night's Dream* we have, at a love moment,

> Transparent Helena! Nature shows art,
> That through thy bosom makes me see thy heart.
> (II. ii. 104–5)

'Nature' is contrasted with 'art', the latter being the medium of soul-recognition. I have noted various uses of 'soul' throughout *Shakespeare's Dramatic Challenge* (27–8, 36–7, 65, 87, 95, 140). A study might be given to Shakespeare's use of it. For my present purpose all we need to recognise, here and elsewhere, is that there is such a reality, beyond brain and all logical thought, and that this makes a large and determining part of what we mean by man and his universe. I have in all my work, from the publication of *Myth and Miracle: on the Mystic Symbolism of Shakespeare* (1929) onwards, taken this into account.

Since our discussion may appear cloudy, I shall next adduce some clarifications forcing us to accept the poetry in Shakespeare as engaging different meanings from ordinary talk. Mark Antony in *Julius Caesar* says:

> I am no orator, as Brutus is,
> But, as you know me all, a plain, blunt man
> That love my friend.
> (III. ii. 221–3)

Nevertheless, his oration has a splendid oratorial quality. Is he being crafty and insincere? Something of this may be involved, but we have little need to suppose so. He says that his oration is empowered by love, as opposed to Brutus' prose speech, relying on reason. It is to this extent spiritualised, and there is the less need to suppose insincerity. Again, Othello addresses the Senators of Venice:

> Rude am I in my speech,
> And little bless'd with the soft phrase of peace;
> For, since these arms of mine had seven years' pith,

Till now some nine moons wasted, they have us'd
Their dearest action in the tented field;
And little of this great world can I speak
More than pertains to feats of broil and battle;
And therefore little shall I grace my cause
In speaking for myself.
(I. iii. 81–9)

His speech however graces his cause nobly; it could not be better. We can say that it is the inward quality, or soul, of his heroic adventures that empowers the poetry. He speaks not as a soldier but as a soldier poetically interpreted or idealised, the essence shown. Throughout the play he employs a particularly noble poetry, all his own: in writing of it, I gave my essay in *The Wheel of Fire* the title 'The Othello Music'. This music is the music of nobility, and without regard to this, analysis of Othello's 'character' is fatuous, and the acting of him misdirected. When angry, he is not an ordinary man happening to speak poetry; he is a poetic man of poetic anger, and the demands on the actor, in voice and gesture, are in accordance.

I offer an example of what is today an all too usual approach to this problem. Jonathan Miller's recent BBC production of *Timon of Athens* presents us with a sensitive account of what may be regarded, hypothetically, as a real man corresponding to Shakespeare's text. In the process, though certain interesting coherences are developed, Timon's dying being ingeniously if not very happily devised, the poetry, for the most part, is discounted and is often muffled and, as poetry, non-existent. The deficiency may be recognised by a comparison with the half-hour of Timon shown in my 'Shakespeare's Dramatic Challenge'. The BBC showed us a Timon overcome and submerged on every level, psychological and physical, by his tragedy; I offered a Timon speaking and acting from *above* his tragedy, scorning it and all its accompaniments in his undeviating course.

Shakespeare, or his inspiring muse, knows what he is doing, and sometimes he may elect not to do it. Exactly the same contrast of eloquence and soldiership occurs in Hotspur and Henry V. Glendower says Hotspur's language lacks all 'ornament', and he replies:

> I had rather be a kitten and cry mew
> Than one of these same metre ballad-mongers;
> I had rather hear a brazen canstick turn'd,
> Or a dry wheel grate on the axle-tree,
> And that would set my teeth nothing on edge,
> Nothing so much as mincing poetry:
> 'Tis like the forc'd gait of a shuffling nag.
>   (*1 Henry IV*, III. i. 128–34)

Paradoxically, he speaks this in verse. In *Henry V*, the contrast is more sharply driven home. When Henry woos Katharine at the end of the play he does not speak the rousing poetry of his address before Harfleur and the 'Crispin' speech, but we find a tongue-tied, rough soldier speaking in prose. Now he has no 'eloquence' or 'cunning in protestation', but just speaks 'plain soldier'; he is not one of those fellows who 'rhyme themselves into ladies' favours'.

If thou wouldst have such a one, take me; and take me, take a soldier; take a soldier, take a king. And what sayest thou then to my love?
                                   (*Henry V*, V. ii. 175)

There we have it obvious enough: his soul is in his soldiership, not in courtly love-making. This helps us to see what is happening in *Othello*, where Iago, lacking nobility, speaks in prose or relaxed poetry. Othello's great poetry, the language of his higher self, reaches its climax, as I have shown in *Shakespeare's Dramatic Challenge*, in the cosmic imaginations of the fifth act.

With *Macbeth* we have a different problem. Commentators are divided as to how far Macbeth's wonderful imaginations are to be attributed to him as a man and how far to Shakespeare's art. Well, to him 'as a man' they perhaps cannot be so attributed; as a poetic fiction they can be. But within this fiction we have an exciting problem. There seem to be two persons functioning, one in thought, the other in action. Macbeth undertakes the murder, as Bradley notes, as an 'appalling duty'; he is in part against it. After it, he speaks lines on Duncan's body:

> Here lay Duncan
> His silver skin lac'd with his golden blood....
>   (II. iii. 118–19)

lines so full of pathos that it would seem that Macbeth had forgotten that he himself had done the deed. He sees the proposed murder of Banquo as a deed of 'dreadful note' (III. ii. 44). Throughout there are these two selves, representing action and conscience, the latter responsible for the air-drawn dagger and Banquo's ghost at the feast, both fantasies impelled by his conscience. At the conclusion he speaks his finest poetry, 'My way of life...', 'Canst thou not minister to a mind diseas'd...' and 'Tomorrow and tomorrow and tomorrow...' (V. iii. 22; V. iii. 40; V. v. 19). He has attained, through self-recognition, a kind of unity, though he remains firm in action. We can say that his soul throughout functions as a critical observer of his behaviour; we are introduced to that soul and made aware of it, as apart from and interpenetrating his other self. We find something of this again in Lady Macbeth's sleep-walking scene: the prose jettings from her subconscious are as her soul trying to get through to us. This interplay of soul and action in *Macbeth* is more complex than elsewhere.

Throughout Shakespeare there is such an interplay taking various forms. Clearly the persons speak for the most part in a way no real person could master; with Greek tragedy and French classical tragedy it is even more obvious. Shakespeare has a greater variety and subtlety. He mixes rhetoric with colloquial intonations even within his poetry; the grandest images are often closely pinned to realism, rising out of it and returning. He always has one foot firmly planted in ordinary life and so tempts us to think of his 'characters' as real rather than fictitious. We are continually forced to raise questions and feel enigmas.

One way to reach some sort of clarity is to inspect certain speeches where the soul-quality is especially evident. There are many. Some may be said to fulfil the functions of a Greek Chorus – those on the burdens of kingship, contrasting them with a humble and simple life, have this quality: *2 Henry IV*, III. i. 4–31, *Henry V*, IV. i. 250–304, and *3 Henry VI*, II. v. 21–54. The national prophecies of John of Gaunt, 'Methinks I am a prophet new inspired' (*Richard II*, II. i. 31) and Cranmer's at the end of *Henry VIII* (V. v. 15–56), 'Let me speak, sir, for Heaven now bids me', are obvious instances; and Wolsey's soliloquy after his fall, followed by his words to Cromwell, claiming to know

> A peace above all earthly dignities
> A still and quiet conscience.
> (III. ii. 380–1)

Many of Richard's long speeches are so attuned: 'Let's talk of graves, of worms and epitaphs' (III. ii. 145), 'I'll give my jewels for a set of beads' (III. iii. 147). Soul-language need not be so religiously inclined. Richard's long meditation in Act V is a purely philosophic adventure, actually forecasting, as I have shown in *The Imperial Theme* (351–67), the progress of Shakespeare's later work. Here the thoughts come from the 'soul':

> My brain I'll prove the female to my soul,
> My soul the father; and these two beget
> A generation of still-breeding thoughts...
> (V. v. 6–8)

The meditation surveys a wide range of life's experiences, as does Jaques' Seven Ages of Man in *As You Like It* (II. vii. 139).

Such speeches may stand out from the speaker's normal behaviour. Lear's address to the storm (III. ii. 1–24) has a new and authoritative poetic energy hitherto quite unsuspected. Hamlet's 'To be or not to be' soliloquy (III. i. 56–88), with its clear contradiction of what we have witnessed in the Ghost scenes, in this sense stands out. It is spoken as though from a wisdom surveying his life's confusions with serenity. Speakers may be temporarily inspired, the soul awakened, as is Berowne in his long speech on Love in *Love's Labour's Lost:*

> And when Love speaks, the voice of all the gods
> Makes heaven drowsy with the harmony.
> (IV. iii. 344–5)

Its transcendental psychology concludes with a New Testament association:

> It is religion to be thus forsworn;
> For charity itself fulfils the law,
> And who can sever love from charity?
> (IV. iii. 363–5)

The speech sits a little strangely on Berowne's 'character'; something similar may be said for Falstaff's speech on sherris-sack (*2 Henry IV*, IV. iii. 92), the prose rising to a semi-medical analysis strange beyond his normal thinking. In all these it is as though a muse of some kind takes over and dictates intellectual or imaginative subtleties beyond the normal; either that or the soul is awakened. Polonius' advice to Laertes in *Hamlet* (I. iii. 55–81) is characterised by an assured wisdom we scarcely attribute to him elsewhere. We hardly expected the superb lines on music from Lorenzo in *The Merchant of Venice*, culminating in thought of the stars, semi-mystically apprehended:

> There's not the smallest orb which thou beholdest
> But in his motion like an angel sings
> Still quiring to the young-eyed cherubins.
> Such harmony is in immortal souls,
> But whilst this muddy vesture of decay
> Doth grossly close it in, we cannot hear it.
> (V. i. 60–5)

Either we can say that the exquisite occasion is more important to the dramatist than Lorenzo's 'character'; or we can say that Lorenzo is temporarily moved beyond himself, his soul awakened.

Portia's description of herself as 'An unlesson'd girl, unschool'd, unpractised' (III. ii. 160) does not prepare us for her rise to the occasion in the trial scene with her 'The quality of mercy' speech (IV. i. 184). So, too, Mercutio in *Romeo and Juliet* speaks well beyond his normal scurrilous wit when he turns to Queen Mab and dreams (I. iv. 55), unless his lewd thrusts may be taken to indicate a scorn of the physical from a spiritual standpoint. However that may be, in attempt to give concrete expression to a soul-reality he conjures up a number of miniatures for comparison: 'in shape no bigger than an agate stone', 'drawn with a team of little atomies', 'wings of grasshoppers', 'the smallest spider's web'; the concrete reality being yet further dissolved into 'the moon-shine's watery beams'. Modern physics might dwell on atoms, electrons and wavelengths, trying to express the intangible. The process is pushed further:

Romeo: Peace, peace! Mercutio, peace!
            Thou talk'st of nothing.
Mercutio: True, I talk of dreams,
            Which are the children of an idle brain,
            Begot of nothing but vain fantasy,
            Which is as thin of substance as the air....
                                    (I. iv. 96–101)

'Nothing' in Shakespeare is often equivalent to a spiritual or soul reality, as in the Queen's forebodings in *Richard II,* where its nature is admirably illustrated. Her 'inward soul' makes her 'with heavy nothing faint and sick'.

Bushy: 'Tis nothing but conceit, my gracious lady.
Queen: 'Tis nothing less: conceit is still deriv'd
           From some forefather grief; mine is not so,
           For nothing hath begot my something grief;
           Or something hath the nothing that I grieve.
                                    (II. ii. 33–7)

Bad news arrives, and the Queen says: 'Now hath my soul brought forth her prodigy' (II. ii. 64). Here the bridge between the spiritual and prophetic 'nothing' and the present actuality is beautifully established. 'Nothing' is clear in *A Midsummer Night's Dream:*

           The poet's eye in a fine frenzy rolling
           Doth glance from heaven to earth, from earth to heaven;
           And, as imagination bodies forth
           The forms of things unknown, the poet's pen
           Turns them to shapes, and gives to airy nothing
           A local habitation and a name.
                                    (V. i. 12–17)

This is, as we see in the 'Queen Mab' speech, the specific nature of poetry: to express the intangible and spiritual in terms of the concrete and physical. Shakespeare's ultimate use of 'nothing' occurs in *Timon of Athens* ('nothing brings me all things', V. i. 193; p. 87 below). See also *The Crown of Life,* III, 82, note; and *The Sovereign Flower,* General Indexes, B. VI, 'Nothing'.

Shakespeare's poetry offers us in varying degrees an idealised, and therefore spiritualised, reading of man. His action is generally distanced, and to that extent romanticised, by being located in the ancient world or Italy. It includes evil persons as well as good: as Keats noted, poetic genius 'has as much delight in conceiving an Iago as an Imogen' (to Richard Woodhouse, 27 October 1818). How can this be? We may suggest that it is the good in Iago that appeals: his skill and wit, his energy and planning, good in essence, though dangerously directed. We can see why, in Sonnets 113 and 114, Shakespeare says that the sublimated love of his friend causes him to see his beauty everywhere:

> To make of monsters and things indigest
> Such cherubins as your sweet self resemble,
> Creating every bad a perfect best
> As fast as objects to his beams assemble....
>
> (114)

That is a perfect key, as I note in *The Mutual Flame* (V, 119–20), to Shakespeare's creative psychology. He is always seeing the positive, and therefore the soul, in man, being inspired by his seraphic ideal.

My use of 'soul' and the 'spiritual' has no necessary implications of morality; it follows rather Edward Carpenter's considerations, which I have already noted, regarding the strange operations of the mind or soul in its subliminal, extrasensory, unbiological, perceptions or activities. Mercutio's 'Queen Mab' speech or the Queen's forebodings in *Richard II* have no moral contacts or affinities. So, in saying that Shakespeare's poetry presents an idealised humanity, I do not exclude evils. Shakespeare's survey ranges from brutality to revenge and war, power-craving and ambition, as well as including the softer values of love, often driving the action to a tragic and sacrificial conclusion. Carpenter follows Goethe's *Faust* in viewing evils as part of the divine plan:

The Devil—*diabolos* the slanderer and the sunderer, the principle of division—reigns. To him, the 'milk and water' heaven of universal but vague benevolence is detestable. He builds up the actual, fascinating, tragic, indispensable world that we know. Selfishness and ignorance, the two great Powers of discord and separation, are his ministers; the earth is his theatre of convulsive hatreds and soul-racking passion. (Carpenter, op. cit., XIII, 245).

He might be describing Shakespeare's imaginative universe. Shakespeare's dramatic world contains a variety of symbolisms; ghosts, black and white magic, storms and earthquake, resurrections and mysterious music. A veritable fairyland of the imagination, and yet insistently close-pinned to actuality, as the rough material that his poetry, in various ways, spiritualises.

Here I point to Nietzsche's reading of man in *Thus Spake Zarathustra*, studied in my *Christ and Nietzsche*. He sees the instinct of power as dominating, but all such instincts, he says, may be variously expressed (*Zarathustra*, I. 22; III. 10). They may take high forms. The book is a laboratory of sublimation and drives its thought towards love (Introductory Discourse, 2, 4; *C & N*, V, 178–83) and the Lady Eternity (III. 16; *C & N*, V. 187–8), to whom his central devotion is offered. He works for a refining rather than a correction of evils and in this refining there may be a great and even moral purpose and, for all we can see, a possible happy ending. In that best-seller at the turn of the century, Ralph Waldo Trine's *In Tune with the Infinite*, we are advised to ally ourselves, in both life and art, to God as the great source of power (1908 edn; 174). So our use of the word 'spiritualises' in respect to Shakespeare need not submit us to a wishy-washy and sentimental morality, though that may have its place, but introduces us to the stronghold of satanic power, regarded as part of God's plan or play. Something like this has for long been my tentative belief.

To return to Shakespeare. Must we not nevertheless regard him as a moral artist? And is he not deeply concerned with 'character'? Such qualities we shall indeed recognise, while never forgetting that Shakespeare's survey includes other realities of equal importance and that at any moment one of these may take control. After Romeo hears of Juliet's supposed death he grows rapidly in stature. He comes, less perhaps as Granville-Barker says, to his 'full height' (*Preface*, 'Characters'), than to a height or depth previously quite unsuspected. His speeches have a quality scarcely 'in character', though not, within the fluid imaginative conception, impossible. His poetry has, as I show in *Shakespeare's Dramatic Challenge,* been gaining in power throughout, and now Shakespeare, concerned with his usual fifth act build-up, allows himself a positive field-day of tragic exploitation. If this be Romeo's 'soul' it takes over with a vengeance. It is so too with Macbeth: they all have their fine conclusions, so much so that Middleton Murry in an early book (*Discoveries,* 1924; 26) thought Macbeth's 'Tomorrow' speech so unsuitable for a criminal that he attributed it to Shakespeare himself, not realising that Shakespeare's people on occasion speak from a height outside or beyond themselves; though in his *Shakespeare* (1936), Macbeth was allowed to keep it. We need not discount morality. Shakespeare observes moral law consistently out of respect for the laws of life itself; that is, he takes morality in his stride. His eyes, however, may be elsewhere fixed, or at least his attention divided. Morality is not our primary concern: we don't pay our money to hear Malcolm's moral summing up.

What Shakespeare is concerned with in his most powerful engagements is, whether he knew it or not, and he probably did not, to present a new dimension of human existence; using, as it were, a poetic X-ray, though the result is no skeletal lessening but an enlargement and enrichment, so that his people are, as the phrase goes, 'larger than life': they have a poetic aura. In Masefield's *The Midnight Folk* (1927; 200) the hero in astral travel enjoys clairvoyant perception of the townsfolk in their sleep, attended by spirits. All poetic drama, though spirits are not directly involved, shows us people with an imaginative aura or halo. In Shakespeare this varies in importance. In Hamlet's 'To be or not to be' soliloquy, Hamlet in meditation is well *above* those personal confusions he turns over, and the speech's difficulty and contradictions (*The Wheel of Fire,* enlarged edn, XV, '*Hamlet* Reconsidered', 304–9), including his words on death 'from which no traveller returns', quite forgetting the Ghost, may be caused by his uneasy contact with a higher, helping power. He only reaches such heights spasmodically, but this is, in varying degrees, what is happening.

We find a similar quality in much high drama, even in
prose. In *Shakespeare's Dramatic Challenge,* I quote Bernard
Shaw's statement in his preface to *Saint Joan* that he has made
his people talk as they would have 'if they had known what
they were really doing'; and Granville-Barker as saying that
persons in poetic drama have to express truth$ about
themselves that, as persons, they *do not know* (*On Poetry in
Drama,* Romanes Lecture, 1937: 34). What is revealed is not
'character' but 'the hidden man' (*Collected Prefaces to
Shakespeare,* 1958; vol. I; 7). In his Preface to *Hamlet* he sees
Shakespeare's imagination beginning to give his persons,
through their poetry, something 'like an immortal soul'.
Again and again our commentators are tempted towards
such categories. C.B. Purdom, in *What Happens in
Shakespeare* (1963), regarded the dramas as timeless visions of
the whole action, viewed by the protagonist, at what he calls
the moment of 'crisis'; which appears to mean a transcendental view, what I have called an 'X-ray', at or after death, in
tragedy; though he applies it too to comedy. I do not follow
it all, but I believe there is something there. Purdom was a
stage authority of consequence, and the author of the
established life of Granville-Barker; and also of a study, *The
God-Man* (1964) of the oriental mystic, Meher Baba. His
views on Shakespeare were passionately held: it is likely that
they contain a truth. I discuss them fully in *Shakespeare and
Religion* (1967). I have always, from my first publication
Myth and Miracle in 1929 onwards, been concerned with this
further dimension. Here we can see the importance of my
recent *Shakespeare's Dramatic Challenge,* sub-titled 'On the
rise of Shakespeare's tragic heroes', showing how in tragedy
the hero's soul is poetically awakened – Macbeth's included –
as though by some inevitable assurance (II, 34–7 and V,
97–103).

III

What I am suggesting has for long been known, if less
challengingly formulated. All dramatic performances, says
Coleridge, are 'ideal', offering us an 'imitation and not the
thing itself'; that is, as he says, a 'likeness', or we might call it

a 'resemblance'. He adduces visual correspondences, comparing the Greek tragedies to statuary and the more inclusive variety of Shakespeare to painting (*Lectures and Notes on Shakespeare,* Bohn Library, 1908; ed. T. Ashe; Lecture II, 1811–12, 53; IX, 122). He wisely notes that Shakespeare gives us an interplay of idealism and realism:

Although I have affirmed that all Shakespeare's characters are ideal, and the result of his own meditation, yet a just separation may be made of those in which the ideal is most prominent... and of those which, though equally idealised, the delusion upon the mind is of their being real. (Lecture IX, Bohn, 132).

This is true; Shakespeare always has one foot in normal realism and that is why we are tempted to a false commentary. Coleridge's 'idealised' means, I take it, 'poetically processed'. Again, thinking of the Greeks: 'The tragic poet idealises his characters by giving to the spiritual part of our nature a more decided preponderance over the animal cravings and impulses than is met with in real life.' ('Poetry, the Drama, and Shakespeare', 1818; Bohn, 189.) He again compares such poetry of the Greeks with statuary, 'where the body is wholly penetrated by the soul', as a 'transparent substance' (Bohn, 189). The ancients, he says, 'idolised the finite', we 'revere the infinite' and so prefer painting (Bohn, 194–5).

Our concentration on the 'ideal' quality, the spiritual essence and controlling power, what Coleridge meant by 'organic form', takes us beyond literary analysis. All art is provisional, determined by our various sense-inlets: it is always hinting at more than itself. Sometimes two arts or more may be used to take us beyond what one can do alone; as when Blake has pictorial designs to supplement his writing. Pope and Rossetti both engaged in painting and Masefield illustrated a presentation copy to the King of *Reynard the Fox* by sketches.

Apart from actual pictures I have discussed the 'spatial' properties of Shakespeare and other literature, especially the massed effects of image and symbolism, building a unity in distinction from the time-sequence alone and corresponding to a more spiritual import. My discussions occur in *The*

Wheel of Fire and *Shakespearian Production;* in the chapter
'Symbolic Eternities' of my study of Pope entitled *Laureate of
Peace,* (erroneously reissued in 1965 as *The Poetry of Pope*); and
in 'Poetry and the Arts', in *Neglected Powers.* The arts are, as it
were, all enslaved to different sense-inlets, and a more
satisfying result can only be reached by blending two or
more of them. No really complete approach to reality could
be had without a reliance on all; or, in so far as they are to be
regarded as a limiting hindrance, as in Marvell's 'Here
blinded with an Eye' (p. 4 above), without a dispelling of
all such limiting opacities and the self somehow opened
beyond them to a more than sense-perceptive confrontation
with the real, knowing no longer 'darkly' but, as St Paul
says, 'face to face' (1 Corinthians, XIII, 12).

Poetry is always hinting through various, often spatial,
effects of stanza, rhyme and image, and even, as L.C.
Knights says, 'silences', at what cannot be plainly 'thought'
(p. 3 above); as in, pre-eminently, the structure as opposed
to the sequences of Shakespeare's long speeches (*Shakespeare's
Dramatic Challenge,* III, 49–53); aiming, that is, to spiritualise
through spatialising itself. This is precisely the reason for
stage performance. The words 'theatre' and 'drama' imply
respectively 'seeing' and 'doing'; so that the spatial atmosphere of a Shakespearian play reacts exactly on visual staging;
on make-up, costume and setting. Now if the actor's
physical performance does not also illustrate the spatial or
spiritual meanings involved it is only doing half its job, or
less.

Apart from acting itself, the most important spatial art in
drama appears to be statuary, used by both Ibsen and
Shakespeare and also Bernard Shaw (*Back to Methuselah,*
p. 107 below), in their final periods; occurring with mystical
intimations in the Resurrection piece of *When We Dead Awaken*
(discussed in my *Ibsen*) and in Shakespeare's *Pericles* and *The
Winter's Tale,* where spatial arts are intimately interwoven
with the transcendental experience of the protagonist, as he
finds life triumphant where death had seemed certain; in
Marina, expert in needlework and statuesquely imagined as
'Patience gazing on kings' graves and smiling extremity out
of act' (*Pericles,* IV. chorus 21–31; V. chorus 3–8; V. i. 140);

and in the elaborately delineated statue and attendant comments of *The Winter's Tale* (V. ii. 1–126, V. iii. 1–141). These I have discussed in *The Crown of Life*, II, 58, 63–7 and III, 116–25; see pp. 99–108 below.

I have recently published a book which goes yet further in this special understanding, as well as illustrating in concrete terms the relation of soul to body. I refer to *Symbol of Man*, composed in 1950–1 and revised for publication in 1979. It has as sub-title 'On Body–Soul for Stage and Studio'. It presents sixteen photographs of pose and action with analyses following the great last century authority, François Delsarte; other authorities include Swedenborg, Blake and Rudolf Steiner. I rely mainly on Genevieve Stebbins' *Delsarte System of Expression* (Dance Horizons, NY; London, Dance Books). I have subsequently been told, by Professor Terrance Fitz-Henry, of Ted Shawn's valuable study of Delsarte, *Every Little Movement* (Dance Horizons, NY; London, Dance Books, revised edn, 1963, reprinted 1974). This I have read with profit and commented on in the 1981 Postscript added to a new American edition of my *Symbol of Man* (University of America Press, Washington, 1981). The photographs are elucidated by consideration of the physical, psychological and spiritual implications in action of various body-parts and limbs. At any moment any part may be physically or spiritually impregnated. The study surpasses the strictly biological limits of Jonathan Miller's seemingly comprehensive study *The Body in Question* (1979), for that takes no account of, and apparently dismisses, the etheric body or soul, which assumes so great an importance throughout Rudolf Steiner's *Eurhythmy as Visible Speech*. Thought and feeling are not biologically analysable; there must be more present which we can call 'mind' or 'soul'. My book offers a visible attempt to pin-point the spiritual mystery functioning in and through the total physical reality. That an inward quality can so function is suggested by Shakespeare's lines on Cressida:

> There's language in her eye, her cheek, her lip,
> Nay, her foot speaks; her wanton spirits look out
> At every joint and motive of her body.
> (*Troilus and Cressida*, IV. v. 55–7)

'Spirits' here are 'wanton', but it is the same with those that
are not. All we need to consider is that there is something of
spiritual, psychological, etheric or mental quality beyond the
biological and incapable of direct analysis and assessment. In
her study of Delsarte, Stebbins remarks: 'It takes many
words to say what a single look reveals' (III. iii. 164).
We are at the heart of, or draw near to, the essence of art.
Oscar Wilde says in *De Profundis,* 'Truth in art is the unity of
a thing with itself: the outward rendered expressive of the
inward; the soul made incarnate; the body instinct with spirit'
(*Works,* ed. G.F. Maine, 1948; 864). At its most ideal, this is
what is offered by Greek statues as Coleridge notes (p. 17
above), and by Michelangelo, and also Delsarte, whose
system is partly based on Greek statuary. In *Symbol of Man,* I
had to break through any diffidence in publishing nude
photographs, realising that our embarrassment at nakedness
is really one with our embarrassment at talk of the soul;
whereas we only feel respectable when safe among the
unavailing complexities and confusions of intellectual abstraction. The purpose is to show the soul variously hidden
and revealed in and through the naked body. That the soul
should be made so readily visible in photography might have
appeared impossible. Each picture has to be interpreted
according to an age-old tradition, today submerged. The
photographs were made first, the commentary, based mainly
on Delsarte, followed. Delsarte himself published nothing,
though his address to the Société Philotechnique is quoted at
length by Stebbins, with other short passages. No earlier
book on him has, to my knowledge, applied his system, in
scope and detail, to life photographs *independently* taken. The
book could only be made by someone who, on dramatic
instinct, made the photo-poses, and afterwards turned to
Delsarte's brilliant understanding to illuminate their significance; if the photographs and poses had been made
subsequently in attempt to *illustrate* his theories, the result
would have been far less convincing.

After scrutinising the photographs and studying the
analyses of *Symbol of Man* we are aware of the physical and
spiritual in perpetual interplay. The same happens with our
reading of Shakespeare, the two principles variously discre-

pant and coalescing. I find this coalescence eminently in Shylock, where a convincing character study touches tragic and poetic heroism. In the great tragedies poetry dominates with less competition. There is however the usual variation, before the heroes die, as I show in *Shakespeare's Dramatic Challenge,* on a crest of poetic achievement, the final plays following naturally. In *Symbol of Man* we are accordingly shown in concrete and visible terms what is in Shakespeare's text: I say 'Shakespeare's text' since surely no other poet-dramatist on record so convincingly blends colloquial phrase with, and often within, high poetry; imaginative idealisation with character; soul with realism.

II   Society and the Cosmos

(from *Critical Dimensions,* ed. Mario Curreli and Alberto Martino; Saste, 1978).

All social concerns within the dramas are subservient to their royalistic allegiance, as best defined in the poetry of *Richard II.* Not that any assured belief in actual kings is conveyed, but the royal principle is left intact, whatever their personal failings. This has all been handled in my *The Sovereign Flower.* My present engagement is, however, limited to a more specifically social reading, together with its further, cosmic extensions, which may finally be grouped with the royal principle as the link between sociology and the divine.

Shakespeare's only full treatment of social revolution comes in Jack Cade's rebellion in *2 Henry VI.* Cade would be ruler of a communist society:

All the realm shall be in common . . . there shall be no money; all shall eat and drink on my score, and I will apparel them all in one livery. (IV. ii. 77–83)

There is to be no more civilisation: legal institutions, records of the past, education – all is to be destroyed: 'my mouth shall be the parliament of England' (IV. vii. 16). It may seem that the revolt is being too comically presented to merit attention, but there is a valuable critique, in that Cade is an autocrat and to that extent contravenes the communism he announces, a point taken up again by Shakespeare in criticism of Gonzalo's ideal commonwealth in *The Tempest.*

Social revolution is not advocated. The mass of lower-class people here, as later in *Julius Caesar,* are regarded as witless and fickle (IV. viii. 58). Shakespeare's main concentration is always on individuals; primarily individuals of leadership and power, though anyone at all, of whatever class, may receive, as an individual, respect and even honour. The second and third parts of *Henry VI* are concerned with civil war; the scene (*3 Henry VI*, II. v. 55–124) between the son who has killed his father and the father who has killed his son drives home the horror of internecine slaughter. Shakespeare does not however forget the mysteries. He is happy with the ambivalences of Joan's witchcraft (*1 Henry VI*, V. iii; iv), with the conjuring of spirits (*2 Henry VI*, I. iv), and with the delirium of the dying Cardinal Beaufort (*2 Henry VI*, III. ii. 368–78; iii. 8–18). Such categories counter any simple social concern. Shakespeare's world is dominated by strong persons entangled in a web of good and evil often with supernatural contacts.

Shakespeare's dramas normally act within a civil community, that should be at peace but suffers disruption from unruly forces. These forces are housed in individuals, who may be powerfully subversive, acting more for themselves than for society. In *Titus Andronicus* the hero starts the macabre action by rashness and cruelty; in response Tamora and Aaron become agents of subversion and violence. Titus in his turn becomes subversive in revenge. Not till the end do we have a restoration to communal order. This is an extreme case, but if it was Shakespeare's first 'tragedy', it shows his instinctive direction.

Richard III is all out for himself and a torment to his community. Ghosts, aroused by his conscience, afflict him; but he ends up delivering a fine speech of patriotism, has tragic stature, and fights with superhuman strength: 'The King enacts more wonders than a man' (V. iv. 2). Richard in *Richard II* starts as an unsatisfactory king, but at the close he wins through to a lonely royalty, at least in his own imagination. Romeo is described for us as shutting himself away from society (I. i. 124–47); love awakens him; but he does not adjust himself socially till the news of Juliet's death, when he attains to sympathy with the Apothecary, before suicide. However the lovers' sacrifice proves socially creative, uniting their families. All these are lonely heroes. They might be called 'outsiders' in their various communities.

In Shakespeare's comedies there are regularly tragic intimations. The conclusion to *Love's Labour's Lost* has sombre, and social, implications (V. ii. 858–79); in *The Two Gentlemen of Verona* the outlaws have a subsidiary, but telling part; in *A Midsummer Night's Dream* the quarrel between Oberon and Titania sets up disturbances in nature with effects on man (II. i. 81–117); social satire is strong in *As You Like It;* in *Much Ado about Nothing* Don John is a background figure of disruption and plotting. In the first half of Shakespeare's work two persons stand out whose incompatibility with social order is powerfully driven home. In *The Merchant of Venice* Shylock the Jew is an outsider in the Christian community and behaves as such. His aloneness is increased by his daughter's betrayal and his firm stand in court, bent on revenge. He is tragically conceived and goes far to dominate the action. Falstaff, in the two parts of *Henry IV,* starts as a comedic figure, but his humour changes, as Dover Wilson has observed, into an anti-social threat, which was there from the start though accepted in terms of humour; the comedy being later reduced, his actions show more clearly their anti-social nature. His rejection by the new king follows inevitably. These two, and we might add Malvolio in *Twelfth Night,* are powerful individualists, and serve to show what unrestful energies are lurking within Shakespeare's most outwardly conformist work.

The comedies do however give us one outstanding and important figure of human insight and social sympathy independent of class: Duke Theseus at the end of *A Midsummer Night's Dream.* A few strokes only, but it is perfect. Class-consciousness is vividly repudiated in *All's Well that Ends Well,* the whole action pivoting on Bertram's rejection of Helena on grounds of class.

In *Julius Caesar* we have a well-intentioned revolution against a reasonably good order. In the symbolism, as I have shown in my essay 'Brutus and Macbeth' in *The Wheel of Fire,* order is subtly handled: Caesar, Brutus, Antony, Cassius all have their different viewpoints which the symbolism enigmatically contains. The plebeian mob is cavalierly treated. Little trust can be placed in it; the action is played out, for good or ill, by individuals. The only person to

uphold the tradition of tragic outsider is Cassius, who fills
the part admirably, and is given a worthy send-off.
Hamlet has a hero who sums up all Shakespeare's lonely
protagonists. Cut off from his society, his only real
companion is the Ghost and this supernatural and in part
infernal association beautifully defines his situation.
Claudius, the King, preserves, and in a sense *is*, social order:

> The single and peculiar life is bound
> With all the strength and armour of the mind
> To keep itself from noyance; but much more
> That spirit upon whose weal depend and rest
> The lives of many. The cease of majesty
> Dies not alone, but, like a gulf doth draw
> What's near it with it; it is a massy wheel,
> Fix'd on the summit of the highest mount,
> To whose huge spokes ten thousand lesser things
> Are mortis'd and adjoin'd; which, when it falls,
> Each small annexment, petty consequence,
> Attends the boisterous ruin. Never alone
> Did the king sigh, but with a general groan.
>   (III. iii. 11–23)

True, Claudius is guilty of an appalling crime; but we are all,
as societies, guilty, and the problem of *Hamlet* is better posed
dramatically by an extreme case. We have to make a
distinction between the individual and society: I mean, we, as
individuals, cannot think in moral terms about such matters
as the millions starving across the globe without coming near
to madness. Hamlet thinks as an individual and becomes a
semi-mad threat. Love, which was Romeo's way, is debarred
from him. Not until his return from his sea journey does he
attain equilibrium with any sort of social connection; as in his
long speech to Laertes, confessing madness, and his formal
behaviour to the King and Queen. In these terms, revenge
follows naturally; most of the leading persons die, and
Fortinbras takes over. It would be a mistake to regard the end
as the play's 'meaning'; the greater part has been a study in
lonely, ghost-impelled, opposition.

In *Measure for Measure* social disorder, so far as vice is
concerned, is rampant. The Duke has left things to go their
own way unchecked. His reason appears to be that, since

each and all of us are guilty, justice is meaningless. His
self-knowledge is emphasised: he is 'one that, above all other
strifes, contended especially to know himself' (III. ii. 252).
When Lucio maddens him by attributing to him various
vices, his irritation may be supposed to be aroused by his
recognition of a psychological truth. Lucio functions as his
conscience, inextricably joined to him: 'Nay, friar, I am a
kind of burr, I shall stick' (IV. iii. 193). Though the Duke is
disguised as a friar, Lucio talks as though he knew who he
was. At the close, the Duke finds it hardest of all to forgive
Lucio.

The play contains a fine passage on the abuse of authority:

> O, it is excellent
> To have a giant's strength, but it is tyrannous
> To use it like a giant ... Could great men thunder
> As Jove himself does, Jove would ne'er be quiet,
> For every pelting, petty officer
> Would use his heaven for thunder; nothing but thunder.
> Merciful Heaven!
> Thou rather with thy sharp and sulphurous bolt
> Split'st the unwedgeable and gnarled oak
> Than the soft myrtle; but man, proud man,
> Drest in a little brief authority,
> Most ignorant of what he's most assur'd,
> His glassy essence, like an angry ape,
> Plays such fantastic tricks before high Heaven
> As make the angels weep; who, with our spleens,
> Would all themselves laugh mortal.
>   (II. ii. 107–23)

That is a comment on the whole. Angelo's fall from grace has
proved the Duke's reasons for clemency right. But what is to
become of vice-ridden Vienna? Well, the Duke's offer to
Isabella may be said to use the happy-ending marriage
convention to indicate a union of clemency and moral
rectitude. Not very satisfactory, and the Duke scarcely seems
cut out for marriage. Beyond this no solution is offered.
Shakespeare does not know the answer.

Troilus and Cressida shows Shakespeare's deep concern
with social order. The Trojans are a harmonious society, but
romantically, almost fancifully, treated; the Greeks, on
whom the main emphasis falls, are in psychological and

social disarray. Achilles, whose personal honour and pride causes him to cut himself off from society, is shown to be behaving illogically (III. iii. 38–242). At one extreme we have Thersites' curses:

Lechery, lechery; still, wars and lechery; nothing else holds fashion. A burning devil take them! (V. ii. 192).

Countering his revulsion is Ulysses' long speech on rule and order. The cosmic scheme, ruled by the Sun, is orderly, but if anything goes wrong with that rule, then its evil affects the earth:

> But when the planets
> In evil mixture to disorder wander,
> What plagues and what portents, what mutiny,
> What raging of the sea, shaking of earth,
> Commotion in the winds, frights, changes, horrors,
> Divert and crack, rend and deracinate
> The unity and married calm of states
> Quite from their fixure!
>   (I. iii. 94–101)

For 'states', see also III. iii. 197–205. Earthly disorder has its origin in the outer cosmos, when the sun's rule has been disturbed. Accordingly we must strive ourselves to remain true to authority and the one harmony, by observing 'degree':

> O, when degree is shak'd,
> Which is the ladder to all high designs,
> The enterprise is sick. How could communities,
> Degrees in schools and brotherhoods in cities,
> Peaceful commerce from dividable shores,
> The primogenitive and due of birth,
> Prerogative of age, crowns, sceptres, laurels,
> But by degree, stand in authentic place?
> Take but degree away, untune that string,
> And hark! what discord follows. Each thing meets
> In mere oppugnancy. The bounded waters
> Should lift their bosoms higher than the shores,
> And make a sop of all this solid globe.
> Strength should be lord of imbecility,
> And the rude son should strike his father dead.

> Force should be right; or rather, right and wrong –
> Between whose endless jar justice resides –
> Should lose their names, and so should justice too.
> Then every thing includes itself in power,
> Power into will, will into appetite;
> And appetite, a universal wolf,
> So doubly seconded with will and power,
> Must make perforce a universal prey,
> And last eat up himself.
>   (I. iii. 101–24)

Humanity 'goes backward' by reason of its very purpose 'to climb'; that is, to assert itself.

We may compare this reading of disorder with that of an ideal order envisaged in *Henry V*:

> For government, though high and low and lower,
> Put into parts, doth keep in one consent,
> Congreeing in a full and natural close,
> Like music.
>   (I. ii. 180–3)

Here too the key is said to be 'obedience'. We follow on with a long speech on the honey bees, whose various and diverse functions act in complete subjection to their 'emperor'. Shakespeare's thought on social organisation is consistent: his whole output is permeated by royalistic thought. The possibly Shakespearian passage in *Sir Thomas More* warning the mob against the dangers of rebellion against the King as God's deputy pursues a similar course.

In *Troilus and Cressida* we have two extremes: an individual's revulsion from human inadequacy, and general disrespect for authority, all characterised, as in Achilles pre-eminently, by 'pale and bloodless emulation' (I. iii. 134); and on the other side due respect for an order whose fountain-head is the king. Between these extremes we have Nestor's speech on tragic endurance and defiance (I. iii. 33–54), by which we can see how in Shakespeare's scheme tragedy exists as a half-way, provisional solution to the enigma; the paradox, that is, of personal assertion and communal necessity.

Four great and sombre tragedies now follow, giving us a

sense of tumultuous anti-social powers unleashed. They possess and control the tragic hero and his actions. They come in part from outside him, as well as from within. We are shown, following the thought of Ulysses' 'order' speech in *Troilus and Cressida,* worlds in disorder and self-conflict. In *Othello* our concern is not with any social disorder, but with an individual and the outer cosmos. Othello is racially an 'outsider', and to that extent insecure. He is precariously balanced; though his disturbance is instigated by Iago, the dark horrors may in part rise from himself. When, as in the last act, there is recovery, it comes less in terms of the social order than in his lonely self-conquest and devotion to an act of sacrifice accompanied by cosmic poetry of sun, moon, stars, and the earth (V. ii. 1–144).

With *Macbeth,* however, we are deeply concerned with social order, both in action and in the accompanying symbolisms of disorder, which are unnatural, like those in *Julius Caesar.* Macbeth's crime is a crime against both nature and society. It is instigated partly from outside, from the anomalous unnatural creatures, the Weird Sisters, who have broken away from Hecate's rule (III, v.; for Hecate see my *The Shakespearian Tempest,* Appendix B), rather like the planets in Ulysses' speech in disobedience to the sun, where, as in *A Midsummer Night's Dream,* disorder in the outer universe precipitates disorder on earth. Macbeth might even be said to be unwillingly executing a grim purpose instigated by supernatural powers; which would explain a lot (see my *Shakespeare and Religion,* 'The Avenging Mind'). The result is wholesale anarchy:

> Though you untie the winds and let them fight
> Against the churches; though the yesty waves
> Confound and swallow navigation up;
> Though bladed corn be lodg'd and trees blown down;
> Though castles topple on their warders' heads;
> Though palaces and pyramids do slope
> Their heads to their foundations; though the treasure
> Of Nature's germens tumble all together
> Even till destruction sicken – answer me
> To what I ask you.
> (IV. i. 52–60)

At the end life is dismissed as merely 'a tale told by an idiot' which signifies 'nothing' (V. v. 26). Disorder is driven to nihilism.

Macbeth poses the question, where does evil originate? Partly, it seems, from beyond the natural order. Alexander Pope considers it all part of the cosmic scheme, the natural and the supernatural being taken together:

> If plagues or earthquakes break not Heaven's design
> Why then a Borgia, or a Catiline?
> Who knows but he, whose hand the lightning forms,
> Who heaves old Ocean, and who wings the storms,
> Pours fierce ambition in a Caesar's mind,
> Or turns young Ammon loose to scourge mankind?
> (*An Essay on Man,* I, 155–60)

'Heaven' is here regarded as the responsible agent.

In *King Lear* the relative play of heavenly prompting and human agency within disorder is forcefully handled in Gloucester's 'These late eclipses of the sun and moon...' speech (I. ii. 115–28), and Edmund's following comments. In the wider action, however, there is no explicit reliance on the abnormal, as there is in the portents in *Julius Caesar* and *Macbeth*. The storm, though said to be of an unprecedented ferocity, and regarded as an implement of judgement, is a natural storm, but the atmosphere generated by these scenes, together with Mad Tom and all his devils, is weird enough to go beyond normality. Lear reacts wildly. Thrust out, and alone but for Kent and the Fool, he welcomes the storm as an agent of destruction:

> And thou, all-shaking thunder,
> Strike flat the thick rotundity of the world!
> Crack nature's moulds, all germens spill at once
> That make ungrateful man!
> (III. ii. 6–9)

From then on, Lear in his lonely mental wanderings, develops to a sense of man's callous lack of care for those in destitution, suffering in rags on such a night as this of the storm (III. iv. 28–36); and thence to bitter satire of man's so-called justice. Human virtue is superficial, sex dominates,

magistrate and thief are interchangeable, the Beadle lusts for
the whore he whips (IV. vi. 121–68):

> The usurer hangs the cozener.
> Through tatter'd clothes small vices do appear.
> Robes and furr'd gowns hide all. Plate sin with gold,
> And the strong lance of justice hurtless breaks;
> Arm it in rags, a pigmy's straw doth pierce it.
> None does offend, none, I say, none.
> (IV. vi. 168–73)

The wider action goes some way to support his words.
Human wickedness abounds.

Timon of Athens comprehends and expands all
Shakespeare's anti-social thinking. It is, as it were, a
rationalisation of earlier tragedies. Timon had aimed at a
society bound together by generosity and friendship. He
finds it a cheat, and at one step has done with it all. Naked,
half-savage and half-prophet, he denounces all human
imperfections.

He starts with a long speech (IV. i. 1–40) imprecating on
man a future of crime, disorder and disease; it is all they are
capable of and deserve. He has lost all social faith:

> Therefore, be abhorr'd,
> All feasts, societies, and throngs of men!
> His semblable, yea himself, Timon disdains.
> Destruction fang mankind!
> (IV. iii. 20–3)

All are, at heart, bad: incontinence, usury, greed, warring
('contumelious, beastly, mad-brain'd war', V. i. 179), all are
condemned. He addresses the Bandits:

> To Athens, go.
> Break open shops; nothing can you steal,
> But thieves do lose it.
> (IV. iii. 452–4)

He is at peace only with the elements. Like Othello in his
fifth act, he concentrates on sun, moon, and earth. And the
sea. He is to be buried by the sea:

> Then, Timon, presently prepare thy grave.
> Lie where the light foam of the sea may beat
> Thy grave-stone daily.
>   (IV. iii. 380–2)

His 'long sickness of health and living now begins to mend' and 'nothing brings me all things' (V. i. 191). He is bound for a kind of Nirvana.

I have elsewhere (*Shakespeare and Religion,* 'New Light on the Sonnets', 263–4) noticed the near simultaneity of the publication of Shakespeare's Sonnets in 1609 and the approximate date of *Timon of Athens.* I hazarded some biographical suggestions. I assumed that Shakespeare wrote the Sonnets' dedication himself, and was behind their publication. *Timon of Athens* I long ago related to the Sonnets (*The Wheel of Fire,* originally 1930; enlarged edn, 211). The Sonnets witness to a homosexual idealism; I intend no physical implications, here or elsewhere, by the word 'homosexual' (= similar in sex). Beside this, is a heterosexual lust, which may be compared with Lear's sexual disgusts and Timon's words to Phrynia and Timandra. Timon has no close and single friend, but that might not have been dramatically easy, though Marlowe succeeded in *Edward II.* The beginning of *Timon of Athens* handles rather the sublimated and socially active instinct, as described by the later Sonnets (*The Mutual Flame,* 104–36). Its early scenes are perhaps the less believable for no such personal concern; we have the white of the egg without the yolk, for which we have to wait until the transition.

I would not press the argument for fear of error, but in justice to the reader I should say that, if pursued, it does not involve any simple anti-feminism. Shakespeare could be in part an anti-feminist in *The Taming of the Shrew,* but his many fine feminine delineations speak for themselves. The truth appears to be that he was so *inside* his women, at least where love is the question, that he drew them perfectly. Perhaps, being himself bisexual, he found it came the more easily in that they were performed by boy actors, so expressing the seraphic dream described by John Cowper Powys in *Rodmoor* (I. 18):

It was neither the form of a boy nor of a girl, and yet it had the nature of both.... It was the kind of form, Nance, that one can imagine wandering in vain helplessness down all the years of human history, seeking amid the dreams of all the great perverse artists of the world for the incarnation it has been denied by the will of God.

Powys handles the matter again in his *Autobiography* (VI, 206–7; IX, 408–10).

Shakespeare's sociology was probably conditioned by a psychological incompatibility with his surroundings. Whatever his external successes, he felt alone and apart. In some moods, he may have been rather like the melancholy Antonio in *The Merchant of Venice,* whose devotion to Bassanio accompanies a repudiation of ordinary love: asked whether he is 'in love', he replies, 'Fie, fie!' (I. i. 46), as though in scorn. The Duke in *Measure for Measure* similarly discounts love:

> Believe not that the dribbling dart of love
> Can pierce a complete bosom.
> (I. iii. 2–3)

He claims to be 'complete', like Christ himself, who does not need a sexual mate; we have to forget about this when he proposes – if that is indeed his meaning – to Isabella.

Now Shakespeare, as man of genius, may have known such lonely constrictions. He was outwardly successful, but his works had been successful mainly as entertainment, their deeper content unrecognised, and that may be why in his fictions he lays so extreme a stress, as in *Timon of Athens,* on ingratitude. Regarded in itself, this emphasis might be too extreme, since to expect gratitude for generous action is not admirable. Gratitude for works of genius is another matter: what they want, and seldom get, is understanding · and encouragement.

Coriolanus shows a vivid confrontation of aristocrat and plebeians. For once, the common people are given a voice. A citizen complains:

Care for us! True, indeed! They ne'er cared for us yet: suffer us to famish, and their storehouses crammed with grain; make edicts for usury, to support usurers; repeal daily any wholesome act established against the rich, and provide more piercing statutes daily to chain up and restrain the poor. If the wars eat us not up, they will; and there's all the love they bear us. (I. i. 83–91).

The thought, and even idiom, is modern. Menenius answers with his parable of the state as a body, the belly for the aristocracy taking in food and deploying it to other members, so that all goes well. Afterwards the Tribunes take over the cause of the plebeians, and Menenius continues as representative of the Senate. Coriolanus' view of the plebeians is utterly scornful, and often ugly. He behaves 'as if a man were author of himself and knew no other kin' (V. iii. 36); his excess of public renown paradoxically severs him from society. The plebeians are on the whole forgiving, and we can attribute the unhappy outcome largely to the Tribunes' intransigence. I discuss more fully the social subtleties of *Coriolanus* in *The Imperial Theme*.

There is little to notice in *Antony and Cleopatra*. *Pericles* has a fine, brief, statement:

> The blind mole casts
> Copp'd hills towards heaven, to tell the earth is throng'd
> By man's oppression; and the poor worm doth die for it.
> Kings are earth's gods; in vice their law's their will;
> And if Jove stray, who dares say Jove doth ill?
> (I. i. 100–4)

That is a sharp enough critique. Pericles decides to flee from the court concerned. Later on, he comes on a starving community in need of help. Cleon of Tarsus speaks:

> O, let those cities that of plenty's cup
> And her prosperities so largely taste,
> With their superfluous riots hear these tears:
> The misery of Tarsus may be theirs.
> (I. iv. 52–5)

'Superfluous' recalls Gloucester's words in *King Lear:*

> Heavens, deal so still!
> Let the superfluous and lust-dieted man,
> That slaves your ordinance, that will not see
> Because he doth not feel, feel your power quickly;

So distribution should undo excess,
And each man have enough.
(IV. i. 67–72)

The thought is Lear's too:

> Take physic, pomp;
> Expose thyself to feel what wretches feel,
> That thou may'st shake the superflux to them,
> And show the Heavens more just.
> (III. iv. 33–6)

Pericles brings the needed help to Tarsus.
A wholly pleasing social order is presented at the sheep-shearing festival of *The Winter's Tale.*
There is little in *Cymbeline,* apart from the national interest. In *The Tempest* we have Gonzalo's dream of establishing himself as king of an ideal commonwealth:

> *Gonzalo:* I'the commonwealth I would by contraries
> Execute all things; for no kind of traffic
> Would I admit; no name of magistrate;
> Letters should not be known; riches, poverty,
> And use of service, none; contract, succession,
> Bourn, bound of land, tilth, vineyard, none;
> No use of metal, corn, or wine, or oil.
> No occupation; all men idle, all,
> And women too, but innocent and pure.
> No sovereignty –
> *Sebastian:* Yet he would be king on't.
> *Antonio:* The latter end of his commonwealth forgets the beginning.
> (II. i. 154–65)

We remember Jack Cade. The dialogue continues:

> *Gonzalo:* All things in common nature should produce
> Without sweat or endeavour: treason, felony,
> Sword, pike, knife, gun, or need of any engine,
> Would I not have; but nature should bring forth
> Of its own kind, all foison, all abundance,
> To feed my innocent people.
> *Sebastian:* No marrying 'mong his subjects?
> *Antonio:* None, man. All idle; whores and knaves.
> *Gonzalo:* I would with such perfection govern, sir,
> To excel the golden age.
> (II. i. 166–75)

In contrast to this impractical dream-world, we have Caliban, who contains in him the human essences of savagery, lust and aspiration. His curses ring true and his actions are violent, unless forcibly controlled by Prospero. Caliban is here the most attractive acting part, like Shylock and Falstaff, for it is in these 'outsiders' that the deeper emotions are engaged. Prospero, following the Duke in *Measure for Measure,* knows that Caliban is part of himself: 'This thing of darkness I acknowledge mine' (V. i. 275).

Prospero finds forgiveness of his main enemies difficult. Ariel's example teaches him:

> Hast thou, which art but air, a touch, a feeling
> Of their afflictions, and shall not myself
> One of their kind, that relish all as sharply
> Passion as they, be kindlier mov'd than thou art?
> (V. i. 21–4)

If Ariel, on one level, corresponds to art, we can say that within Shakespeare's own artistry was an element that made him counter his anti-social furies with calm and consideration; it seems that such an element must have been present or he could not have placed them in works so admirably ordered.

Though social conformity came, if it did come, with difficulty, there was no such difficulty with patriotism. That there is a difference between the two may be seen from the socially-disruptive Richard III being given as fine a patriotic speech (V. iii. 315) as any in Shakespeare; a contrast appearing again with Cloten in *Cymbeline* (III. i). Through patriotism Shakespeare could make terms with society. At the conclusion to *King John,* civil and other disturbance gives place to English patriotism. The rebel barons return to their allegiance:

> Now these her princes are come home again,
> Come the three corners of the world in arms
> And we shall shock them. Nought shall make us rue,
> If England to itself do rest but true.
> (V. vii. 115–18)

Richard II (II. i. 40–68) has John of Gaunt's extended speech on 'this sceptred isle', England. Henry V assures peace at home by engaging in a foreign war. There are close patriotic contacts in *Macbeth,* through Banquo and the show of future kings; and in Edward the Confessor. *King Lear* has little, but in *Cymbeline,* with a pattern not unlike that of *King John,* we have a firm national statement. *The Tempest* can be related to English colonisation. It is not a matter for surprise that Shakespeare should have ended his writing career with *Henry VIII;* a play of peace, in which Shakespeare made his peace with society through patriotism. It concludes with Cranmer's prophecy over the child, Elizabeth:

> She shall be lov'd and fear'd; her own shall bless her,
> Her foes shake like a field of beaten corn
> And hang their heads with sorrow. Good grows with her:
> In her days every man shall eat in safety
> Under his own vine, what he plants; and sing
> The merry songs of peace to all his neighbours.
> God shall be truly known; and those about her
> From her shall read the perfect ways of honour,
> And by those claim their greatness, not by blood.
>   (V. v. 31–9)

Under James I this harmony is to continue: 'peace, plenty, love, truth, terror' are to be his, and his greatness shall 'make new nations'; as indeed we have seen. There is a touch of Jack Cade and Gonzalo's 'golden age' about this prophecy, which may be best read, as is all such prophecy, as lying ahead of us still. Shakespeare appears to have written *Henry* VIII with a deliberate will to self-transcendence; subjecting his personal quest, with all its social revulsions and anarchic terrors, to a work of Christian love and patriotic faith.

In *Henry VIII* we have the culmination of Shakespeare's royalistic thoughts. Despite earlier denigrations, the seething London crowd enjoys significant honour on this festive occasion. The King, or Duke, is one with social order and links it to the cosmos and thence the divine.

Revolt against authority, it is true, forms a large part of Shakespearian drama. There is nevertheless a purpose within the anarchic furies displayed, which themselves derive from a non-social origin. In both *A Midsummer Night's Dream* and Ulysses' speech on order, earthly disruption comes from a supernatural or cosmic source; so does it in *Hamlet* and

Macbeth; in *King Lear* it is accompanied by mad Tom's ravings and natural disorders of unprecedented ferocity, and in *Othello* and *Timon of Athens* the hero is finally at home only with the elements, the heavenly bodies and the sea. We must beware of studying Shakespeare's sociology without attending to the imponderables.

III Folklore and Spiritual Healing

(based on lectures to the Folklore Society, London 1975; and to the Folklore section of the Exeter Devonshire Association, 1982)

I

Why do we study folklore? Beyond our natural interest in it, I believe certain basic truths are involved, which Shakespeare helps us to understand. George Peele's *The Old Wives' Tale* (c. 1590), which I have defined in *The Golden Labyrinth* as 'a strangely satisfying medley of country life, romance, a bad magician, and a kindly ghost', sets the tone, with variations, for much of Shakespeare's use. 'Old', as in this title, is a recurring thought. After discussion with our Exeter Secretary, Major A.A. Anderson, I have decided to limit my present enquiry in the main to folklore in spoken tradition; for certain more arcane book sources I would point to Professor Kenneth Muir's article in a recent issue of *Folklore* (London, 1981). So, though much of Shakespeare has a folk origin, where his direct sources are books, I shall not enquire further. Often he refers to tales or spoken accounts within his text. He may start with folklore, but his handling regularly transmutes it.

Herbs and flowers and their properties are important, in Friar Laurence's skills in *Romeo and Juliet,* in the flower connotations of Ophelia's mad scene in *Hamlet* and the flower dialogue of *The Winter's Tale;* these I pass over. My main concern will be Shakespeare's references to magic, witchcraft, devils, ghosts and in general the darker elements, together with his regular surpassing, or transcending, of these to happier pointings.

II

Shakespeare's early first part of *Henry VI* gives us a study of
Saint Joan, called 'La Pucelle'. We first hear her claiming to
perform wonders inspired by divinity. She succeeds, but
after a while, her powers failing, she calls on 'fiends', who
actually appear. She is willing to make a Faust-like compact
with them, being ready to endure any sacrifices to preserve
their assistance, which however is denied. The fiends shake
their heads and, without speaking, depart (V. iii. 1–29).

At her trial, though, fearing the fire, she finally claims to be
with child, she has in its process given a remarkable defence:

> First, let me tell you whom ye have condemn'd;
> Not me, begotten of a shepherd swain,
> But issu'd from the progeny of kings;
> Virtuous and holy; chosen from above,
> By inspiration of celestial grace,
> To work exceeding miracles on earth.
> I never had to do with wicked spirits
> But you – that are polluted with your lusts,
> Stain'd with the guiltless blood of innocents,
> Corrupt and tainted with a thousand vices –
> Because you want the grace that others have,
> You judge it straight a thing impossible
> To compass wonders but by help of devils.
>   (V. iv. 36)

This is not logical: we have *seen* her 'fiends'. The stage
directions might be faulty, but in the text they were, as
'familiar spirits' (V. iii. 10), conceived according to the beliefs
of folklore. Is this defence a deception? Surely it rings too
true and is too aptly phrased for that. What we are witnessing
is, somehow, the will to find in or behind the beliefs of
folklore a greater truth, corresponding to the denial of such
diabolical reliance by Jesus in the New Testament or to
modern spiritualist controversies: the lines might have been
spoken in our time. In historic fact, Joan's defence was
justified by her later rehabilitation in 1456, well before
Shakespeare, and final canonisation in 1920. The result is that
Shakespeare's treatment is ambiguous if not contradictory,
partly perhaps because patriotic motives forced a certain
hostility; and it may be that Joan's defence is a later addition,

trying to state a necessary reversal: our text of *Henry VI* is from the Folio of 1623, some years after the original composition.

This will to lighten or transcend a dubious folklore is usual in Shakespeare. We get it in the Welsh scene of *1 Henry IV*. Owen Glendower's magical powers, the natural cataclysms that he claims to have accompanied his birth, are such as we normally do not believe. Hotspur, a down-to-earth realist, does not, and infuriates Glendower with his caustic comments:

> *Glendower:* I can call spirits from the vasty deep.
> *Hotspur:*   Why, so can I, or so can any man. But will they come
>   when you do call for them?
> (III. i. 53)

We have a Welsh song and Glendower offers a musical accompaniment:

> *Glendower:* And those musicians that shall play to you
>   Hang in the air a thousand leagues from hence,
>   And straight they shall be here; sit and attend.
> (III. i. 226)

It happens; Glendower's magic powers are proved authentic. Hotspur has at first a good reply: 'Now I perceive the Devil understands Welsh.' But, after listening, he admits: 'By'r Lady, he's a good musician' (III. i. 233). Here magic clearly wins.

In this otherwise firmly realistic play, the Welsh scene stands out as an oasis, a window to other dimensions. First, it is true, countered as superstitious, but then a greater power, through Shakespeare's favourite expedient for expression of such imponderables, is revealed in the music. We are certainly glad to have such a scene, most appropriately in Wales, in such a play. Somehow we are even at home with the superstitions; with a warm, cosy feeling, such as is regularly given us by ghost stories or the supernatural. Strange, but true; and the psychology of it may point to a greater truth. Here it is the music.

There may have been folklore behind the literary sources and story of Helena in *All's Well that Ends Well;* but if so it is folklore worked up to great positive significance in the healing of the king. This is so important that I append it as a separate item (see pp. 57–9 below).

Mercutio's 'Queen Mab' speech in *Romeo and Juliet* is based on popular belief of the fairy queen as purveyor of dreams to man, the various dreams being here regarded more or less cynically; but cynicism is later countered by Romeo's transcendental dream, which is, as I have shown in *Shakespeare's Dramatic Challenge,* dramatically vital. Again, we have the balance, the further pointing.

In *The Merry Wives of Windsor* we have a fine example of popular superstition engagingly put to a humorous purpose. It is reported as an 'old tale':

> There is an old tale goes that Herne the Hunter,
> Sometime a keeper here in Windsor Forest,
> Doth all the winter-time at still midnight
> Walk round about an oak, with great ragg'd horns;
> And there he blasts the tree and takes [= infects with disease] the cattle,
> And makes milch-kine yield blood, and shakes a chain,
> In a most hideous and dreadful manner.
> You have heard of such a spirit, and well you know
> The superstitious idle-headed eld
> Receiv'd and did deliver to our age
> The tale of Herne the Hunter for a truth,
> (IV. iv. 29–39)

They get Falstaff to disguise himself with horns as Herne the Hunter, and arrange for children and others, disguised as fairies, to come in and mock him with pinches in punishment of his lusts.

We have, as elsewhere, superstition and age involved: 'the superstitious idle-headed eld'. The dramatic purpose is farcical but within the comedy we can watch folklore being given a moral purpose, with another variation on our usual balance.

The fairies recall A *Midsummer Night's Dream,* and Herne's witchcraft Puck's more mischievous tricks. Puck is one who 'frights the maidens in the villagery', upsets the housewife's

labours, and misleads night-wanderers. He goes by various
names: Robin Goodfellow, Hobgoblin, Sweet Puck:

> Thou speaks't aright,
> I am that merry wanderer of the night,
> I jest to Oberon and make him smile
> When I a fat and bean-fed horse beguile,
> Neighing in likeness of a filly foal,
> And sometimes lurk I in a gossip's bowl
> In very likeness of a roasted crab,
> And when she drinks, against her lips I bob,
> And on her wither'd dewlap pour the ale.
> The wisest aunt, telling the saddest tale,
> Sometimes for three-foot stool mistaketh me,
> Then slip I from her bum, down topples she,
> And 'tailor' cries, and falls into a cough,
> And the whole quire hold their hips and laugh...
> (II. i. 42–55)

Puck is pure folklore artistically trimmed. Oberon and
Titania with their fairies are nature-spirits, and sometimes
more than that. Oberon in especial is a superlative creation.
Shakespeare's source-origins confuse us, but this matters
little; he is newly conceived and splendid. His own poetic
tendency is contrasted with Puck's folklore reminders:

> *Puck:* My fairy lord, this must be done with haste,
> For night's swift dragons cut the clouds full fast,
> And yonder shines Aurora's harbinger
> At whose approach ghosts, wandering here and there,
> Troop home to churchyards: damned spirits all,
> That in cross-ways and floods have burial,
> Already to their wormy beds are gone,
> For fear lest day should look their shames upon.
> They wilfully themselves exile from light
> And must for aye consort with black-brow'd night.
>
> *Oberon:* But we are spirits of another sort.
> I with the morning's love have oft made sport,
> And, like a forester, the groves may tread,
> Even till the eastern gate, all fiery-red,
> Opening on Neptune with fair blessed beams,
> Turns into yellow gold his salt-green streams.
> (III. ii. 378–93).

The contrast is here of what we may call 'white magic' against the witchery and dark black magic beliefs of so much folklore. But Puck, too, speaks beyond the more crude beliefs. We shall observe that the 'damned spirits' of his speech themselves stay damned 'for shame' and so 'wilfully exile themselves': which is strikingly true to spiritualist teaching as known today. If there were a spark of higher will, it could lift them on; if they fail, they remain in darkness. Oberon stands apart from these darker concerns. He is a being at home with dawn, the dawn to which we are impelled through Shakespeare's darker involvements. Our whole play most brilliantly enacts the breaking of dawn on dream-like confusions.

The same balance recurs at the play's conclusion, when the fairies come in to bless the marriages. First Puck, again the voice of folklore, in which the dark hours are always fearful:

> Now it is the time of night
>   That the graves, all gaping wide,
> Every one lets forth its sprite
>   In the churchway paths to glide.
>   (V. ii. 9–12)

This is followed by Oberon's entry with his fairy company, blessing the dark hours and looking for dawn:

> Now until the break of day
> Through this house each fairy stray.
> To the best bride bed will we
> Which by us shall blessed be;
> And the issue there create
> Ever shall be fortunate...
> With this field-dew consecrate
> Every fairy take his gait,
> And each several chamber bless
> Through this palace, with sweet peace.
>   (V. ii. 31–48)

Nature's dew is one with consecration. *A Midsummer Night's Dream* enjoys pre-eminence as Shakespeare's most loved comedy precisely because, though firmly based on folklore and all its fears and fun of 'night-time' confusion, it so firmly enacts the dawn of their transcendence.

III

We pass to the Tragedies. Here we can see very clearly how Shakespeare gains by his knowledge and use of folklore. Some seventeenth-century dramatists, particularly in the Restoration period, are rich in paranormal treatment semi-scientifically handled. Their approach is such as could win acclaim today. In contrast, Shakespeare appears to be far nearer to popular superstition. Why are the lesser poets sound while the great poet appears fraudulent? For a very good reason. Drama hooks on to our deep instincts; we have ingrained in us folklore and its superstitions; we are not creatures of pure reason. Poetry, and still more drama, exists to give us, not thoughts so much as experiences. The Ghost in *Hamlet* may or may not be unbelievable; but dramatically he exists in firmest reality, and this dramatic existence is prior to, and independent of, belief. Horatio addresses it:

> I'll cross it, though it blast me. Stay, illusion!
> If thou hast any sound or use of voice
> Speak to me:
> If there be any good thing to be done
> That may to thee do ease and grace to me,
> Speak to me:
> If thou art privy to thy country's fate,
> Which happily foreknowing may avoid,
> O! speak:
> Or if thou hast uphoarded in thy life
> Extorted treasure in the womb of earth,
> For which, they say, you spirits oft walk in death,
> Speak of it: stay, and speak!
> (I. i. 127–39)

'They say': a reminder of popular superstition. Now in this first scene we find the same development as we have found in other examples. Though the Ghost is first seen in terms of darkness and folklore, it gives rise to thoughts of dawn and sanctity:

> Bernardo: It was about to speak when the cock crew.
> Horatio: And then it started like a guilty thing
> Upon a fearful summons. I have heard

The cock, that is the trumpet to the morn,
Doth with his lofty and shrill-sounding throat
Awake the god of day; and at his warning,
Whether in sea or fire, in earth or air,
The extravagant and erring spirit hies
To his confine; and of the truth herein
This present object made probation.

Marcellus: It faded on the crowing of the cock.
Some say, that ever 'gainst that season comes
Wherein our Saviour's birth is celebrated,
The bird of dawning singeth all night long.
And then, they say, no spirit can walk abroad;
The nights are wholesome; then no planets strike,
No fairy takes [= infects with disease]
          nor witch hath power to charm
So hallow'd and so gracious is the time.

Horatio: So have I heard, and do in part believe it.
But look: the morn in russet mantle clad,
Walks o'er the dew of yon high eastern hill.
                              (I. i. 147–67)

'Some say', 'I have heard': round the appearance of the Ghost, these various reports cluster. Horatio 'in part' believes all this. But the Ghost was dramatically real enough: the more real for all these doubts and questions. And we lead up to the bird of dawning, which I take to be the lark (as in *Romeo and Juliet*, III. v. 6, and *Cymbeline*, II. iii. 22), and to a grace beyond witchery. The subtleties are manifold.

On the Ghost's second appearance, when he speaks to Hamlet, the conception is less folklorish than orthodox; he seems to be in a sort of Purgatory; it remains enigmatic. Hamlet later wonders whether it could have been the Devil, though we, as audience, have good reason to suppose that it has told the truth.

The plot of *Othello,* however domestic, turns on magic. Othello was at the start falsely accused by Brabantio of using 'spells and medicines bought of mountebanks' to win Desdemona's love (I. iii. 61); but this false suspicion of a disreputable practice is countered later by a far greater magic in which Othello deeply believes; the magical handkerchief given him by an Egyptian, sometimes supposed to be a 'gipsy', who was a 'charmer' and one able to read thoughts.

Othello had given it to his wife, and he now describes its powers as a marriage pledge which, if lost or given away by her, will automatically turn his love to hate. Why he had not told her all this before, is not revealed:

'Tis true. There's magic in the web of it.
A sybil that had numbered in the world
The sun to course two hundred compasses
In her prophetic fury sew'd the work...
                                    (III. iv. 70–4)

Now, the handkerchief lost, Othello's extraordinary behaviour goes far to prove the superstition correct. When he storms at her and goes off in fury Desdemona's 'Sure, there's some magic in this handkerchief' shows, as Middleton Murry was the first to point out, her recognition of its actual and suddenly revealed powers dominating Othello. We may assume that Othello too believes in their inevitability. Pope in *The Rape of the Lock* (v. 105–6) indicates its importance:

Not fierce Othello in so loud a strain
Roar'd for the handkerchief that caus'd his pain.

It is the handkerchief, more than anything else, that makes Othello's agony and determines his subsequent behaviour: he refers to it continually; he falls in a fit after spasmodic gaspings: 'Confess! Handkerchief! O devil!' (IV. i. 44). Probably we too should follow its influencing effect with at least Coleridge's 'suspension of disbelief'. We may even suppose that its magic-in-action motivates or otherwise causes Emilia's strange silence till the end, when she at last summons courage to break through its powers and speak out. In his *Conversations of Lord Byron* Thomas Medwin reports that Byron observed how apt its use was because 'the handkerchief was the strongest proof of love, not only among the Moors, but all Eastern nations.' Centuries of Oriental folklore are accordingly behind it. We must feel the magic as effective until dispelled by a stronger power in Emilia's simple honesty. And yet the magic had done its work. It had forced Othello up to what, as I have explained in *Shakespeare's Dramatic Challenge,* may be regarded as his

finest sacrificial hour: 'This sorrow's heavenly; it strikes
where it doth love' (V. ii. 21).

In *Macbeth* we have a field-day of popular superstitions.
The Weird Sisters are in the first scene as elemental beings
but they have their familiar spirits, 'Graymalkin' and
'Paddock', and at their second appearance are obviously
conceived as witches according to traditional beliefs. One
tells how she will avenge an insult:

> I'll drain him dry as hay:
> Sleep shall neither night nor day
> Hang upon his pent-house lid;
> He shall live a man forbid
> Weary se'nnights, nine times nine,
> Shall he dwindle, peak and pine,
> Though his bark cannot be lost
> Yet it shall be tempest-tost.
> (I. iii. 18–25)

The rhymes become an incantation:

> The Weird Sisters, hand in hand,
> Posters of the sea and land,
> Thus do go about, about:
> Thrice to thine, and thrice to mine
> And thrice again to make up nine –
> Peace! the charm's wound up.
> [I. iii. 32–7).

They prophesy Macbeth's future and instigate his crime.

The Cauldron scene recalls the spirit-raising scene of 2
Henry VI and its folklorish introduction:

> Bolingbroke: Patience, good lady: wizards know their times:
> Deep night, dark night, the silent of the night,
> The time of night when Troy was set on fire;
> The time when screech-owls cry, and ban-dogs howl,
> And spirits walk, and ghosts break up their graves,
> That time best fits the work we have in hand.
> (I. iv. 18–23)

A spirit is conjured up and makes prophecies. The invoca-
tion, following occult lore, is traditionally normal.

Macbeth gives us a far subtler development. True, the

Witches' gruesome collection of hideous objects for their Cauldron follows traditional beliefs, but, the charm having been concocted, they produce three Apparitions from it and we are aware of conventional superstitions being used to create symbols of high artistic and metaphysical quality well beyond folklore. The three Apparitions, The Armed Head, the Bloody Child, and the Child crowned with a Tree, must be understood on two levels; one for the story and one, of more ultimate significance, dramatising powers of death and life in conflict, with life and nature victorious. They arise from the Cauldron and, though their origins would appear tainted with evil, they actually signify the exact opposite; again a transcendence. And when Macbeth demands to know whether Banquo's descendants will reign, the Witches are reluctant; the Apparitions have already gone far to falsify their apparent values, and Macbeth is invoking a, to them, positively suicidal pageant, which they are nevertheless constrained to present, with a line of Kings leading to the union of realms under James I. The whole Cauldron scene is a grand paradox. Though we deplore its basis we have to applaud its results in which evil is being forced, despite itself, to envisage and display good, flowering out to this last towering statement of national prophecy for Shakespeare's England.

The Witches had from the first made accurate prophecies (I. iii. 50, 65–7), which later on, in the Cauldron scene, appear to come from their 'masters' (IV. i. 63). It seems that the Witches' arts, though distasteful, can manipulate revelations from beings of an order superior to themselves.

Here we may also place against the Macbeth-evil the English king's miraculous powers of healing, as described by Malcolm (IV. iii. 147–59).

Hecate appears as the goddess of witchcraft. She was mentioned earlier: 'Witchcraft celebrates pale Hecate's offerings' (II. i. 52). Her actual appearance may seem to jar with the Witches in that she speaks a rather different sort of verse, more lilting, perhaps less ominous. Hecate has often been supposed an interpolation. I have in *The Shakespearian Tempest* (Appendix) given a possible reason for her presence as showing a harmony behind the evil in *Macbeth*. Hecate blames the Witches for having dangerously tried to mix different orders of reality, so making a disharmony:

> How did you dare
> To trade and traffic with Macbeth
> In riddles and affairs of death;
> And I, the mistress of your charms,
> The close contriver of all harms,
> Was never call'd to bear my part
> Or show the glory of our art?
> (III. v. 3–9)

This certainly lends itself to a metaphysical interpretation of evil; the wrongness is due to a faulty relation. Pure evil would be a harmony, a secret 'art'. The Witches are themselves conceived as hybrids, anomalous, and they have tried to implant on human affairs an art not attuned to life. Though Hecate associates herself with 'harms', that is perhaps not quite the same as 'evils'; or we could say that 'harms' only become 'harmful' if wrongly placed. We can at least see Hecate as an attempt, once again, to raise folklore to a higher status. This we have already seen done in the artistic manipulation of symbols, but in Hecate it is rendered explicit. Her appearance may, like Joan's defence, be a later addition, as though the author were trying to place *Macbeth* in his usual sequence in which, because of the absolute nature of its 'evil', *Macbeth* otherwise stands solitary, as I note in *The Wheel of Fire* (157, 267–8).

In *King Lear* we have our most obvious and prolonged dramatic enactment of what we could call active folklore: I refer to Edgar in disguise as Tom O'Bedlam. True, it is all pretence, but pretence for an artistic purpose within the drama's pattern. As Mad Tom, Edgar is what Lear calls his 'philosopher' (III. iv. 158, 176). Lear leaves the Fool for Edgar as more attuned to his own madness. Tom acts Lear's madness, calling on his own possessing devils: Smulkin, Frateretto, Hopdance, Flibbertigibbet:

This is the foul fiend Flibbertigibbet: he begins at curfew and walks till the first cock; he gives the web and the pin, squints the eye, and makes the hare-lip; mildews the white wheat, and hurts the poor creature of earth. (III. iv. 118)

The folklore suggestion is the more cogent for Tom's words involving a country setting, nature, and village-life, as in his repeated 'Still through the hawthorn blows the cold wind' (III. iv. 99), and this passage:

Poor Tom! that eats the swimming frog, the toad, the tadpole, the wall-newt and the water; that in the fury of his heart, when the foul fiend rages, eats cow-dung for sallets; swallows the old rat and the ditch-dog; drinks the green mantle of the standing pool, who is whipped from tithing to tithing, and stock-punished and imprisoned; who hath had three suits to his back, six shirts to his body, horse to ride, and weapon to wear.

But mice and rats and such small deer
Have been Tom's food for seven long year.

Beware my follower. Peace, Smulkin! peace, thou fiend. (III. iv. 132)

That it is all Edgar's pretence does not affect the argument; it is dramatically real. Edgar's darting movements and naked presence, together with his talk, act the storm scenes of Lear's progress. This is the best example of massed folklore playing a part within a spiritual progress. There is an ascending advance: from Lear's pagan curses in Act I and Mad Tom's devils to Lear's reunion with Cordelia, his use of the word 'God' at V. iii. 17, together with the medieval tonings of the combat of Edgar and Edmund, to the final climax (p. 63 below).

Timon of Athens, Shakespeare's most universal and philosophic play, contains a unique passage on animals, including strange folklore connotations with reference to animal behaviour:

If thou wert the lion, the fox would beguile thee; if thou wert the lamb, the fox would eat thee; if thou wert the fox, the lion would suspect thee, when peradventure thou wert accused by the ass; if thou wert the ass, thy dulness would torment thee, and still thou livedst as a breakfast to the wolf; if thou wert the wolf, thy greediness would afflict thee, and oft thou shouldst hazard thy life for thy dinner; wert thou the unicorn, pride and wrath would confound thee and make thine own self the conquest of thy fury; wert thou a bear, thou wouldst be killed by the horse; wert thou a horse, thou wouldst be seized by the leopard; wert thou a leopard, thou wert german to the lion and the spots of thy kindred were jurors on thy life; all thy safety were remotion and thy defence absence. What beast couldst thou be that were not subject to a beast? (IV. iii. 329)

The animals are presented strangely, some of it drawn from folklore beliefs. But the main statement is clear: an animal's plight is, for the most part, hazardous. Why, in this most philosophically profound of Shakespeare's works, must he fall back on old superstitions? In prose, too. Partly, perhaps, through a wish to penetrate, as we normally cannot, the animal's consciousness. This being impossible, we fall back on ancient beliefs as, at least, a second-best. There may be a better answer, but I have not discovered one.

IV

The early scenes of *Pericles* may arise from a folklore origin; after that we have mainly new intuitions. Cerimon's medical artistry is in descent from Friar Laurence's herbalist skills and Helena's spiritual assurance. The whole five-act story is given, as it were, a folklorish frame in the choruses spoken in suitable old-world style by Gower. It is at first to be accepted as, to use Peele's title, an 'old wives' tale'; but from this, wonders enough spring to new life.

Its companion piece is given a corresponding title: 'The Winter's Tale'. 'Winter' recalls Herne the Hunter and Richard II's:

> In winter's tedious nights sit by the fire
> With good old folks, and let them tell thee tales
> Of woeful ages long ago betid....
> (V. i. 40)

That is the key-tone of our play's opening: a wintry tone.[1] It is emphasised by the attractive boy, Mamillius, far more attractive than young Macduff or Coriolanus's son, who is to entertain the ladies with a tale. What shall it be? 'A sad tale's best for winter,' he says, 'I have one of sprites and goblins.' He starts: 'There was a man dwelt by a churchyard. .' (II. i. 24). His tale is interrupted; fate singles him out for an early death.

It may appear strange that the tale is a boy's; usually such tales are thought of, as in our *Richard II* quotation, as long-ago tales from old people. And yet it is true that our persistent love of Gothic-style stories is shared by children; indeed, they perhaps love them most. Among Shakespeare's plays *Macbeth* is a favourite of young schoolboys. The second part of *The Winter's Tale* is springlike and happy: a vivid contrast. We have Perdita's folklore impregnated flowers with her words on the power of unadulterated nature as against artificial grafting; and though the issue is left unsettled, Perdita's insistence is indirectly here relevant to the strength of natural powers working within all our beliefs. But these powers may nevertheless be transcended, as Polixenes tells us:

Perdita: For I have heard it said
          There is an art which in their piedness shares
          With great creating nature.
Polixenes: Say there be;
          Yet nature is made better by no mean
          But nature makes that mean; so, over that art,
          Which you say adds to nature, is an art
          That nature makes.... This is an art
          Which does mend nature, change it rather, but
          The art itself is nature.
          (IV. iii. 86–97)

Even so the dark substances of folklore are to be not rejected, but rather understood, transformed and reorientated.

Of these powers the entertaining rogue Autolycus may bear witness. His various deceptions appeal to our comic insights. When he appears at the sheep-shearing festival as a pedlar selling ballads he takes on, in the rustic setting, a protagonist stature. The shepherdesses Mopsa and Dorcas are fascinated. One of his ballads tells of a miser's wife who gave birth to money-bags, and another of a sexually cold woman who was transformed into a fire. 'Is it true, think you?' they ask, wide-eyed. And he replies: 'Why should I carry lies about?' One he claims was supported by 'Five justices' hands' (IV. iii. 262–84). A glorious comic variation on our dubious tales.

And so to the amazing end, Shakespeare's most precise penetration into the beyond-tragedy mystique. We ask, like the girls, 'Is it true?' Hermione has, we are assured, died; her figure has appeared to Antigonus in a dream. A famous sculptor, sixteen years later, has made a statue of her for Paulina. Then we are to watch it, in a chapel and to music, come alive, like Pygmalion's in the Greek myth. It moves; at last it speaks. It is 'warm': Hermione is living. The whole action is controlled by Paulina.

Has she kept Hermione aside, in secret, all these years? Outwardly, the story may be thought to assume this. But it does not fit the earlier events, nor the dream, nor the lengthy descriptions of what is regarded as Julio Romano's all but miraculous artistry; of the same sort, it seems, as Helena's divinely prompted skills in *All's Well that Ends Well*, which are 'able to breathe life into a stone' (II. i. 76). Or is it a spiritualistic manifestation, with Paulina as medium? We have three choices: which is it to be?

Our final statement is Leontes' to Paulina:

> Thou hast found mine;
> But how, is to be questioned, for I saw her,
> As I thought, dead.
> (V. iii. 139–41)

Hermione just says that she has 'preserved' herself: by what means? The one person who knows the full truth is presumably Paulina. She tells us:

> That she is living,
> Were it but told you, should be hooted at
> Like an old tale; but it appears she lives....
> (V. iii. 115–17)

Were they just *told* the news, people would greet it, as they do folklore tales, with 'hoots', that is guffaws of mockery. On such questions second-hand narration is always ineffectual.

The phrase not only reminds us of both our play's title and Mamillius's interrupted 'tale', but the choric Gentlemen, describing Leontes' reunion with his supposed dead daughter, use it twice: 'so like an old tale that the verity of it is in strong suspicion', and 'like an old tale still' (V. ii. 30,67). The secret is not revealed (pp. 62, 107–9 below). And yet the black magic, the 'wicked powers', of so much folklore is here transcended into a 'holy' engagement (V. iii. 89–91, 96, 104, 111).

In *The Tempest* Prospero's power evolves less from folklore than from what are designated the 'liberal arts' (I. ii. 73–4); it is certainly based on reading and books. With it he masters and directs nature's powers, rather like a modern scientist. When Caliban tells us that the spirits 'all do hate him as rootedly as I' (III. ii. 105), we can suppose nature in revulsion at our own ecological tyranny. At the end, he renounces his magical powers:

> Ye elves of hills, brooks, standing lakes and groves,
> And ye that on the sands with printless foot
> Do chase the ebbing Neptune and do fly him
> When he comes back. You demi-puppets that
> By moonshine do the green-sour ringlets make
> Whereof the ewe not bites...
> (V. i. 33–8)

Such folklore elements he has subdued, but he now renounces his art and will 'drown' his 'book', his means of control.

He is cruel, not only to Caliban but to Ferdinand, though in pretence only. During the play his actions are harsh. Bonamy Dobrée well argued that there is no warmth in his forgiveness. Despite the riches of nature brought by the classical goddesses in the Masque, the play as a whole, certainly in so far as it is dominated by Prospero, strikes us surely as rather cold in comparison with *A Midsummer Night's Dream*. And this coldness is partly due to its apparent lack, or denigration, of folklorish elements or atmosphere. Shakespeare for once had no sources; much is his own invention, and there is a corresponding loss in human appeal and warmth.

Or rather this would be so were it not for Caliban. With him we feel at home. As for folklore, he has an honourable descent; his mother was Sycorax, called a 'witch', who was bent double by 'age and envy' (I. ii. 258). We hear that she would have been condemned to death but for 'one thing she did'. What that was we are not told. It may in some way correspond to that within folklore which we must preserve and cherish. 'There is some soul of goodness in things evil', as we are told in *Henry V* 'would men observingly distil it out' (IV. i. 4).

Caliban responds to his slavery under Prospero with curses:

> As wicked dew as e'er my mother brush'd
> With raven's feather from unwholesome fen
> Drop on you both!... All the charms
> Of Sycorax, toads, beetles, bats, light on you!
> (I. i. 321–40)

When he plans to kill Prospero we can at least understand; though, remembering our civilisation, we ponder.

We certainly tend to *like* Caliban better. He is nature personified; his vices are nature's vices; and being so close to nature he is close to folklore. And it is just because he is all this that he can hear and respond to the cosmic music. He is visited by dreams. Prospero tells us that the whole manifested creation will dissolve, and that we are all no better than 'dreams':

> We are such stuff
> As dreams are made on and our little life
> Is rounded with a sleep.
> (IV. i. 156–8)

The thought is impressive, but remains rather negative. Caliban in contrast hears voices and music beyond our normal perception, and has wondrous dreams:

> Be not afeard: the isle is full of noises,
> Sounds and sweet airs, that give delight and hurt not.
> Sometimes a thousand twangling instruments
> Will hum about mine ears; and sometime voices,
> That, if I then had wak'd after long sleep,
> Will make me sleep again: and then, in dreaming,
> The clouds methought would open and show riches
> Ready to drop upon me; that, when I wak'd,
> I cried to dream again.
> (III. ii. 147–55)

We can choose, between Prospero who tyrannises over nature and appears to denigrate dreams, and Caliban, who grows out of nature and has dreams of glory. Caliban's faults are shown to have their reverse, their silver lining. His folklorish origin is one with his utterance of the most marvellous lines in Shakespeare.

We must not deny Prospero his rights. That would be to make the play nonsensical. Prospero's world is, for most of us, *our* world, of civilisation, science and politics. Prospero's renouncing of his magic and taking up his ducal responsibilities corresponds to Shakespeare's retiring from his more personal artistic quest and composing *Henry VIII*. Not much folklore there, except possibly for Norfolk's description of the Field of the Cloth of Gold with its superlative figures that tended to support belief in the mythological hero, Bevis of Southampton (I. i. 38); with a faint reflection perhaps in Cranmer's reference to the 'merry songs of peace' in his concluding prophecy (V. v. 36), where 'merry' does not quite suit our inquiry, since Shakespeare's folklore suggestion is so often dark. But I have tried to show how the grimness not only holds within it a salutary and comforting element, but is also balanced with happier pointings, transcending the fearsome substances from which they flower.

The importance of this folklore element in Shakespeare may perhaps be best appreciated by noting its rarity in later British drama and how, when brilliantly handled, as it is today in Francis Berry's poetic narrative *Murdock,* it attains a maximum of power. It is all there, as in Shakespeare: village life embedded in folklorish fears and ghostly midnight presences; the terror faced; and then the achieved victory, commensurate to the depth, into ascent and harmony. The expanding development in *Murdock* of folklore terror to a great and over-ruling consummation is exactly Shakespearian.

V: Spiritual Healing

(from *Link,* Newsletter of National Spiritualist Church, Exeter, March, 1977; republished in *The Spiritual Healer,* Burrows Lea, Shere, August, 1980).

Harry Edwards has told us that spirit-healing comes about through the enlisting of spirit help to allow the body's natural resources to effect a cure. Shakespeare in *All's Well that Ends Well* (II. i) gives us a description of an exactly similar process. Helena is the humble daughter of a famous doctor. Her powers are said to be such as to 'breathe life into a stone' (as in *The Winter's Tale*) or raise the dead (76–80). She determines to cure the King of France, who suffers from a seemingly fatal disease. She has her father's secret prescription which was given to her to be preserved as a 'triple eye', more 'dear' to her than the other two. This is the Third Eye, well known to occult teaching, and said to be used by healers.

The King at first refuses:

> We thank you, maiden,
> But may not be so credulous of cure,
> When our most learned doctors leave us, and
> The congregated college have concluded
> That labouring art can never ransom nature
> From her inaidable estate.
>   (117)

'The labouring art' of orthodox medicine, as in our time, is contrasted with such practices. So the King would not 'stain our judgement' and bring 'our great self and our credit' into disrepute by putting trust in 'empirics'; that is, in methods unknown to science. Helena replies that God can work through the 'weakest minister', and mentions examples. She urges that human science does not exhaust reality, but only deals in what is known to sense-perception, or through appearances:

> It is not so with Him that all things knows
> As 'tis with us that square our guess by shows.
> But most it is presumption in us when
> The help of heaven we count the act of men.
> Dear Sir, to my endeavours give consent,
> Of heaven, not me, make an experiment.
>   (152)

She describes the nature of the proposed cure:

> What is infirm from your sound parts shall fly.
> Health shall live free, and sickness freely die.
>
> (170)

There is, as in spirit-healing today, no antidote, but rather a reliance on 'health', on the existent life-powers, which are restored to freedom, obstructions being dissolved. The King gives way: 'Methinks in thee some blessed spirit doth speak.' He is cured.

Lafeu, a lord, comments (II. iii):

> They say miracles are past; and we have our philosophical persons to make modern and familiar things supernatural and causeless. Hence is it that we make trifles of terrors, ensconcing ourselves into seeming knowledge when we should submit ourselves to an unknown fear.

He calls it 'a showing of a heavenly effect in an earthly actor.... In a most weak and debile minister, great power, great transcendence.' It should, he says, be of 'further use' than the healing of the King alone. It should be more 'generally', that is widely, recognised.

It appears that Shakespeare, or his inspirers, had an exact understanding of what is involved in spirit-healing.

A more comprehensive study of Helena's personality is given in my essay 'The Third Eye' in *The Sovereign Flower*.

Note

[1] A recent production of *The Winter's Tale,* if correctly reported, starts with rumbustious comedy: my reaction is, as they say on television, 'No comment'. The sign of an assured Shakespearian production will be faultless truth to all details, stated or poetically suggested, within the text. If a myriad moments of truth pile up, one is, or would be, aware of a brilliant production. This, in my limited experience since I do not now attend often, is today seldom if ever offered to us, whereas tricks totally unrelated to, or contradicted by, the play, are presented again and again; and often enough praised. The worst instances make one suffer agonisingly, like biting on a painful tooth. In this matter we seem to be in darkness, or at the best in fog. The normal clarity of Shakespeare is not respected.

IV Gloucester's Leap

(from *Essays in Criticism,* XXII, 3, July 1972)
On certain problems raised during two lectures on Shakespearian tragedy at the Dulwich College Literary Society and at the Latymer Foundation Upper School, on 4 and 5 October 1971.

A young Dulwich questioner, Tony Cohen, remarked that the peculiar event in *King Lear* (IV. vi) of Gloucester's attempted suicide was like nothing else in Shakespeare. Could I explain its deeper meaning? This almost comic flirtation with the terrors of sudden death is certainly unique. It reminds one, perhaps, of Webster's bizarre pictorial charades, though it is more intricate and purposive, being so elaborately organised by Edgar to dissuade his father from suicide. And yet the extraordinary stage action exerts, for better or worse, an effect far in excess of any rational argument: if the action itself is not in some way profound, it is clumsy. I had no satisfactory answer.

At Latymer Upper School I was asked whether I thought Othello's suicide an ignoble 'escape'? Shakespeare's valuations on suicide depend partly, but not entirely, on period. In the Roman plays it is honourable: Hamlet, as a Christian, knows that it is forbidden; and yet Othello's suicide in a Christian setting is regarded by Cassio as a sign of greatness. At the lecture I stated that according to modern Spiritualism (that is, according to the teaching of spirit-guides speaking through trance mediums), suicide as escape is wrong and anyway useless, since one finds oneself directly after death in all essentials the same person as before and with the same problems; a reading of survival very exactly followed by T.S. Eliot in *The Cocktail Party* and *For the Indian Soldiers who died in Africa* (the passages, 'the first five minutes after a violent death' and 'the moment after death', are discussed in my *Neglected Powers, 397*). See p. 64 below. As for suicide, we may not choose our time of dying. As Edgar puts it:

Men must endure
Their going hence, even as their coming hither.
Ripeness is all.
(V. ii. 9–11)

That means, men must await patiently their proper hour.

I now suggest that what Shakespeare shows us in Gloucester's Leap is not only Edgar's way of dissuading him from suicide, but also a remarkable dramatisation in terms of earthly action of what everyone experiences at death. Only a most carefully devised concurrence of events could establish the needed analogy. The old man's blindness is as the blindness of us all when we regard death as a fall into nothingness. Edgar's long, and otherwise scarcely relevant, speech describing the mind's dizziness in looking down on the sea creates an analogy to the bottomless nothing of death as usually apprehended. But it is all false; we who watch know that there is no cliff or sea. Cliff, sea and dizziness are similarly used in *Hamlet* (I. iv. 69–78) in association with the Ghost, madness and presumably death, Horatio's phrase 'some other horrible form' corresponding to the horrible fiend described by Edgar. The description (IV. vi. 70–3), involving vast nature, is truly horrific.

My conclusion is that in Gloucester's Leap Shakespeare has dramatised in earthly terms the truth of death. This he has done for us who watch, though not so precisely for Gloucester who thinks that he has fallen and been saved by a miracle; nor even for Edgar himself, who, thinking in normal terms, fears lest the shock might kill his father. I do not assert that Shakespeare knew that he was doing what I have suggested, but simply that he appears to have done it.

In my two lectures, concentrating on the positive powers of Shakespearian tragedy, I was at pains to emphasise the final dignity, as though in some way poetically and spiritually enriched, of each tragic hero, even Macbeth, in turn. This reading had been developed in my *Shakespearian*

Production (enlarged edn 1964) and also, for the best discussion of *Macbeth*, in the chapter 'The Avenging Mind' in *Shakespeare and Religion* (1967); subsequently expanded throughout *Shakespeare's Dramatic Challenge* (1977). The easiest way to drive home my argument is to adduce Marlowe's diametrically opposite approach, comparing the end of *Edward II* with that of *Richard II*, or of *Doctor Faustus* with *Macbeth*. I am not claiming that Shakespeare was offering an explicit doctrine, but am concerned rather with what shines through his human artistry.

It is the same with the last plays, *Pericles* and *The Winter's Tale*. In calling these 'myths of immortality' I was never claiming for them a point by point and faultlessly logical dramatisation of a doctrinal philosophy, but simply pointing out that Shakespearian narrative was here so manipulated and toned that what seemed certainly dead is found, to the hero's and our own amazement, alive. The human story remains a basis: in *The Winter's Tale*, though the logic of drama has clearly directed us through Antigonus's account of his dream (III. iii. 15–45) to assume that Hermione has died, yet when she appears at the play's conclusion she bears signs of age that suggest that she has not. The final explanations (V. iii) only confuse us. Polixenes wonders whether she has been living somewhere, or, if not, how she has 'stolen from the dead'. Her survival, says Paulina, would, were it not patent, be 'hooted at like an old tale'. Hermione says simply that she has 'preserved' herself to see her child. Leontes remains quite baffled. She obviously *is* living,

> But how, is to be question'd; for I saw her,
> As I thought, dead.
>   (V. ii. 139)

On that note we are left: it is as though the poet himself is baffled. We could, of course, call all this unfair, but it is safer to recognise that in being impelled to wrestle with facts which Hamlet calls (I. iv. 56) 'beyond the reaches of our souls', great poets may have to involve themselves in contradictions and enigmas. Vergil did. So does the New Testament, and also its derivative in Christian dogma. What we have to do is to respond accurately not only to the words but even more to the action or actions, and to what, to use my earlier phrase, 'shines through'.

My treatment of Gloucester's Leap goes beyond my normal practice of direct interpretation; but since, as my questioner rightly remarked, the incident sticks out so awkwardly in Shakespeare's world, it may be allowed to force a peculiar handling. A possible support to my reading comes in Lear's reunion with Cordelia where, though the event is earthly, the tonings, 'Thou art a soul in bliss', 'You are a spirit, I know; when did you die?' (IV. vii. 46, 49), suggest the transcendental. Adrian Abbotts has suggested to me that Cordelia may be equated with Lear's 'soul', so we have here a mutual spirituality.

Additional Note, 1981

I believe Lear's words at Cordelia's death derive from sight of her soul-body released:

> Do you see this? Look on her, look, her lips,
> Look there, look there!
> (V. iii. 312)

True, he is thinking of the feather (V. iii. 267); but that thought blends into sight of her soul-body released, giving us the final exclamation, his eyes lifted. 'Look there' resembles Macbeth's words on Banquo's ghost: 'Prithee, see there! behold! look! lo!' (III. iv. 69). It would, it seems, be an artistic error on Shakespeare's part to end such a drama as *King Lear* with the hero dying in a state of complete delusion; surely his final words must make some sort of sense. After Lear's death, Kent believes Lear is calling on him to follow.

Besides these surrounding thoughts in *King Lear*, suggesting survival, to which I have already drawn attention in *Shakespeare's Dramatic Challenge* (V. 110–11), we can point to other passages on the soul's release. In *Richard II*, Bolingbroke addresses Mowbray:

> By this time, had the king permitted us,
> One of our souls had wander'd in the air,
> Banish'd this frail sepulchre of our flesh...
> (I. iii. 194–6)

Richard at his death thinks in the same terms:

> Mount, mount, my soul! Thy seat is up on high,
> Whilst my gross flesh sinks downward, here to die.
> (V. v. 112)

Romeo conceives similarly:

> Now, Tybalt, take the villain back again
> That late thou gav'st me, for Mercutio's soul
> Is but a little way above our heads,
> Staying for thine to keep him company.
> (III. i. 131–4)

This belief in a lately-departed soul existent near and from above appears to be a normal Shakespearian acceptance. At the least, we could say that the conception is certainly no alien intruder. See also *The Wheel of Fire*, VIII, 168.

We may appear to have departed too far from Gloucester's Leap and for a nearer analogy I could point to Ibsen's sculptured Resurrection piece in Act I of *When We Dead Awaken*. The figure is shown 'awakening' on Resurrection Day:

Not marvelling at anything new and unknown and undivined; but filled with a sacred joy at finding herself unchanged – she, the woman of earth – in the higher, freer, happier region – after the long dreamless sleep of death.

Here time is assumed to lapse before the awakening, but the result conforms. For a closer analogy we have already pointed to T.S. Eliot's statement in the poem *For the Indian Soldiers who died in Africa* (in *Of Books and Humankind, Essays and Poems Presented to Bonamy Dobrée*, ed. John Butt, 1964; 174) that a full and comprehensive consciousness is active at 'the moment after death'. A similar view is present in a passage of my own *Atlantic Crossing* (I. 27), in description of a well-known optical illusion, the scene being a ship in the St Lawrence River, near Quebec.

'Look, Mother – can you see?' The bridge looks very low, the mast terribly high, and the nearer we get the more impossible it seems. 'It can't possibly,' she says, enjoying the fun. 'Don't talk nonsense.' Now the mast springs up, taller, taller, and the whole ship's speed seems to increase second by second, the mast leaps higher, swiftly towards disaster, just twice as high as the bridge, like a man instant by instant approaching death, which, as he sees it coming, spells necessary dissolution – and next, smoothly, easily, serenely, the masthead glides beneath with leisurely assurance, many feet to spare, and the big ship sails queenly down the river as before.

Whatever be the ultimate truth, that passage appears to convey the exact intuition from which Gloucester's Leap was somehow devised.

V   *Timon of Athens*

(i) Shakespeare on the Gold Standard

(from *Saturday Night* (Toronto), 17 February 1940)

Why should a play so poignantly relevant to present conflicts as Shakespeare's *Timon of Athens* have been consistently neglected? Perhaps the inwardness of its more profound suggestions echoes too distantly on the twentieth-century mind. A famous English critic, William Hazlitt, once wrote in *The Characters of Shakespeare's Plays: 'Timon of Athens* always appeared to us to be written with as intense a feeling of his subject as any one play of Shakespeare. It is one of the few in which he seems to be in earnest throughout, never to trifle nor go out of his way. He does not relax in his efforts, nor lose sight of the unity of his design'. Nevertheless, it remains seldom read and scarcely ever performed.

Timon, a wealthy lord, wholeheartedly devoted to a life of friendship, patronage and glittering generosity, finds his riches exhausted and himself forthwith deserted by his friends. His love is replaced by loathing of an ungrateful and money-ridden society. Retiring to a state of hermit savagery by the sea shore, he finds gold while digging for food, and becomes again sought-after, both for that and the value of his name and experience in the defence of Athens against Alcibiades. But he remains steadfast in his refusal to return.

We must, of course, look deeper than the supposedly historical interest. The play, based on a short account in Plutarch's *Antonius*, impregnates an old story with fresh and expansive meaning. Shakespeare writes at a period when the feudal order was disintegrating before a rising commercialism. Something of a high value breaks in the passing of an old aristocracy, while the acquisitive instincts, free from traditional checks, are felt waiting to push civilisation towards chaos. In Timon's imprecation of disasters on a people rotting with greed and ease we may therefore feel the future bourgeois civilisation of Europe summoned to account.

The attack, levelled primarily against a vicious insincerity, is as old as the Gospels: but in our age *Timon* also stands ancestral to a long line of satire, with Pope as its closest kin, but the main attacks of Swift and Byron also contained while also forecasting Tolstoy's and Nietzsche's uncompromising repudiations. Moreover, Timon's return to nature, his resting back on the vastness of earth and ocean, moon and sun, his desert cave and seashore burial, variously forecast not only aspects of Prospero in *The Tempest* and *Robinson Crusoe*, but all later nature retreats of Romantic poetry, the mountainous solitudes of Goethe, Wordsworth and Byron, and impassioned searchings of Lawrence. America provides two powerful analogies: Melville coined the word 'Timonism' for his own very similar experience; and today Robinson Jeffers, both in his work and life, traces out the rhythms of Timon's story on the shores of the Pacific. Shakespeare's play compasses the two main pulses, satiric and Romantic, the negative and positive energies of European poetry.

There is today a tendency to diagnose root evils in terms of economics, while the dramatic literature of the past, being comparatively silent on economic theory as such, might seem of scant assistance; though its concentration on those forms of the personality lying behind and finally determining all currencies of merchandise and wealth points indirectly towards a solution. Now *Timon*, perhaps alone in dramatic history, has powerfully fused these realms, imposing on the crude fact of monetary greed the mighty periods of great poetry. Timon, in self-chosen banishment from man, addresses the gold dug from the earth as the 'common whore of mankind', that 'puts odds among the rout of nations'. Again:

O thou sweet king-killer and dear divorce
'Twixt natural son and sire; thou bright defiler
Of Hymen's purest bed, thou valiant Mars,
Thou ever young, fresh, lov'd, and delicate wooer,
Whose blush doth thaw the consecrated snow
That lies on Dian's lap! thou visible god
That solder'st close impossibilities
And mak'st them kiss; that speak'st with every tongue
To every purpose: O thou touch of hearts,
Think thy slave man rebels, and by thy virtue
Set them into confounding odds, that beasts
May have the world in empire!
(IV. iii. 384–95)

Which may be referred to contemporary world confusions.

Now Alcibiades, the warrior, a man in whom honour burns proudly, is first antagonised by the cold, smugly reasoned, justice of the capitalist Senate; his patience exhausted, he leads an army against Athens; is next aided with Timon's new-found gold and empowered by his righteous curse; and last, like Fortinbras in *Hamlet*, establishes the new order. Contemporary Fascism scores a point, especially if it chooses to quote from Spengler's *Decline of the West:* 'A power can be overthrown only by another power, not by a principle, and no power that can confront money is left but this one. Money is overthrown and abolished only by blood.' 'Blood', here meaning racial instinct, is however a dangerously ambiguous word. Timon's loathing of 'contumelious, beastly, mad-brain'd war' is bitter as Swift's, and when he hopes Alcibiades and Athens will plague each other to exhaustion, the modern communist might, in his turn, nod a generous approval, and he could, indeed, urge that the action proves the inherent unwisdom of private ownership, disastrous alike in a Timon's expenditure and his friends' selfishness.

But, though including these suggestions, the play as a whole transcends such partialities. It condemns no system, but rather men as individuals, found incapable of handling private wealth which is, finally, equivalent to personal responsibility and personal power. Until so capable, they cannot properly assume public responsibility either, national and international problems being even more complex. Social regeneration must therefore be expected, if at all, to mature from a reversal in human personality. We are accordingly shown as central the resplendent personality of Timon, conceived as unwise but not *essentially* at fault, and more finely tuned than the bold executor of military violence, Alcibiades. Though Timon can only turn savage and curse, yet within each curse lies a supreme positive, each accent is barbed by truth and winged by a fierce love; while the gold he finds, addresses in bitterness, yet hands with imprecations to all who come, symbolises, too, something of that soul worth in himself which Athens has rejected.

Oedipus was banished from Thebes that his city might survive; but our Athens has cast out Timon, sullied its own golden powers, and remains unclean. For Timon is the inmost genius of man unwanted, cast out, and embittered by his own degraded social consciousness. He is all but poetry incarnate, his story mirroring the lot of genius throughout the centuries, while the main guilt of our society is, as Shelley saw, an imaginative lack, a denial of the poetic essence, a stifling or poisoning of that more subtle virility Spengler missought in the bond of 'blood'. Once money, wealth, mechanical inventions, learning, or any other good, ceases to function as a sacrament of the heart's gold it becomes suicidal. This *Timon of Athens* says with no less authority and much of the tone of Hebraic prophecy; and our neglect hitherto measures, perhaps, our unwillingness to dig out its riches in ourselves.

(ii) Isaiah in Renaissance Dress

(from *The Trinity University Review*, February, 1940)

Arise, my God, and strike, for we hold Thee just!
Strike dead the whole weak race of venomous worms,
That sting each other here in the dust,
We are not worthy to live.
(Tennyson, *Maud*, XXIII, ii. 10–13)

Our destiny, our being's heart and home
Is with infinitude and only there.
(Wordsworth, *The Prelude*, VI. 604–5)

In *Timon of Athens* we have the very essence of Shakespearian, perhaps of all, tragedy. Ingratitude is Shakespeare's primary human aversion and the persistent theme, raised to titanic, almost grotesque, proportion, rises here to a condemnation of man and all his works of oppression, idolatry and greed, with imprecations of war. The diagnosis is likely to prove important for the age succeeding the present (1940) European disturbances. It is no mere denial: for within the poetry lies, though as yet unread, and at depths far below social or political analysis, the one necessary wisdom which we await.

The long falling movement is inwardly conceived, is indeed less a human narrative than a cosmic exploration, like Shelley's *Prometheus* or *The Book of Job*. We have seen the individual soul prove unable to realise perfection in social intercourse; and beyond Swiftian rejections looms the yet darker record of a complete mental and emotional severance from all temporal commitments whatsoever, calling down through a succession of mighty speeches that sense of the numinous, of other-wordly powers and presences – what Nietzsche called the Dionysian as opposed to the Apollonian – usually attending only the final impact of great tragedy. Timon's hate is always nearer prophecy than neurosis. His denunciations, like those of Isaiah, Jeremiah and Ezekiel, are Hebraic. At the last he is, like Wordsworth's Newton, felt as 'voyaging through strange seas of thought, alone'; more truly at one with a wild nature, a surging ocean, and imagery of sun and moon, than human purposes. Into such vast infinities his story fades.

The action is general, not particular. The protagonist sums all Shakespeare's tragic heroes and forecasts those many examples of a like literature who retire from man's civilisation to nature. The New Testament shows Christ likewise withdrawing from city life to sea or mountain, with phrases of lonely disquietude or bitter prophecy. The comparison is, indeed, twice hinted in Shakespeare's phraseology. Timon is a universal lover and, in the last scenes, endures a slow crucifixion. He is as a Christ who cannot, at the last, forgive.

The play must be given a sympathetic hearing to be understood. It has not the intimacy of *Hamlet,* the human warmth of *Othello,* the subtlety of *Lear.* Timon's expansive generosity may seem as unreasonable as his subsequent loathing. The artistic structure at times approaches that of the morality plays in stiffness of symbolic intention; at others, it is vast and Aeschylean. The emotional meanings rise in rough-hewn slabs and blocks. It is probably Shakespeare's greatest single tragic statement. As certainly as *Hamlet* – which preceded, as this concludes, the succession of sombre plays – it stands central in Shakespeare's life work, as a heart in a body; that is to say, central in the prophetic literature of Renaissance Europe.

VI   *Timon of Athens* and Buddhism

(from *Essays in Criticism*, XXX, 2, April 1980)

Timon of Athens is Shakespeare's only play of deliberate philosophic planning. With others we have philosophy suggested through symbolism and atmosphere, but here it seems to be consciously planned. The text is unrevised and at times faulty, as though Shakespeare put it aside unfinished. Its thought draws close to Indian teaching and in especial Buddhism.

It has a prologue in the Poet's speech describing the theme the drama is to develop. It is conceived as inoffensive and impersonal. 'My free drift', he says, 'halts not particularly':

> No levell'd malice
> Infects one comma in the course I hold,
> But flies an eagle flight, bold and forth on,
> Leaving no tract behind.
> (I. i. 48–51)[1]

Its flight is to be powerful, courageous and direct, challenging the future rather than regarding the past.

Timon is a bounteous and benevolent patron enjoying a brilliant social communion. We have a sumptuous feast with a Masque introduced by Cupid who honours Timon as lord of the senses:

> The five best senses
> Acknowledge thee their patron.... Th'ear,
> Taste, touch, smell, pleas'd from thy table rise;
> They only now come but to feast thine eyes.
> (I. ii. 131–5)

'They' (or 'These' if we emend) refers to the ladies as Amazons, who enter as part of the show.

Contrasted with Timon is the surly and ascetic philosopher, Apemantus, who despises sensuous pleasure and serves to point, though with a difference, the direction Timon is to take. For when Timon's wealth is exhausted and his friends refuse to help him, his eyes are opened to the viciousness of men and in disgust he breaks from society and retreats to the wilds.

The Buddha's rejection of the high social status into which he was born, together with all its sensuous enjoyments, followed by his embracing of poverty and religious devotion, is different from Timon's; but there are certain similarities. Buddha's famous Fire Sermon attacks sense-impressions; he sees the eye, tongue, ear, nose, the whole body as on fire with sensation; and more, with passions; and comprehensively with birth, age, disease and death. This torment of existence his sermon opposes. The Fire Sermon gave T.S. Eliot the heading to Part III of *The Waste Land* which ends with

> Burning burning burning burning
> O Lord Thou pluckest me out
> O Lord Thou pluckest
> burning

Timon's burning sense of ingratitude may seem slight reason for a wholesale repudiation, but it serves as a dramatic excuse – one near to Shakespeare's heart, because it is reiterated in his work – for getting him to a state like that of The Fire Sermon. This is the transition:

> Burn house! Sink Athens! Henceforth hated be
> Of Timon man and all humanity.
>   (III. vi. 115)

Hatred is not counselled by the Buddha, but a degree of repudiation or renunciation is. It is the nature of drama to deal in forceful kinetic action; Buddhism, unlike Christianity, is not a dramatic religion, and indeed *Timon of Athens* itself has been criticised for the undramatic quality of its settled revulsion during the later acts.

In his first ascetic practices the Buddha lived in extreme

want and sometimes in nakedness (M.S. Sangharakshita: *The Three Jewels, an Introduction to Buddhism,* Chapter III, 14. All references to this book refer to the second edition after the letter *J;* see note 2). According to Indian tradition this was usual. Nakedness could be a sign of holiness; in the Bible both Isaiah (XX. 2–4) and Micah (1.8) used it to empower their messages. Gandhi's appearance in London incurred, if I remember correctly, Winston Churchill's aspersion on him as 'a naked savage'. There may be a meaning in it that goes beyond asceticism. In C.B. Purdom's study of the mystic Meher Baba we find an extreme example of self-exposure, as reported by Gandhi of Upasni Maharaj (*The God-Man,* 1964, III. 95).

Timon conforms to the practice:

> Nothing I'll bear from thee
> But nakedness, thou detestable town!...
> Timon will to the woods, where he shall find
> The unkindest beast more kinder than mankind.
> (IV. i. 32–6)

During the later acts Timon wears, presumably, a loin-cloth. It may suggest degradation, as in Flavius's 'Is yon despised and ruinous man my lord?' (IV. iii. 468). Apemantus, speaking of his 'slave-like' and 'sour-cold' dress, says that if not forced but done to 'castigate thy pride', it might have been reasonable; 'pride' here suggesting sexual potency (IV. iii. 206; 240–2). One thinks of naked Edgar in *King Lear,* the 'poor, bare, forked animal' that is 'unaccommodated man' (*King Lear,* III. iv. 109). Such phrases correspond to the 'rags' often referred to in descriptions of Indian asceticism, but there is another side to be considered. That other side is in the Buddhist hero:

Despite the emphasis on compassion the Bodhisattva is no mere sentimentalist. Nor, for all his tenderness, is he an effeminate weakling. He is the Great Hero, the embodiment not only of Wisdom and Compassion, but also of *virya* or Vigour, a word which like the etymologically equivalent 'virility' signifies both energy and masculine potency. This aspect of the Bodhisattva's personality is prominent in the well-known Ahicchatra image of Maitreya, with its powerful torso, massive yet graceful limbs, and clinging nether garment that covers without concealing his evident masculinity. (*J,* XVI. 170–1)

This corresponds to the visible power that should character-
ise Timon when he says:

> Who dares, who dares
> In purity of manhood stand upright
> And say, 'This man's a flatterer'? If one be
> So are they all.... Therefore be abhorr'd
> All feasts, societies and throngs of men.
> His semblable, yea himself, Timon disdains.
> (IV. iii. 13–22)

Timon scorns all humanity, including himself. This resembles the Buddhistic will to surpass human existence. During
his words Timon should look as physically strong and
aesthetically pleasing as may be. Timon rejects human
existence at its best. From now on, having done with the
perceptual universe, he is to strip away all but essentials,
ending with life itself. He first passes to a forest. I have
perhaps stressed this less in my productions than I should
have done; but the atmosphere I also used of a sea coast is
simultaneously helpful.

Timon, as we have seen, says he is going to 'the woods'.
As You Like It forecasts *Timon* in its persons' retirement to
the Forest of Arden, where nature is, as in *Timon,* said to be
kinder than man (II. vii. 174–93). In the forest the
melancholy Jaques is a clear precursor of Timon, describing
his satiric attack in equivalent terms (II. vii. 44–87); and we
have the 'old religious man' living in the forest who converts
the villain (V. iv. 167). The word 'forest' is reiterated, as it is
in Indian philosophy. In his introduction to my book *The
Wheel of Fire,* T.S. Eliot makes reference to 'the Forest
Philosophers of India'. He used *'The Sacred Wood'* as a title.

Trees certainly hold here some deep significance. Buddha's
first experience of enlightenment came to him while sitting
under a tree, and he next sat under 'various other trees'
nearby, assimilating the truth he had discovered (*J,* III. 15).
A tree somehow helps: an initiate is told to live on alms and
wear rags, and 'live at the foot of a tree' (*J,* XVII. 211–12;
and see 222). It counters temptation, as one sits in its 'cool
shade' apart from all 'pleasure of the senses' (*J,* XIII. 119).
The Buddha is pictured under a tree 'with eyes half closed'
while women vainly exhibit their charms (*J,* XIII. 126). The

Bodhi tree, scene of his enlightenment, is accordingly regarded as holy, primitive tree-worship thus being incorporated into Buddhism (*J*, XIX. 246, 249). It is all part of an age-old regard of 'dense forests and remote mountain caves' for an anchorite's existence (*J*, XVII. 224). An authoritative text says that those 'who practise asceticism and faith in the forest' are favoured by the gods (Paul Deussen, *The Philosophy of the Upanishads,* trans. A.S. Geden, 1906, I. 69).

Timon's retirement 'to the woods' is accordingly placed. In my own production I put less emphasis on trees than on rocks and sea coast, but trees are important in the poetry: Timon's friends

> That numberless upon me stuck as leaves
> Do on the oak, have with one winter's brush
> Fell from their boughs and left me open, bare
> For every storm that blows.
> (IV. iii. 264–7)

Before that Apemantus in a fine passage compares Timon's ascetic life with his past luxury:

> What! think'st
> That the bleak air, thy boisterous chamberlain,
> Will put thy shirt on warm? Will these moss'd trees,[3]
> That have outliv'd the eagle, page thy heels
> And skip when thou point'st out?... Call the creatures
> Whose naked natures live in all the spite
> Of wreakful heaven, whose bare unhoused trunks,
> To the conflicting elements expos'd
> Answer mere nature, bid them flatter thee...
> (IV. iii. 222–32)

Notice the ingrained sympathy with animal life (as too in *As You Like It,* II. i. 21–68). This is characteristic of Buddhism, which has compassion for all living things. It is not spoken by Timon himself, but he has a notable speech on animals, strangely worded, and relying on folklore as well as fact:

If thou wert the lion, the fox would beguile thee; if thou wert the lamb, the fox would eat thee; if thou wert the fox, the lion would suspect thee, when peradventure thou wert accused by the ass; if thou wert the ass, thy dulness would torment thee, and still thou livedst but as a breakfast to the wolf; if

thou wert the wolf, thy greediness would afflict thee, and oft thou
shouldst hazard thy life for thy dinner; wert thou the unicorn, pride and
wrath would confound thee and make thine own self the conquest of thy
fury; wert thou a bear, thou wouldst be killed by the horse; wert thou a
horse, thou wouldst be seized by the leopard; wert thou a leopard, thou
wert german to the lion, and the spots of thy kindred were jurors on thy
life. All thy safety were remotion, and thy defence absence. What beast
couldst thou be, that were not subject to a beast? (IV. iii. 329)

Animal creation is seen as universally suffering; by voracity
and hazard, nature being, as Tennyson has it, 'red in tooth
and claw' (*In Memoriam,* LVI); and by mental inadequacy and
fierce passions. The strange beliefs here incorporated from
folklore are used presumably as a rough pretence to being
inside the animal consciousness, which is for ever debarred
from us. The general result is clear; man may be suffering,
but it is worse for the beasts. Buddhism has sympathy not
only for man but for all sentient life. Its view is that of St
Paul: 'To this day, we know, the entire creation sighs and
throbs with pain' (Romans, VIII. 22). Animal life is to be
included in our survey.

Timon, like the Buddhist, is a vegetarian, living on 'roots':

> Common mother, thou
> Whose womb unmeasurable and infinite breast
> Teems and feeds all; whose self-same mettle
> Whereof thy proud child, arrogant man, is puff'd,
> Engenders the black toad and adder blue,
> The gilded newt and eyeless venom'd worm,
> With all the abhorred births below crisp heaven
> Whereon Hyperion's quickening fire doth shine,
> Yield him who all thy human sons doth hate,
> From forth thy plenteous bosom, one poor root.
> (IV. iii. 178–87)

When Thieves come to him saying that they are 'men that
much do want', he replies:

> Your greatest want is, you want much of meat.
> Why should you want? Behold, the earth hath roots;
> Within this mile break forth a hundred springs;
> The oaks bear mast, the briers scarlet hips;
> The bounteous housewife, nature, on each bush
> Lays her full mess before you. Want! Why want?
> (IV. iii. 422–7)

One answers:

> We cannot live on grass, on berries, water,
> As beasts and birds and fishes.
> (IV. iii. 428)

Though in the earlier scenes (e.g. III. vi. 85 and elsewhere)
Timon's feasting included 'meat', he has changed, following
Buddhist practice.

Timon, digging for 'roots', finds gold:

> What is here?
> Gold! yellow, glittering, precious gold! No, gods,
> I am no idle votarist. Roots, you clear heavens!
> Thus much of this will make black white, foul fair,
> Wrong right, base noble, old young, coward valiant.
> Ha! you gods, why this? What this, you gods? Why, this
> Will lug your priests and servants from your sides,
> Pluck stout men's pillows from below their heads;
> This yellow slave
> Will knit and break religions...
> (IV. iii. 25–34)

Timon sees himself as a 'votarist', meaning a religious
devotee.

He sees gold as subverting all valuation and morality; and
yet this new gold is clearly god-given. The thought is
repeated (IV. iii. 533). Later Timon addresses it as ambiva-
lent, as itself a 'visible god that solder'st close impossibilities'
(389), dangerous and yet miraculous in potency:

> O thou touch of hearts!
> Think thy slave man rebels, and by thy virtue
> Set them into confounding odds, that beasts
> May have the world in empire.
> (IV. iii. 392–5)

It is a power, in itself; and it may be good. To his faithful
servant Flavius, Timon says:

> Thou singly honest man,
> Here, take: the gods out of my misery
> Have sent thee treasure.
> (IV. iii. 532–4)

'Misery': the gold may be called 'tragic gold'. The name 'Timon' indicates worth, and his new gold helps to reestablish his position; his dramatic status is now raised; he is still wanted. He hurls gold to Alcibiades and the Thieves accompanied by imprecations. Gold and rich metals throughout literature and the human story exert magical radiations; and this magic is in Timon. Though he urges Alcibiades to ruthless war he is answered by, 'I'll take the gold thou giv'st me, not all thy counsel' (IV. iii. 130). Formerly, Alcibiades spoke callously of the slaughtered on a battlefield: 'So they were bleeding new, my lord, there's no meat like them' (I. ii. 81); but now he is strangely softened by Timon's imprecations, whose words, accompanied by what I call his 'tragic gold', induce not evil but good. In the event, at the conclusion, he is merciful. This is clearer when Timon scatters gold to the Thieves, telling them to 'cut throats' and 'break open shops', since those they steal from are themselves all thieves; and then, speaking to each other, one says, 'He has almost charm'd me from my profession by persuading me to it', and another, 'I'll believe him as an enemy and give over my trade' (IV. iii. 457–62). 'Charm'd': Timon is a 'charmer', like the Egyptian who gave Othello the magical handkerchief (*Othello*, III. iv. 58). Though there is no explicit statement to this effect, the gold clearly acts as an externalisation of Timon's spiritual power. Timon is a magical personage, like Oedipus in Sophocles' *Oedipus at Colonus*, and he, like Oedipus, is finally wooed by his city to return, as a saviour. The early acts are a-glitter with wealth and references to gold; in his tragic gold that richness is re-awakened. From start to finish Timon has a golden aura.

What has such gold-magic to do with so seemingly abstract and spiritual a religion as Buddhism? Rich metals, especially jewels, are symbolically as important in Buddhism as in Shakespeare (see *Othello*, V. ii. 143, 346). Sangharakshita's book is itself called *The Three Jewels,* the 1977 publication having an appropriate cover design by Upasaka Devaraja. 'Wherever the Three Jewels are revered' (*J*, XIX. 261) is a natural Buddhist designation. The three jewels signify Enlightenment, Doctrine and Community (*J*. Preface ix). We hear of 'the Jewel Ornament of Liberation' (*J*, XVI. 175).

Though poverty is a high value for Buddha's followers, both jewels and gold exercise normal imaginative functions in their iconography, corresponding to the tragic, god-given gold in *Timon*. The Buddha is given a robe of 'cloth-of-gold' (*J*, III. 24); other Buddhas are pictured with 'golden aureoles' (*J*, XVIII. 239); 'gilded' structures are typical in Asian Buddhism (J, XIX, 248). Sacred scriptures are written on 'tablets of gold' and enclosed in a box made of gems (*J*, XIX. 251, and see 252). Bodies of the dead are gilded (*J*, XIX. 260). Ceremonial is golden, as when'Long lines of yellow-robed monks sweep past in procession bearing, amidst a glitter of gold and jewels, and with royal pomp, a sacred image or relic from one shrine to another' (*J*, XIX. 254). Early Buddhism may have been simpler and less ornate, but it developed sumptuously. In a BBC production, *The World About Us* (17 June 1979), we were shown a Buddhist monastic community in the Himalayas. The robes of the monks and ceremonial insignia gave a massed impression of the golden. It is the same with Timon: both before and after his retirement, the play glitters with gold. In both, an inward meaning expresses itself in golden terms.

I have before now written of Timon as confronting society by two positive powers: first his naked body, that is, essential humanity; and second, by his new-found gold. These two I have grouped together, speaking of the 'golden powers of the human form' (*Christ and Nietzsche*, VI. 228). His loin-cloth can be supplemented by a gold cord. Under lights, with suntan or make-up, his body can, and should, look golden. For a darker coloured Indian this may not be possible; golden or orange garments serve instead, with other decorations. It may seem that the Greek feeling for the body is absent; the Greeks have been called the first people to see significance in the human form, and yet it appears that Indian art could do that too.

Buddhism has a name, Bodhisattva, for 'one who is on the way to the perfect attainment of knowledge, a future Buddha' (S. Radhakrishnan, *Indian Philosophy*, 1923, revised 1929; X, 600). A chapter of *The Three Jewels* entitled 'The Glorious Company of Bodhisattvas' contains an interesting description of Arahants (= Worthy Ones; *J*, XV. 151) and Bodhisattvas:

Iconographically the 1250 Arahants are depicted as elderly shaven-headed monks, clad in yellow robes and holding a begging-bowl or a staff; they stand stiffly, with compressed lips, and their attitude seems not altogether free from strain. The Bodhisattvas, by way of contrast, are all beautiful young princes. Gem-studded tiaras sparkle on their brows, while their nobly proportioned limbs are clad in light diaphanous garments of coloured silk. They wear gold bracelets and strings of jewels, and round their necks hang garlands of fragrant flowers. Their expression is smiling, their poses graceful and easy. (*J*, XVI. 168)

'These splendours' symbolise 'spiritual riches'. We are to 'keep steadily in view the transcendental insight' by which 'the glorious figure of the Bodhisattva stands as against a background of gold' (*J*, XVI. 174). The term Bodhisattva seems to be used for both earthly devotees and transcendental saints. One important Bodhisattva may be variously depicted, but 'usually he manifests as a beautiful youth, sixteen years old, golden in hue, richly clad in the silks and ornaments of a Bodhisattva and wearing at the parting of his hair and over his ears three blue lotuses' (*J*, XVI. 190). A Bodhisattva's well known image 'is that of a slenderly built young prince in a high jewelled headdress who, with body gracefully bent, stands bearing a lotus in his left hand and making the gesture of bestowing alms with the right, while his beautiful face is alive with tenderness and compassion' (*J*, XVI. 193). These are to be understood as imaginative and spiritualised conceptions.

In the first passage we have a contrast of world-weary age, and the seraphic ideal such as I have shown as percolating throughout British drama in *The Golden Labyrinth;* and it appears to be equally active in the East. In the West it descends from the Greek, where we have a contrast of the ill-favoured yet spiritually attuned Socrates and his visual ideal of youth as described in the *Phaedrus* and the *Symposium*. We have the same balance in Shakespeare's Sonnets, wherein the poet is depicted as old (Sonnet 73) and sees his ideal as a youth, who is addressed, as Leslie Hotson has argued (*Mr. W.H.*, i.e., *Master W.H.*, II. 26–41), not as a young lord but as a sovereign. In two of our Buddhist quotations the Bodhisattvas appear as princes.

Timon of Athens derives from the same life-view as the Sonnets. Together, as I have argued in 'New Light on the Sonnets' in *Shakespeare and Religion* (XX), they may be regarded as Shakespeare's main personal statements. *Timon* is dated about 1608, near the year that the Sonnets (which were probably composed much earlier, though they may have been revised) were published. Both are concerned with male friendship, the female sex being less pleasantly treated, as with the Dark Lady and Sonnet 129 on lust; and, in *Timon,* the ladies who accompany Alcibiades, called 'whores' (IV. iii. 140). Before that, we have only the Amazons of the Masque. Timon himself, we may assume, had not been sexually involved; he is probably conceived as bisexual, and once called a 'Phoenix' (II. i. 32). Lusts are, in both works, repudiated, and women regarded, as in so much Oriental thought, as a danger. In *Timon* the whores are told to 'burn' men with their 'fire' as a punishment for their general sins (IV. iii. 140–4); fire being strangely used, since water imagery is more usual for sexual lusts; but it conforms to the Buddha's fire sermon, which is primarily attacking *mental* lust, where fire imagery is more appropriate. The Buddha was averse from admitting women to his Order. There are, nevertheless, Buddhist nuns to balance male communities; the main concern is – as too in Christianity – for devotees of either sex to keep clear of sexual temptation. Sexual feeling in both the Sonnets and *Timon of Athens* conforms to Buddhist practice.

But what of the Buddhist command that we should exercise compassion? How does that compare with Timon's invectives? Timon's first long soliloquy after the crash, with its nihilistic repudiations of 'the whole race of mankind' (IV. i. 1–40), harking back to Ulysses' 'order' speech in *Troilus and Cressida* (I. iii. 109–24), is a passionate realisation, at once condemnation and abandoned evocation, of human iniquity. It is, we must suppose, ironic; but there is more than irony to it; the passionate diatribe is far from easy to explain.

The key perhaps lies in its passion. Timon's long interview with Apemantus (IV. iii. 198–398) registers his disgust at any settled and rational negations, unpowered by the heart. His complaint throughout is that without the heart's gold man is doomed. For Timon even war, terrible though it be, is not the worst; as with the whores, it is to be viewed in terms of a vicious race. Though in the past he had been a fine soldier himself, he now addresses Alcibiades and his childish war ritual with scorn: 'I prithee, beat thy drum, and get thee gone' (IV. iii. 96). Hearing that he wars against Athens, Timon replies:

> The gods confound them all in thy conquest
> And thee after, when thou hast conquer'd.

Alcibiades: Why me, Timon?
Timon: That, by killing of villains thou wast born to
> conquer my country:
> Put up thy gold – go on – here's gold – go on.
> Be as a planetary plague, when Jove
> Will o'er some high-vic'd city hang his poison
> In the sick air: let not thy sword skip one.
> Pity not honour'd age for his white beard...
> Put armour on thine ears and on thine eyes
> Whose proof nor yells of mothers, maids nor babes
> Nor sight of priests in holy vestments bleeding
> Shall pierce a jot. There's gold to pay thy soldiers.
> Make large confusion; and thy fury spent
> Confounded be thyself!
> (IV. iii. 104–29)

A strange speech. Timon, like a Hebrew prophet, sees war as God's justice on man's vice; but he blames equally the conqueror and the conquered, with a universal condemnation; and, while saying all this, there is pity active within, or beneath, his phrases. Pity and horror; what else could have composed the thought, 'nor sight of priests in holy vestments bleeding'?

When the Senators at the end come to Timon imploring his help as a saviour, he turns them down:

> But if he sack fair Athens
> And take our goodly aged men by the beards,
> Giving our holy virgins to the stain
> Of contumelious, beastly, mad-brain'd war,
> Then let him know, and tell him Timon speaks it,

> In pity of our aged and our youth,
> I cannot choose but tell him that I care not,
> And let him take't at worst.
>   (V. i. 176–83)

Here again there is horror: the words 'fair', 'goodly', 'holy', 'pity' are balanced against 'contumelious, beastly, mad-brain'd war'. The lines are fraught with pity, agonised pity; but Timon does not give way to it; he speaks 'in pity' but yet as a voice *above* pity; at the end he is said, by Alcibiades, to have *scorned* human tears, as from a higher dimension (V. iv. 76–8). After giving gold to Flavius, he adds:

> Go, live rich and happy,
> But thus condition'd: thou shalt build from men;
> Hate all, curse all, show charity to none,
> But let the famish'd flesh slide from the bone
> Ere thou relieve the beggar.
>   (IV. iii. 534–8)

Again, the lines hold compassion: only compassion could have made them. Within this very hate of mankind burns a love, more infectious than many sermons; and this, and not the supposed argument, gets across; to us, as to Alcibiades and the Thieves, who, as I have already noted, are charmed to mildness, overpowered as by magic.

One way, not exactly to explain the paradox, but to understand what is going on, is to adduce the example of Nietzsche. In *Thus Spake Zarathustra,* we are told that 'God hath died of his pity for men', and that 'all great love is raised above its pity; for it seeketh to *create* that which it loveth' (*Zarathustra*, 'Of the Compassionate', II. 3). 'As deep as man looketh into life, so deep he looketh into suffering'; 'courage' is needed (III. 2). 'Compassion' is regarded as Zarathustra's 'last sin', and is at the conclusion surmounted (IV. 20). Nietzsche knew only too well what compassion was, and what he could counsel as a prophet he could not live as a man; his first overt action of so-called insanity was his bursting into tears and embracing a horse that was being brutally ill-treated. Honesty is needed. Sanity depends on the surmounting of pity. Even Timon's lines to Flavius make good sense when we think of the thousands who starve or the animals suffering in laboratories, while we are carefree. We forget. Perhaps we are right to forget; otherwise, as Nietzsche did, we might go mad.

In Buddhism striving for enlightenment comes first, and then compassion; as in the New Testament's two commandments, reverence to God precedes love of man (Matthew, XXII. 36–40; Mark, XII. 28–31). *Timon of Athens* is, it is true, more drastic. Its attacks are nearer the Hebraic than the Buddhist, though even so scarcely approaching the terrifying threatenings of Ezekiel in the Old Testament. Buddhism is more passive, more pacific. In drama, however, we must have the main thrust isolated and defined through opposition. Timon's curses are as near to compassion as is safe; more, and there would be no detonation; we should be left with a moral sermon. It is for the actor to decide how much irony his voice should reflect. Timon's words must always be felt as part only of the whole visual impact, including his naked power and god-given gold. And he ends more serenely:

> Commend me to them;
> And tell them that, to ease them of their griefs,
> Their fears of hostile strokes, their aches, losses,
> Their pangs of love, with other incident throes
> That nature's fragile vessel doth sustain
> In life's uncertain voyage, I will some kindness do them;
> I'll teach them to prevent wild Alcibiades' wrath.
> (V. i. 202–8)

His solution is suicide, as in Hamlet's 'To be or not to be' soliloquy, where we also hear of 'pangs of dispriz'd love' (III. i. 72).

Timon means this, for others and for himself. A true Bodhisattva, filled with compassion, defines life's sufferings:

I have made the vow to save all beings. All beings I must set free. The whole world of living beings I must rescue, from the terrors of birth, of old age, of sickness, of death and rebirth, of all kinds of moral offence, of all states of woe, of the whole cycle of birth-and-death, of the jungle of false views, of the loss of wholesome dharmas (i.e. doctrine), of the concomitants of ignorance – from all these terrors I must rescue all beings .... I walk so that the kingdom of unsurpassed cognition is built up for all beings. (*J*, XVI. 172)

The tone of this is less hard than Timon's offer, but in both there is an equivalent rejection. Buddhism, I take it, disapproves of suicide, though, if death were annihilation, its logic would, as Hamlet says, be evident. Radhakrishnan writes: 'In the whole history of thought no one has painted the misery of human existence in blacker colours and with more feeling than Buddha' (*Indian Philosophy* VII. 362). Existence is bad, so we must surpass existence. The difference is that Timon reacts with defiance and Buddhism with acceptance.

Timon, bound for death, wishes to be buried by the sea:

> Then, Timon, presently prepare thy grave.
> Lie where the light foam of the sea may beat
> Thy grave-stone daily. Make thine epitaph
> That death in me at others' lives may laugh.
> (IV. iii. 380–3)

The elemental powers of sun, moon and earth are emphatic in the later acts, but the sea, acting as a symbol of an expanse beyond living, is yet more important. Death is a happiness in which Timon can mock at life; it is like the Nirvana of Buddhism.

What is this Nirvana? An interesting analogy appears in John Cowper Powys's *Rodmoor*. The hero, Adrian, is composing a book on destruction as the key to existence. Death's 'nothingness' is the name for 'What lies beyond life', where life becomes 'nothing'. It is 'as a blinding white light', or rather neither light nor darkness, but just 'cool and deep and empty'. There he will be united with its 'angel', the book's idealised youth, Baptiste (XXI. 324–6). Adrian dies by the sea, like Timon, in a dream 'of white mists and white vapours and the reflection of white stars in dark waters'; moving towards an elemental infinitude beyond both life and death, a 'Nothingness' that is an 'escape', dwarfing humanity and its gods. He cries 'Baptiste', and dies (XXVII. 456–8).

Powys's thought here corresponds closely to what Buddhist philosophy calls Nirvana. Nirvana is a paradoxical and ambiguous concept. The Buddha is reported in W.Y. Evans-Wentz's *The Tibetan Book of the Dead* as saying:

There is, disciples, a Realm devoid of earth and water, fire and air. It is not endless space, nor infinite thought, nor nothingness, neither ideas nor non-ideas. Not this world nor that is it. I call it neither a coming nor a departing, nor a standing still, nor death, nor birth; it is without a basis, progress, or a stay; it is the ending of sorrow. (3rd edn, 1957; Introduction, XII. 68)

In it 'the false powers of the finite mind cease to exist' and 'the natural forces of the True Reality alone work' (Addenda, 'Reality', 226). It would seem to be variously regarded as personal and impersonal. The negative emphasis is sometimes strong, and after ploughing through the various ambiguities of Radhakrishnan's *Indian Philosophy,* the mind is often baffled. There is one firm and comforting statement, that 'to think that Nirvana is annihilation is according to Buddha "a wicked heresy"' (Part II, VII. 449–50). We do best to rely on symbols, such as the sea in Shakespeare and Powys, for the ocean of being. Sangharakshita refers to 'the infinite ocean of Nirvana' (*J,* XIII. 124), and when he says, 'Nirvana is the Cool Cave, the Island in the Floods, the Farther Shore, the Holy City' (*J,* XIV. 144), or refers to the 'cool shade of the rose-apple tree, aloof from pleasures of the senses' (*J,* XIII. 119), the phraseology recalls Powys.

So much by way of introduction to what I take to be the one perfect expression of what is, or should be, meant by Nirvana. It is Timon's

> My long sickness
> Of health and living now begins to mend,
> And nothing brings me all things.
> (V. i. 191–3)

Never was the paradox more crisply and comprehensively, and here without any reliance on symbolism, stated. Not a word too many, and yet it is all there. Though in perfect 'health', Timon knows that, because 'living', he is sick. Life now 'begins to mend'; it is a gradual unfurling towards a beyond–life maturity. No exact cause of his death is stated. Death is, as in Powys, a 'nothing'; and yet it somehow 'brings *me*', personal advantage being involved, 'all things'. Much depends on the ending. How different this is from Richard II's at first sight similar

> Nor I nor any man that but man is
> With nothing shall be pleas'd till he be eas'd
> With being nothing.
>   (V. v. 39–41)

The important ending here is negative; in Timon, positive.[4]
Whatever Nirvana is, it must have an over-balance of the
positive or it could hardly exert so universal an appeal. And it
must be, surely, in some undefinable way, personal.

Timon's statement is a simple unit. Later, we return to
ocean symbolism:

> Come not to me again, but say to Athens,
> Timon hath made his everlasting mansion
> Upon the beached verge of the salt flood,
> Who once a day with his embossed froth
> The turbulent surge shall cover. Thither come
> And let my grave-stone be your oracle.
> Lips, let sour words go by and language end:
> What is amiss, plague and infection mend!
> Graves only be men's works and death their gain!
> Sun, hide thy beams! Timon hath done his reign.
>   (V. i. 219–28)

Timon has now done with bitterness and with 'words'. For
all that is 'amiss', for all the ills of mortal flesh deplored by
Buddhism, let man's ailments be the natural remedy. Making
graves is his best activity and death the final reward. Let the
sun be obscured: sense-perception is blacked out as, like
Antony in *Antony and Cleopatra,* 'O sun, thy uprise shall I see
no more' (IV. x. 31), Timon leaves the manifested creation
for the mystery. Since he broke from the riot of the five
senses, from hearing, taste, touch, smell and sight (I. ii.
131–5), and all human conviviality and social pleasure, it has
been a straight progress, 'an eagle flight, bold and forth on' (I,
i. 50), of ever more total rejection in one who is 'no. idle
votarist' (IV, iii. 27); through nature, nakedness and the
elements, to the non-perceptual and all-embracing finality
crowning existence.

I have not attempted a complete review of *Timon of Athens,*
and still less of the manifold ramifications of Buddhism, for
which, anyway, I lack qualification. I have merely noted

some points of contact. The Buddhist doctrine of compassion is no more than implicit in Timon, while Buddhism correspondingly lacks the dramatic impact of Hebrew prophecy and Christianity. *Timon of Athens* might be called a blend of Buddhism and the Hebraic: its Hebraic affinities are noted in my essay 'Isaiah in Renaissance Dress' (p. 69 above). Certainly in no other Shakespearian work do we find so sustained and comprehensive a philosophy. Shakespeare may have been uneasy about the attempt, leaving it unrevised with loose ends, which however matter little. Timon forecasts Byron's life, as I have shown in *Byron and Shakespeare*. His end resembles that of Oedipus in Sophocles' *Oedipus at Colonus;* in both the magical hero endures a mysterious dissolution or ascension that is not fully explained. The causes of Timon's death and burial are of set purpose left mysterious, the soldier who finds his tomb remarking:

> Timon is dead who hath outstretch'd his span;
> Some beast rear'd this; here does not live a man.
> (V. iii. 3–4)

I here follow Warburton's emended reading.

As for Timon's three lines on death, they may be called our one supreme expression of the central enigma not alone of Buddhism but of religious inquiry throughout the human race.

Additional Note

Nirvana cannot be defined verbally but something of it may be acted. My own performance of Timon's death in my dramatic recital is described in *Shakespeare's Dramatic Challenge* (1977, 163–5). I now have an improved variation, dating from 1979.

No sex-covering is worn. After 'Let my grave-stone be your oracle', Timon starts to turn up stage, and during the turn loosens his loin-cloth while speaking the words 'Lips, let sour words go by and language end' (no *words* can really describe what is being visually enacted). At 'What is amiss, plague and infection mend', he waves it triumphantly in his left hand, and throws it down. At the following 'Graves only be men's works and death their gain!' his hands are out to the ocean, and come back on his eyes at 'Sun, hide thy beams.' From this back view no sex-covering is needed and so there is no elastic waistband to obtrude. This was my original reason for the variation, which is certainly an improvement. The fade-out and rising surf are as before, the sound blending finally into an ever-so-faint suggestion of melody.

For a comparison and in part contrast of my reading of Timon's end with the Crucifix in Christianity, see *Shakespeare's Dramatic Challenge,* 165–6; also my Postscript to the American edition of *Symbol of Man* (University Press of America, 1981). In the latter, this Shakespearian climax is also elaborately discussed as a profound and universal example of 'transition', as defined on p. xvi above.

Notes

[1] My quotation avoids engaging in the crux, 'wax' or 'tax' in line 48. For a commentary see the Penguin edition (149–50) ed. G.R. Hibbard, noting especially his reference to *As You Like It* (II. vii. 70–87).

[2] Many of my quotations are drawn from Maha Sthavira Sangharakshita's fascinating book, *The Three Jewels:* an Introduction to Buddhism (Windhorse Publications, 119 Roman Road, London E2, 1977; first published by Rider (1967), under the author's name 'Bhikshu Sangharak-shita (Sthavira)'. My references apply to the second edition (1977), after the letter *J*.

I am most grateful to the author for granting me permission to quote from the work.

The volume was presented to me by the Friends of the Western Buddhist Order (Surrey) at Purley, after a performance arranged for them of my 'Shakespeare's Dramatic Challenge' (20 May 1979). This chapter originated from impressions received during this performance and was written in gratitude for their, and Mr Stephen Parr's, kindness.

[3] The Oxford edition accepts the emendation 'moss'd' for the Folio's 'moyst', which elsewhere in Shakespeare carries only the modern connotation, but here scarcely relevant. For a close comparison similarly associating 'moss'd' with age, we may adduce *As You Like It*, IV. iii. 106: 'Under an oak whose boughs were moss'd with age.' See also *Titus Andronicus*, II. iii. 94–5:

> The trees, though summer, yet forlorn and lean,
> O'ercome with moss and baleful mistletoe...

In the eighteenth century, Walter Whiter, *A Specimen of a Commentary on Shakespeare* (ed. Alan Over and Mary Bell, London 1967) gives reasons for accepting 'moyst'. John Lawlor, *The Tragic Sense of Shakespeare*, 1960, 131 ff., defends 'moist', the reading adopted by Peter Alexander's edition.

[4] 'Nothing' in Shakespeare may hold deep meanings. In *Richard II* it is used for an indefinable foreboding (II. ii. 9–40); in *A Midsummer Night's Dream* for what is behind poetic composition (V. i. 16). See *The Sovereign Flower*, Shakespearian Themes, B, VI, 317. The word's ubiquitous use as witnessed by a Concordance, is itself significant. For Powys's use, see my *The Saturnian Quest*, Index C, 'Nothingness'.

VII Visual Art in Kyd and Shakespeare

I

Thomas Kyd's *The Spanish Tragedy* has much in common with Shakespeare's *Titus Andronicus,* and indeed with Shakespeare in general. It has the same surge and subsidence of passion in a blank verse of Shakespearian affinity. The tone is Shakespearian as Marlowe's never is. It dates from about 1588, but in 1602 certain additions, mainly concerning visual art, were made to the text. For them there is some faint evidence of Ben Jonson's authorship; but Charles Lamb thought otherwise, and suggested Webster. Coleridge thought they must have been by Shakespeare. Francis Berry, in his *The Shakespeare Inset; Word and Picture* (1965, USA 1971; VIII, 132), refers to the 'superbly fine' additions to the text. He writes well on Kyd's visual artistry throughout, seeing to it 'that something was visually happening all the time, that the stage-picture was continually changing' (III. 33). In these additions the dialogue with the Painter, our present concern, stands out powerfully. (Act and scene are given in the Temple Dramatists edition, Dent, ed. J. Schick, 1926, as III. 12A. In the following pages I give line references only.)

Distraught by the murder of his son, who had been found stabbed and left hanging on a tree, Hieronimo, now standing by that tree, hears of a Painter's approach.

> Bid him come in and paint some comfort,
> For surely there's none lives but painted comfort.
> (74–5)

Painting is to act as a 'comfort'. He hears that the Painter's son had also been murdered, and we have a fascinating dialogue. The problem posed by it is that of Lessing's *Laocoon,* weighing the rival attributes, kinetic and motionless, of poetry and painting. Hieronimo wishes that the terrible discovery of his son's murder should be given permanence in art. This will serve as a comfort, presumably as an eternalising of his grief, as verbal description cannot. The story is to be established in a series of picturings done, for depth, in rich oils. 'Come,' he says, 'let's talk wisely now' (104): which implies that Hieronimo's words are to involve a deep meaning. Then, with reference to the Painter's own dead son:

Hieronimo:	How dost take it? art thou not sometimes mad? Is there no tricks that comes before thine eyes?
Painter:	O Lord, yes, sir. (106–8)

Hieronimo has moments of vision ('tricks'), which may be madness, but as the dialogue progresses, assume method. Such moments he wishes recaptured.

Hieronimo:	Art a painter? Canst paint me a tear, or a wound, a groan, or a sigh? Canst paint me such a tree as this?
	(109–10)

Hieronimo wishes to include sounds, but finds they cannot be actualised in paint.

Hieronimo:	Look you, sir, do you see, I'd have you paint me for my gallery, in your oil-colours matted, and draw me five years younger than I am – do ye see, sir, let five years go; let them go like the marshal of Spain – my wife Isabella standing by me, with a speaking look to my son Horatio, which should intend to this or some such-like purpose: 'God bless thee, my sweet son'; and my hand leaning upon his head, thus, sir; do you see? – may it be done?
Painter:	Very well, sir,
Hieronimo:	Nay, I pray, mark me, sir: then, sir, would I have you paint me this tree, this very tree. Canst paint a doleful cry?
Painter:	Seemingly, sir.

Hieronimo: Nay, it should cry; but all is one. Well, sir, paint me a youth run through and through with villains' swords, hanging upon this tree. Canst thou draw a murderer?

Painter: I'll warrant you, sir; I have the pattern of the most notorious villains that ever lived in all Spain.

Hieronimo: O, let them be worse, worse: stretch thine art, and let their beards be of Judas his own colour; and let their eye-brows jutty over: in any case observe that. Then, sir, after some violent noise, bring me forth in my shirt, and my gown under mine arm, with my torch in my hand, and my sword reared up thus, and with these words:
      'What noise is this? who calls Hieronimo?'
      May it be done?

Painter: Yea, sir.
      (114 ff)

The 'doleful cry' can only be done 'seemingly', though Hieronimo wants art to match life itself. Then:

Hieronimo: Well, sir; then bring me forth, bring me through alley and alley, still with a distracted countenance going along, and let my hair heave up my nightcap. Let the clouds scowl, make the moon dark, the stars extinct, the winds blowing, the bells tolling, the owls shrieking, the toads croaking, the minutes jarring, and the clock striking twelve. And then at last, sir, starting, behold a man hanging, and tottering and tottering, as you know the wind will wave a man, and I with a trice to cut him down. And looking upon him by the advantage of my torch, find it to be my son Horatio. There you may show a passion, there you may show a passion! Draw me like old Priam of Troy, crying: 'The house is a-fire, the house is a-fire, as the torch over my head!' Make me curse, make me rave, make me cry, make me mad, make me well again, make me curse hell, invoke heaven, and in the end leave me in a trance – and so forth.

Painter: And is this the end?

Hieronimo: O no, there is no end: the end is death and madness! As I am never better than when I am mad: then methinks I am a brave fellow; then I do wonders: but reason abuseth me, and there's the torment, there's the hell. At the last, sir, bring me to one of the murderers; were he as strong as Hector, thus would I tear and drag him up and down.
      (145 ff)

In his madness or semi-madness he attacks the Painter. He here admits to madness which he had earlier denied, but claims to be 'better' when mad. From madness these speeches are composed. If he is really 'better', then there must be some sense in it. There must be some meaning conveyed apart from sounds. What he seems to be searching for is that which makes of pictorial art a consolation; it cannot be described in words; it can only be shown. Somehow it is to be a *living* transcending of actuality. There must be a truth here, otherwise how can we account for the extraordinary prices paid for some great master's work? There must be some instinct in us recognising, however dimly, that the picture is a kind of telescope through which some further dimension of existence is focused.

Whoever composed these passages, and they certainly do not feel like Jonson's, they go deep, and may serve as an introduction to Shakespeare's handling of visual artistry.

II

At first sight we might accuse Shakespeare of a limitation in that his normal view of painting is limited to realistic imitation; but I think this accusation arises from a limitation of our own. Consider Bassanio's reaction to Portia's portrait in *The Merchant of Venice:*

Bassanio: What find I here?
           Fair Portia's counterfeit! What demi-god
           Hath come so near creation? Move these eyes?
           Or whether, riding on the balls of mine,
           Seem they in motion? Here are sever'd lips,
           Parted with sugar breath: so sweet a bar
           Should sunder such sweet friends. Here in her hairs
           The painter plays the spider, and hath woven
           A golden mesh to entrap the hearts of men,
           Faster than gnats in cobwebs: but her eyes –
           How could he see to do them? having made one,
           Methinks it should have power to steal both his
           And leave itself unfurnish'd. Yet look, how far
           The substance of my praise doth wrong this shadow
           In underprizing it, so far this shadow
           Doth limp behind the substance.
                        (III. ii. 114–29)

The artist must have been a 'demi-god', creating life itself. Bassanio thinks of an exact copy, but one really quite impossible. The eyes move. Is it through Bassanio's own seeing? They certainly 'seem' in motion, and even 'breath' is half-felt. The copy finally fails, since it is only a 'shadow' of the 'substance' (for 'shadow', compare *A Midsummer Night's Dream* V. i. 215–17, 'The best in this kind'; also *Antony and Cleopatra,* V. ii. 97–100, 'Nature wants stuff', discussed in *The Imperial Theme,* VII. 260). There is a desire to get more from painting than painting can give: the picture aims at, but cannot quite achieve, life itself. This is far from any contentment with a mere photographic exactitude. Warm life itself is glimpsed, through art. The poetry attempts to say this, as best it may.

In so crucial a matter as the balance of visual artistry and poetic description we turn naturally to Shakespeare's one self-consciously philosophic drama, *Timon of Athens.*[1] The play opens with a discussion between a Poet and a Painter. The Poet is meditating on a poem he has composed, reading to himself the lines:

> When we for recompense have praised the vile,
> It stains the glory in that happy verse
> Which aptly sings the good.
> (I. i. 15–17)

He firmly repudiates flattery. Their dialogue is fascinating. We observe that each is diffident regarding his own work. The Poet says it came 'idly' or spontaneously, arising, as Keats said poetry should, 'as naturally as the leaves to a tree' (to John Taylor, 27 February 1818). Shakespeare uses a similar metaphor. It 'oozes' like a gum, being self-nourished from an undefined source, stimulating 'itself':

> *Poet:*   A thing slipp'd idly from me.
> Our poesy is as a gum, which oozes
> From whence 'tis nourish'd: the fire i' the flint
> Shows not till it be struck; our gentle flame
> Provokes itself, and like the current flies
> Each bound it chafes.
> (I. i. 20–5)

He asks to see the Painter's picture, which, though the artist himself is suitably diffident, he praises highly:

Poet: Let's see your piece.
Painter: 'Tis a good piece.
Poet: So 'tis: this comes off well and excellent.
Painter: Indifferent.
Poet: Admirable: how this grace
Speaks his own standing! What a mental power
This eye shoots forth! how big imagination
Moves in this lip! to the dumbness of the gesture
One might interpret.
         (I. i. 28–36)

Its poise 'speaks'. Its 'dumbness' invites verbal interpretation. There seems a 'mental power' in the eye 'shooting' rays of thought; and 'imagination' is conveyed by the 'lip', as though on the brink of utterance. To the Poet, adept in words, there is naturally a desire for verbal interpretation.

The Painter, secure in his non-verbal accomplishment, can afford to be objective and technical:

Painter: It is a pretty mocking of the life.
Here is a touch; is't good?
Poet: I'll say of it,
It tutors nature: artificial strife
Lives in these touches, livelier than life.
         (I. i. 36–40)

The art shows a dramatic interplay ('artificial strife'; for 'strive' applied to art, see *Cymbeline,* II. iv. 73). The Poet sees it as going beyond life, adding a dimension, as great art should, to appearance. But the lines mean rather more than any usual respect to genius. The picture is not only factually true, like a photograph, nor just profoundly infused by genius, but seems actually and immediately and dramatically living, with a life 'livelier than life', surpassing Portia's life-like portrait. Painting is regarded as taking us beyond actuality. Such a mad, non-rational apprehension was perhaps behind Hieronimo's wish to have his grief represented. There are no words really to express what is meant.

The Poet next describes his poem. Though he had said it

came 'idly', it is clearly a considered work, aimed at Timon,
even though he claims now that it is impersonal:

Poet: My free drift
                Halts not particularly, but moves itself
                In a wide sea of wax:² no levell'd malice
                Infects one comma in the course I hold;
                But flies an eagle flight, bold and forth on,
                Leaving no tract behind.
                        (I. i. 46–51)

The emphasis is on freedom and power. His further
description arouses the Painter's interest in its pictorial
possibilities:

Poet: Sir, I have upon a high and pleasant hill
                Feign'd Fortune to be throned: the base o' the mount
                Is rank'd with all deserts, all kind of natures,
                That labour on the bosom of this sphere
                To propagate their states: amongst them all,
                Whose eyes are on this sovereign lady fix'd,
                One do I personate of Lord Timon's frame,
                Whom Fortune with her ivory hand wafts to her;
                Whose present grace to present slaves and servants
                Translates his rivals.
Painter: 'Tis conceived to scope.
                This throne, this Fortune, and this hill, methinks,
                With one man beckon'd from the rest below,
                Bowing his head against the steepy mount
                To climb his happiness, would be well express'd
                In our condition.
Poet: Nay, sir, but hear me on.
                        (I. i. 64–78)

Being now excited by his own narrative, the Poet is
impatient at interruption. After he has described his hero's
tragic fall, deserted by his former friends and dependants, the
Painter comments, rather unkindly:

Painter: 'Tis common.
                A thousand moral paintings I can show,
                That shall demonstrate these quick blows of Fortune's
                More pregnantly than words. Yet you do well
                To show Lord Timon that mean eyes have seen
                The foot above the head.
                        (I.i. 90–5)

The balance of the two is neatly held. At first they are diffident, but when their professional pride is in question there is some opposition. The Painter is right to claim that there is a fine opportunity for visual artistry in depiction of Fortune enthroned; he is rather discourteous with his 'thousand moral paintings'; but finally agrees that the Poet has done a reasonable and useful job.

When the Poet and Painter reappear in Act IV, they are there to be satirised and may be regarded as almost different persons. The Poet, we remember, had earlier been at pains to disclaim flattery. Timon's view of humanity has suffered a complete reversal, and their later presentation is, for our present purpose, irrelevant.

The Poet's description of Fortune suggests visual art. So, after their fashion, do the three Apparitions in *Macbeth*. They are raised in a kind of materialisation séance by the Witches, or Weird Sisters. Their appearance is striking: an Armed Head, a Bloody Child, and a Child crowned with a Tree in his Hand. Their symbolic meanings go deep, as I have shown in *The Shakespearian Tempest* and *The Christian Renaissance,* signifying Death, Conflict and Life Triumphant. In stage performance they should be given exact visual attention. It is to be observed that Macbeth makes a mistake usual in us all in such matters of being more responsive to their words than to their appearance; attending to their speech without being aware of what we see. There is a lesson for us here.

Not until the last plays do we have a full development of visual artistry. As I show in *The Crown of Life, Pericles* has a pervading and elaborately presented use of the visual in ceremonial, a memorial statue, and Marina's embroidery. Once the statuesque attains direct spiritual power. The newly-discovered Marina is to Pericles as a 'palace' wherein 'crowned Truth' dwells (V. i. 123). She is like a statue:

> Thou dost look
> Like Patience gazing on kings' graves, and smiling
> Extremity out of act.
> (V. i. 139–41)

That is, victorious over tragedy in happy assurance, so rendering 'extremity', which suggests compactly long ages

of extreme suffering, futile; as in Pericles' later words, on
finding Thaisa:

> No more, you gods! Your present kindness
> Makes my past miseries sport.
>   (V. iii. 40–1)

With Pericles' words on 'Patience' we may compare Viola's
less powerful description in *Twelfth Night* of her supposed
sister sitting 'like Patience on a monument, smiling at grief'
(II. iv. 116). In *The Crown of Life* I have adduced other
relevant comparisons.

Pericles' lines on 'Patience' may be compared with Byron's
even more powerfully compacted, 'Love watching Madness
with unalterable mien' (*Childe Harold,* IV, 69–72; *Poets of
Action,* V. 193).

III

In *Pericles,* Shakespeare is as a moth nearing the candle of a
fascinating, but artistically dangerous attempt at actually
dramatising the union of art with that which is beyond art. In
The Winter's Tale he plunges boldly ahead. In the flower-
dialogue in Act III, nature and human art are exactly
balanced. Perdita supports nature, but Polixenes argues that
human artistry is itself part of nature:

> This is an art
> Which does mend nature, change it rather, but
> The art itself is nature.
>   (IV. iii. 95–7)

With Hermione's statue we are on more difficult ground. It is
described by one of the Gentlemen, who serve as a kind of
chorus:

Third Gentleman: The Princess hearing of her mother's statue, which
                      is in the keeping of Paulina, a piece many years in
                      doing and now newly performed by that rare Italian
                      master, Julio Romano, who, had he himself eterni-
                      ty and could put breath into his work, would
                      beguile Nature of her custom, so perfectly he is her

ape: he so near to Hermione hath done Hermione,
that they say one would speak to her and stand in
hope of answer. Thither with all greediness of
affection are they gone, and there they intend to
sup.

Second Gentleman: I thought she had some great matter there in hand;
for she hath privately twice or thrice a day, ever
since the death of Hermione, visited that removed
house. Shall we thither and with our company piece
the rejoicing?

First Gentleman: Who would be thence that has the benefit of access?
Every wink of an eye, some new grace will be
born.

(V. ii. 105 ff)

There are hints of Paulina's visits to a living Hermione, yet it
is also clearly asserted by the Gentleman functioning as choric
commentator that, though the piece has been many years in
the making, it has now been finally perfected by the brilliant
Italian sixteenth century executant, Julio Romano. The glar-
ing anachronism may perhaps be attributed to Shakespeare's
passionate engagement at this moment with the actuality of
the art in question.

The description follows Shakespeare's earlier handling in
The Merchant of Venice and *Timon of Athens*. The work is a
near perfect replica of Nature ('her ape'), lacking only
'breath'; which recalls the 'breath' of Portia's portrait. It is so
vivid, you expect her to talk. It is art, but more than what we
expect of art: in such passages Shakespeare is again expecting
an art beyond all reason.

Paulina is equally high in her valuation:

> As she liv'd peerless
> So her dead likeness, I do well believe,
> Excels whatever yet you look'd upon
> Or hand of man hath done; therefore I keep it
> Lonely, apart. But here it is: prepare
> To see the life as lively mock'd as ever
> Still sleep mock'd death: behold: and say 'tis well.
>
> (V. iii. 14–20)

It is unique, beyond what the 'hand of man' has hitherto
accomplished, almost supernatural; and therefore Paulina has

preserved it secretly. The last lines are difficult. Does 'mock'd' imply scorn or does it simply imply resemblance ? Both uses of the word are Shakespearian. Either way the sense is clear. The statue's livingness surpasses life, as the Poet in *Timon* said of the Painter's picture, calling it 'livelier than life' (p. 97 above). It resembles the relation of sleep to death, as observed in *Measure for Measure* (III. i. 17–19) and *Macbeth* (II. iii. 83). Sleep has a dimension of livingness above death; therefore the statue has a dimension of livingness beyond life. It represents a greater life. This is what the words appear to say.

I have hitherto reviewed the mystical properties of *The Winter's Tale* in relation to Shakespeare's progression in dramatic composition and insight; here for the first time I am highlighting references drawn from his thoughts on the visual arts. Those, in so far as they suggest that fine artistry comes near to self-transcendence by creating a life-reality beyond art or even, as in *Timon of Athens,* life itself, are clear pointers to the complex development we are discussing. They tread the borderline of mysticism or miracle.

But we may also suppose that Hermione may have been living throughout. The Gentleman refers to Paulina's visits, and we hear later, as though to suit this supposition, that Hermione's present age has been taken into account by the sculptor:

> *Leontes:*   But yet, Paulina,
> Hermione was not so much wrinkled; nothing
> So aged as this seems.
> *Paulina:* So much the more our carver's excellence;
> Which lets go by some sixteen years and makes her
> As she lived now.
>   (V. iii. 27–32)

If Paulina has been making all this up to deceive there would be no further problem. Hermione looks older simply because she is older. Our laboured speeches on artistry, which we thought so important, would then have to be regarded as irrelevant. Little of the drama's power would be left.

We have another, third, choice. Paulina, at Hermione's original collapse, swore that she was unquestionably dead

(III. ii. 204–8). Antigonus's dream of Hermione's apparition in Act III (iii. 15–45) is related by him to 'spirits of the dead' and as such he accepts it. This is his first news of Hermione's death. It conforms to the well-established fact of such appearances bringing news of death at or soon after it, as described by F.W.H. Myers in his chapter 'Phantasms of the Dead' in *Human Personality and its Survival of Bodily Death* (abridged ed, 1927, VII). Dramatically the dream must be taken to support what we have hitherto gathered: that Hermione is dead. In the resurrection scene, as I point out in *The Crown of Life,* religious and mystical tonings abound. It occurs in a chapel, is repeatedly distinguished from unholy magic, is dependent on the 'faith' of those who watch, and Hermione is finally 'redeemed into life'. We have a new art, music: 'Music, awake her: strike!' (V. iii. 98). Poetry, sculpture and music are all engaged. Leontes' repentance is also constituent, and this may be why Paulina, who has acted as his conscience throughout, says: 'for the stone is mine' (V. iii. 58), like Prospero acknowledging Caliban (*The Tempest,* V. i. 275). It all recalls Helena's art-skills in *All's Well that Ends Well* that were said to be 'able to breathe life into a stone' or raise the dead (p. 58 above). Again, we are near to the miraculous.

If we do not wish to go so far, we might adduce some known facts of Spiritualism. Hermione's revival has certain points in common with what is known as 'materialisation', Paulina acting as medium. Materialisation is formed of ectoplasm drawn from the medium and moulded, by a kind of artistry, by spirit-powers; it is sometimes compared with sculpture. Since the materialised form, though only a copy, is said to appear in every respect like the original, sense is made of Leontes' tantalising reply when Paulina hints that the statue may move:

> Let be, let be,
> Would I were dead, but that, methinks, already –
> What was he that did make it? See, my lord,
> Would you not deem it breath'd, and that those veins
> Did verily bear blood?
> (V. iii. 61–5)

This is, as Elias Schwartz says in his valuable discussion (*The Mortal Worm*, 1977), 'a curious speech'. Is Leontes, as he supposes, thinking of being with Hermione? Why does he first crave for death and change to acceptance of the present in 'already' as though what will exist beyond earthly life were now beside him? And why, at this moment, does he ask, in strangely vague yet forceful manner, what kind of being can possibly have made it?

Hermione is exactly as a living person:

> O, she's warm.
> If this be magic, let it be an art
> Lawful as eating.
> (V. iii. 109–11)

Shakespeare, or his inspirers, seems to be fighting the battle Spiritualism is always fighting, insisting on natural law and denying miracle and black magic (V. iii. 89–91, 96, 104, 111), relying only on the 'great creating Nature' (IV. iii. 88) which dominates *The Winter's Tale*. Here we can certainly point to a similarity with spiritualistic phenomena. As with them, power is in part generated by 'faith' (V. iii. 95), or at least absence of scepticism, from those present; music functions as with the hymns or other music at a séance; and even Paulina's 'the stone is mine' may be related to the medium's ectoplasm. Materialisation, which is not permanent, cannot however be supposed to cover the whole story. The most I would suggest is that reports of materialisations may have been known to Shakespeare, for it would be wrong to think that they cannot have happened, necessarily in secret, long before the nineteenth century. Being in his mind, his creative powers (or his inspirers) made use of them.

Of all these approaches the least satisfactory, least interesting, and least dramatic, is the obvious one that Paulina has kept Hermione alive in seclusion. If we accept it with so little corroborative evidence within the drama, we are like those who regard the rational solution to a Gothic novel as a satisfying key; whereas it is the ghostly subject-matter that precedes it that has attracted us, and the ending comes as little more than a concession to our beliefs. Somewhat similarly, in *The Winter's Tale,* we are dramatically transfixed, as also in *Pericles,* by the experience of life where death seemed certain.

In his final period Shakespeare's work shows an access of the visual: dramatic ceremonial, arts of design, sculpture, divine appearances. Beyond *Pericles* and *The Winter's Tale* these cluster in *Cymbeline, The Tempest* and *Henry VIII.* The story is covered in my *The Crown of Life.*

Shakespeare appears to have been fascinated by the silence, which he calls dumbness, of such artistry. In *Richard III* a speechless crowd is 'like dumb statuas or breathing stones' (III. vii. 25); 'breathing' suggests life, though silent. The Poet in *Timon* referred to the 'dumbness' of the yet significant gesture in a painting (p. 97 above). Of the sculpted figures in *Cymbeline* we hear:

> The cutter
> Was as another nature, dumb; out went her
> Motion and breath left out.
> (II. iv. 83–5)

Of the strange figures that serve the Banquet in *The Tempest:*

> I cannot too much muse,
> Such shapes, such gesture, and such sound, expressing –
> Although they want the use of tongue – a kind
> Of excellent dumb discourse.
> (III. iii. 36–9)

In *The Crown of Life* (V. 248) I have called them 'plastic or pictorial art incarnate'. They arise from some intuition of non-verbal communication, like the Ancients in Shaw's *Back to Methuselah,* or reports of life in higher spheres. To this dumbness *The Winter's Tale* attempts to give dramatic development, in words and action; almost as the gods in *Troilus and Cressida* (III. iii. 200) are said to 'unveil' men's thoughts 'in their dumb cradles'. The attempt necessarily fails: one cannot easily ally the supposedly god-like artistry of Julio Romano with the living Hermione. The paradox is stated:

> *Leontes:*   Still, methinks,
> There is an air comes from her: what fine chisel

> Could ever yet cut breath? Let no man mock me
> For I will kiss her.
> (V. iii. 77–80)

So it is not a statue – and yet it is! Paulina follows with:

Paulina: Good my lord, forbear.
The ruddiness upon her lip is wet.
You'll mar it if you kiss it; stain your own
With oily painting.
(V. iii. 80–3)

We are constantly reminded that the statue *is* a statue, until religious tonings take over and it is awaked by music. Sculpture, religion, music, all are constituents to this extraordinary dramatic event. If she is a person, you would expect Hermione to come forward readily, but even after the music sounds she does not, and has to be urged by Paulina, as though some power were being invoked without which she was helpless. Nor does she speak at first: 'If she pertains to life, let her speak too', says Camillo (V. iii. 113). The statue's dumbness has to be broken down. There is something here quite beyond rationality. Paulina, who alone is in full possession of the facts, indicates that the truth, if told, would be unbelievable:

> That she is living,
> Were it but told you, should be hooted at
> Like an old tale; but it appears she lives
> Though yet she speak not.
> (V. iii. 115–18)

She introduces Perdita. Then at last Hermione speaks, saying that she has 'preserved' herself to see her daughter, without further explanation. We are left with Leontes' final statement that Paulina has 'found' Hermione, 'but how, is to be questioned, for I saw her, as I thought, dead' (V. iii. 138).

We may observe that the two outstanding dramatists of the modern world, Shakespeare and Ibsen, both in their late work turn to sculpture and spiritualistic resurrection. Having wrung from humanity all it can say and do, both envisage an art beyond words. Ibsen's last drama was *When We Dead*

Awaken, with as hero and heroine Rubek and Irene, sculptor and model, and at its heart the Resurrection piece. We may note also W.B. Yeats's reiterated line 'The heart of the statue is beating' in his play *Resurrection.*
This points on to G. Bernard Shaw's *Back to Methuselah* (standard edn, 1931), in which human destiny is shown as bound for 'eternity'. Within the process lies art, and primarily sculpture, where the human form is impregnated by mind. But it lacks life: 'What fine chisel could ever yet cut breath?' (p. 106 above). The next stage shows a sculptor infusing life into his statues, but the result is a kind of Frankenstein monster, crude and dangerous.
As one advances in age, sleep, as we are told of the spirit world, is unneeded (Part V, 204). Beyond is a life of pure mind in the immortality of thought, and to this the Ancients aspired: the Ancients are like Spirits, their minds control and even create material objects. They converse telepathically and, as we are told of higher spirits, find it hard to lower their thinking to normal converse: they have to 'put things crudely' to make themselves 'intelligible' (248). Spiritualism is throughout suggested and becomes explicit in the thought that early man 'dreamed of what he called an astral body' (248). All this I discuss in *The Golden Labyrinth* (XV. 349). It seems that in the Pygmalion myth, Shakespeare, and Ibsen we have adumbrated in terms of sculpture a step that Shaw attempts in similar terms to define.
In Peter Redgrove's *The Sleep of the Great Hypnotist* (1979) a complex development of attempts at spiritualistic materialisation, hypnotism and technology revolves about a central statue.

IV

What is our conclusion? Shakespeare, with the help of the visual arts, has touched a truth beyond tragedy. The matter of bodily resurrection cannot adequately be discussed without a firm belief in a soul-body interpenetrating the physical whose presence I have demonstrated throughout *Symbol of Man.* This is, according to St Paul, the 'spiritual body' of the resurrection (1 Corinthians, XV. 42–9). It is also the etheric body, released at death from the physical, of Spiritualism. Such a concept, though it does not resolve all the difficulties of *The Winter's Tale,* makes some sense of them. Shakespeare, or his inspirers, are trying to get some great truth home in terms of his own limited mental stock-in-trade, which included fascination with visual artistry, itself on the borderline always of the supernal, together with a reliance on religious terminology and belief. This may be called a rough-and-ready method, but all spiritualistic investigations are so determined. The New Testament and Christian dogma are equally provisional. We have to be content with the best that the spirit-powers can do with man's present opaque consciousness. John Cowper Powys tells us in *Mortal Strife* (1942, VII. 113):

When we are dead, life and death, according to this present dimension, cease; and something else substitutes itself for them. Of the nature of this something else it is not only now impossible to obtain the faintest clue; it must of necessity always be impossible, simply because Time and Space get in the way.

That may be going too far: 'clues' are to hand, in St. Paul, in Spiritualism, in Vergil (*Aeneid* VI), and in *The Winter's Tale.* But when faced by 'thoughts beyond the reaches of our souls' (*Hamlet,* I. iv. 56), no easy intellectual satisfaction can be expected.

The responses of certain early critics have been reviewed by Kenneth Muir in 'The Conclusion of *The Winter's Tale*', *The Morality of Art* (ed. D.W. Jefferson, 1969). His conclusion is that, whatever the doubts experienced by the reader, no problem is raised in the theatre. I cannot quite – though I do in part – agree that this settles the issue: the discrepancies are too sharp. Something similiar happens in the treatment of Helena's healing art in *All's Well that Ends Well,* blending a doctor's prescription with spiritual power; and also with the Ghost in *Hamlet,* where, instead of supporting a single reading of the event dramatised, the author has crammed various possibilities together, with a handling less selective than holistic. In *The Winter's Tale,* this is some evidence of the seriousness he brings to it; the solution is quite deliberately left 'in the air'; as when Vergil in *Aeneid* VI leaves his hero's visit to Elysium clouded by a half-worded suggestion that it may all have been a false dream. *The Winter's Tale* is pointedly named, and the real truth, says Paulina, would, if reported, be mocked as superstitious, like an old folklore tale. And that is just how we, as readers or as audience, would also react; so the poet decides not to commit himself.

Or perhaps he, as an inspired author, is not himself sure of what happens. I am reminded of John Cowper Powys's *A Glastonbury Romance* (XXIX, 1100, 1051), where, after Tom Barter's murder, the author renounces for once his expected omniscience and suddenly interrupts his narrative by himself coming forward to admit that whether or not, or for how long, the murdered man's consciousness survived, he does not know. Perhaps Shakespeare did not know; though his inspirers probably did.

Notes

[1] Strangely omitted by Arthur H.R Fairchild in his otherwise comprehensive *Shakespeare and the Arts of Design* (University of Missouri Studies, XII. 1), which I reviewed in *The Modern Language Review* (January 1938, XXXIII. 1, 68); the review reprinted in my *Shakespeare and Religion*, App. B, 356.

[2] For the reading of 'tax' instead of 'wax', see note on p. 90, above.

VIII   Caliban as a Red Man

(from Shakespeare's Styles: *Essays in Honour of Kenneth Muir*, ed. P. Edwards *et al.*, Cambridge 1980)

For my Red Indian material I rely on the following books: John G. Neihardt, *Black Elk Speaks* (London, 1974; 1961); Frank Waters, *Masked Gods* (New York, 1973); Ralph T. Coe, Catalogue of the 'Sacred Circles' Exhibition, Hayward Gallery, London, October 1976–January 1977 (Arts Council of Great Britain, 1976); Carlos Castaneda, *The Teachings of Don Juan* (Harmondsworth, 1976; 1968); Francis Parkman, *The Oregon Trail* (Harmondsworth, 1949; 1849); T.C. McLuhan, *Touch the Earth* (London, 1973; 1st edn 1972).

As a contribution to a book on Shakespeare's style, this paper may at first seem inappropriate though, as it develops, its placing should appear more assured. I am to point to certain analogies between Caliban and the Red Men of America. We cannot say what Shakespeare knew about them, but he probably heard accounts. Some aspects of Caliban, especially what others say of him, I do not stress, being concerned rather with Caliban's own outlook. In pursuance of this argument, I rely primarily on a stylistic judgement.

As his first entry he addresses Prospero and Miranda:

> *Caliban:* As wicked dew as e'er my mother brush'd
> With raven's feather from unwholesome fen
> Drop on you both! A south-west blow on ye
> And blister you all o'er!
> *Prospero:* For this, be sure, to-night thou shalt have cramps,
> Side-stitches that shall pen thy breath up; urchins
> Shall, for that vast of night that they may work,
> All exercise on thee; thou shalt be pinch'd
> As thick as honeycomb, each pinch more stinging
> Than bees that made them.

110

Caliban: I must eat my dinner.
This island's mine, by Sycorax my mother,
Which thou tak'st from me. When thou cam'st first,
Thou strok'dst me and mad'st much of me, wouldst give me
Water with berries in't, and teach me how
To name the bigger light, and how the less,
That burn by day and night; and then I lov'd thee,
And show'd thee all the qualities o' th' isle,
The fresh springs, brine-pits, barren place and fertile.
Cursèd be I that did so! All the charms
Of Sycorax, toads, beetles, bats, light on you!
For I am all the subjects that you have,
Which first was mine own king: and here you sty me
In this hard rock, whiles you do keep from me
The rest o' th' island.
                    (I. ii.321–44)

That is our introduction.

Nature is Caliban's mental stock-in-trade. It may be impregnated by the evil charm of his mother Sycorax, who is conceived as a witch of great power, as one

That could control the moon, make flows and ebbs,
And deal in her command without her power.
                    (V. i. 270–1)

That means, presumably, she could use the moon's power without herself possessing it. Prospero calls her practices 'earthy' and her sorceries 'terrible', though 'for one thing she did / They [the people of Argier or Algiers] 'would not take her life' (I. ii. 263–73); what that was, we are not told. Such is Caliban's descent. Prospero addresses him as 'thou earth', 'tortoise', 'poisonous slave', 'hag-seed' (I. ii. 314, 316, 319, 365). He threatens Caliban with more torments.

At first all had gone smoothly till Caliban tried to violate Miranda. He had been taught language and introduced to the higher heavenly powers. Caliban in his turn showed earth – nature to Prospero, 'all the qualities o' th'isle'. He is uniquely at home with earth-nature. His curses are weighted with it, and even in his slavery he is imprisoned by Prospero 'in this hard rock' (I. ii. 343).

Caliban bears certain traces of savages as they were viewed

by colonial adventurers. Their talk would often have been
considered meaningless. In his *Shakespeare* Mark van Doren
says that Caliban's language comes with difficulty, as though
speech is hard for him.[1] Prospero refers to the time

> When thou didst not, savage,
> Know thine own meaning, but wouldst gabble like
> A thing most brutish.
> (I. ii. 355–7)

However brutish he may have been, his closeness to nature
demands respect. He is one with the heavier elements of earth
and, to some extent, water, and his contacts cover nature's
springs and fertility. Most important of all for our immediate
comparison is his claim that the island is *his;* as the Red Men
of America, to this hour, are persistent in their claim that
they have been robbed of their land. Their land, to the Red
Men, was as a living entity of which they were part.

We next meet Caliban with a burden of wood, collected
for Prospero, whom he still curses:

> All the infections that the sun sucks up
> From bogs, fens, flats, on Prosper fall, and make him
> By inch-meal a disease!
> (II. ii. 1–3)

There is thunder which Caliban, as indeed did the Red Men,
regarded as coming from the spirits:

> His spirits hear me,
> And yet I needs must curse. But they'll nor pinch,
> Fright me with urchin-shows, pitch me i'th' mire,
> Nor lead me, like a firebrand, in the dark
> Out of my way, unless he bid 'em; but
> For every trifle are they set upon me;
> Sometime like apes that mow and chatter at me,
> And after bite me; then like hedgehogs which
> Lie tumbling in my barefoot way, and mount
> Their pricks at my footfall; sometime am I
> All wound with adders, who with cloven tongues
> Do hiss me into madness.
> (II. ii. 3–14)

We have a new variation on animal life. As in Caliban's curses, the animals are still spiritually impregnated, but this time by spirits controlled by Prospero. Here Caliban is aware of spirits within animal forms, as the Red Men felt through animal life to spirits. This spiritual apprehension somehow, as through his curses earlier, does not prevent the animals being real to us as animals. We feel the clustering and thickly inhabited jungle, with the noise of apes and its dangerous serpents. Caliban is vividly aware of spirits in animal or human form. At Trinculo's entry he thinks him, too, a spirit, as savage tribes sometimes do when confronted by strangers. The term is used by Caliban when he first sees the whole new community of strangers from the ship: 'These be brave spirits indeed' (V. i. 261).

Our Indian comparisons have verbal support, though whether Indians of east or west is intended is not clear. When Stephano enters he finds Caliban and Trinculo hiding together under Caliban's 'gaberdine', and, seeing limbs only, thinks it some trick of 'savages and men of Ind' (II. ii. 61). Trinculo had earlier associated Caliban with a 'dead Indian': he had a 'fish-like smell' but was 'legg'd like a man, and his fins like arms' (II. ii. 35).

We shall next inspect passages which will show Caliban as a nature force. Whether as spirit-powers or as their ordinary selves, he is one with earth's creatures; 'all the qualities o' th' isle' (I. ii. 337) come to us unmediated by any particular 'style' of expression; or we might say we have the perfection of style in its apparent absence. In Caliban's words we shall find a close-up of nature, and this apparent closeness seems to be unique in Shakespeare's nature poetry. He has always a vast resource at his disposal. There are nature-spirits in *A Midsummer Night's Dream* and there is Perdita's flower dialogue in *The Winter's Tale*. His tragedies have elemental tempests, and references to fierce animals, lion, bear, wolf and boar. There is pretty nearly every sort of nature, located or atmospheric, in reference or setting; but all are, in the comparison I am now making, used for a literary or dramatic purpose, and so in a way distanced. Even the stallion in *Venus and Adonis,* the boar and hunted hare, yes, and the wonderful snail (ll. 1033–6), might be called descriptive triumphs and are to that extent lacking in spontaneity. I am thinking on the lines of Tolstoy's final tenets, wherein he repudiated all artistic sophistication. Caliban's nature has an actuality beyond the literary; he speaks as one embedded in it, as sophisticated man cannot be. This embeddedness somehow gets across to us in his words; it may be called a matter of 'style' but if so it is a style that does not submit to analysis; even the term 'transparent' is inapposite. The literary surface is absent and reality presented as though beside us, as in a close-up, again the best phrase I can think of to give the quality of Caliban's talk.

Comparison with the Red Men is obvious. With them, animal and elemental life is throughout emphatic. They bear animal and elemental names: Black Elk, Sitting Bull, Crazy Horse, Red Cloud, Shooting Star. In their ritual dances they wear animal disguises (Waters, *Masked Gods,* Part Two). In trance they converse with talking animals (Neihardt, *Black Elk Speaks,* III, 28–9, 42). Animals and spirits are felt in unison, or identification. The earth and higher elements are remembered; in their names, in prayers and invocations, in their belief in the supernal powers of lightning and thunder. To Earth's stones and rock they attribute vitality. Like Robinson Jeffers, they felt reality rising from 'earth's stony core'. When they made a treaty, they used to call on Earth, pounding it with a staff: 'What has the earth got to say?' (Murray Hickey Ley, Papers lodged at the University of Notre Dame, South Bend, Indiana, USA, *Introductions* (booklet), 24, 27). One's feet should be able to 'hear the very heart of Holy Earth' (McLuhan, *Touch the Earth,* 90). Caliban's earthiness is, by the Red Men's standards, wholly honourable.

We now have a trio: Stephano and Trinculo, a drinking servant and a jester, who both speak in prose, and Caliban, who speaks almost wholly in poetry, the difference in style reflecting their status. Caliban is trembling with fear of what he regards as spirits sent by Prospero to torment him, and given drink by Stephano to calm him. The drink works rapidly upon him:

These be fine things, an if they be not sprites.
That's a brave god, and bears celestial liquor.
(II. ii. 125)

I'll swear upon that bottle to be thy true subject, for the liquor is not earthly. (II. ii. 134).

He thinks Stephano has dropped from heaven (II. ii. 147). Here he corresponds exactly to the Red Men, who were easily dominated, often to their ruin, by European drink despite the knowledge of drugs, such as mescalin, in certain tribes; and they smoked freely (for drugs, see Castaneda, *The Teachings of Don Juan*). Caliban's phrase 'celestial liquor' corresponds to the Red Men's name for whisky, which they called 'holy water' (Neihardt, *Black Elk Speaks*, X, 100).

The drink at first seems to loosen Caliban's speech to a new freedom, so that his innate feeling for nature is unleashed. He will show Stephano 'every fertile inch o' th' island' (II. ii. 160). Again:

I'll show thee the best springs, I'll pluck thee berries;
I'll fish for thee, and get thee wood enough.
A plague upon the tyrant that I serve!
I'll bear him no more sticks, but follow thee,
Thou wondrous man.
(II. ii. 173–7)

Trinculo's comment is: 'A most ridiculous monster, to make a wonder of a poor drunkard.' True: Caliban has no intellectual judgement; his gifts are of another order. Next, with growing pride in his expertise:

I prithee let me bring thee where crabs grow;
And I with my long nails will dig thee pig-nuts;
Show thee a jay's nest, and instruct thee how
To snare the nimble marmoset. I'll bring thee
To clust'ring filberts, and sometimes I'll get thee
Young scamels from the rock.
(II. ii. 180–5)

What 'scamels' are is not known: 'seamews' has been suggested. Here his nature poetry is at its best. W.H. Clemen observes the amount of 'sensuous and concrete detail' contained in these lines (*The Development of Shakespeare's Imagery*, London 1951; XIX, 187). Caliban has pleasure and just pride in revelation of nature's secrecies, her ways and habits.

Caliban's kinship with animals does not preclude hunting them. The Red Men were characterised by their simultaneous love of nature in trees and in animals together with control and use of natural resource. In that classic document of Red Indian life and culture, Longfellow's *Hiawatha* (VII), trees are cut down and shaped for a canoe. Sympathy is accorded their complaint, but they finally agree. When a woman, to make a basket, cuts the roots of a tree, she prays to it not to be angry (McLuhan, *Touch the Earth*, 40). These are compact miniatures of the Red Men's nature philosophy. In hunting, they used every part of the buffalo, each for a special purpose, observing full respect for the creature they had killed. There was normally no hunting for pleasure and no wanton destruction of arboreal life. In human affairs they could both inflict and endure suffering; they seem to have been unique among races in acceptance, without sentimentality, of the conditions of incarnate life, both its wonders and its agonies. Caliban's words breathe natural kinship, sympathy and understanding; but also mastery, through man's place in the created scheme.

In *The Oregon Trial*, Francis Parkman notes

a curious characteristic of the Indians, who ascribe intelligence and a power of understanding speech to the inferior animals; to whom indeed, according to many of their traditions, they are linked in close affinity; and they even claim the honour of a lineal descent from bears, wolves, deer or tortoises. (XV, 210)

The drink intoxicates Caliban. Wildly he chants his new freedom. He has in Stephano a new master, and will desert Prospero. There will be no more unwilling labour but instead

> 'Ban, 'Ban, Ca-Caliban
> Has a new master – Get a new man!
> (II. ii. 197)

He is quite drunk. The fall of the Red Men is often regarded as due to their having given way to the 'fire-water' brought by Europeans (McLuhan, *Touch the Earth*, 83, 102, 104, 141, 161). In 1849 Francis Parkman wrote:

> With the stream of emigration to Oregon and California, the buffalo will dwindle away, and the large wandering communities who depend on them for support must be broken and scattered. The Indians will soon be abased by whisky and overawed by military posts; so that within a few years the traveller may pass in tolerable security through their country. Its danger and its charm will have disappeared together. (*The Oregon Trail*, XIV, 176).

That is at least honest. Parkman also refers often to the treachery of the Indians. He might be thinking of Caliban who now plans, perhaps because he is under the influence of the drink, to get Stephano to murder Prospero:

> I am subject to a tyrant, a sorcerer, that by his cunning hath cheated me of the island. (III. ii. 49)

Prospero's 'sorcery' corresponds – in our admittedly quite arbitrary comparison – to gunpowder and European technology in general, which the primitive mind certainly regarded as a kind of magic.

Again the reiterated – and just – complaint:

> I say, by sorcery he got this isle;
> From me he got it.
>   (III. ii. 62)

The general case of the Red Men as against white robbery is well stated in the many Indian complaints compiled by T.C. McLuhan in *Touch the Earth* (85, 87, 91–2, 96–7, 107, 131, 156, 169). Caliban continues:

> I'll yield him thee asleep,
> Where thou may'st knock a nail into his head.
>   (III. ii. 70–1)

His murderous thoughts are crude and ugly:

> Why, as I told thee, 'tis a custom with him
> I' the afternoon to sleep; there thou may'st brain him,

> Having first seiz'd his books; or with a log
> Batter his skull, or paunch him with a stake,
> Or cut his wezand with thy knife. Remember
> First to possess his books; for without them
> He's but a sot, as I am, nor hath not
> One spirit to command: they all do hate him
> As rootedly as I.
>   (III. ii. 98–106)

Caliban knows that Prospero relies on his 'books'; without them he is powerless. His magic is to this extent a magic of learning, not so far away from European science; which may indeed be supposed to be covered by his early use of the term 'liberal arts' (I. ii. 73), in which what we should call 'science' was embryonic. He commands spirits tyrannically and that they resent it may be true: Ariel cries for freedom. We may suppose that Prospero's command of nature spirits and nature in general is of the same order as western callousness in using nature for our immediate ends, regardless of consequences. Today the Red Men assert regularly that they have never been guilty of ravaging, despoiling and pollution. Respect for the rights of the environment was intrinsic to the Indian way of life. In comparison our own record is appalling. Prospero is to Caliban a callous slave-master: 'They all do hate him as rootedly as I.' That is how nature may feel under the tyranny of technology. Indians assert that the white man's greed 'has blinded him to the pain he has caused Mother Earth by his quest for what he calls natural resources' (Letter by a group of Indians to President Nixon, quoted in McLuhan, *Touch the Earth,* 170).

Caliban and his companions go ahead, bent on murder. Prospero, knowing their purpose, has set out a rich array of 'glistering apparel' to distract them. Stephano and Trinculo are ravished by it. We have an indirect correspondence to the Europeans' greed for gold, which the Red Men saw as a kind of worship, driving them 'crazy' (Neihardt, *Black Elk Speaks,* II. 18) and they suffered grimly because of it, being driven from land where gold could be found. When Trinculo first sees the 'glistering' show, Caliban's scorn registers his superiority: 'Let it alone thou fool; it is but trash.' His accent exactly corresponds to the Red Men's inability to understand the Europeans' gold-lust. He warns them a second time:

'What do you mean/To dote thus on such luggage?' (IV. i. 226–33).

They are now trapped: '*A noise of hunters heard. Enter divers Spirits, in shape of dogs and hounds, hunting them about.*' Prospero uses animals, or spirits as animals, for harsh purposes; there is no evidence in him of a kindly approach to animal life. We heard earlier of his punishing Caliban with the sting of bees (I. ii. 329–30), and Caliban describes at length other instances, as we have seen. The hounds are sympathetically viewed, but then they are half-humanised and used for a cruel purpose; the joy of a hunt is innately cruel. We are given their names:

> *Prospero:* Hey, Mountain, hey!
> *Ariel:* Silver! there it goes, Silver!
> *Propero:* Fury, Fury! There, Tyrant, there! Hark, Hark!
> (IV. i. 258–60)

Two of Prospero's names are harshly toned, but Ariel's corresponds with his own quicksilver quality. The pleasure and excitement of a hunt is before us. They are hunting human beings; we may remember that hounds were used to track runaway slaves. Prospero has more torments in store:

> Go, charge my goblins that they grind their joints
> With dry convulsions, shorten up their sinews
> With aged cramps, and more pinch-spotted make them
> Than pard or cat o' mountain.
> (IV. i. 261–4)

Another callous reference to animals, very different from the ingrained sympathy of Caliban's 'nimble marmozet' (II. ii. 183), or his later exquisite:

> Pray you, tread softly, that the blind mole may not
> Hear a foot fall.
> (IV. i. 194–5)

This is perhaps Caliban's best natural close-up. Prospero speaks from a superiority to, Caliban from an identity with, the animal creation.

The Tempest is full of spirits in one shape or another, but if we concentrate on Caliban, my sole present purpose, we can say that he is sometimes aware of spirits in animals and sometimes speaks of nature direct. In both modes, the animals, as animals, are vividly present, and probably more so than when others speak of them, in *The Tempest* or elsewhere in Shakespeare. The style has an authenticity beyond that of Shakespeare's style of reference elsewhere, which may be called at the lowest 'fanciful' and at the best 'literary'.

Now what I am leading up to is this: *exactly the same applies to Caliban's style in respect of extrasensory perceptions.* In *The Tempest* spirits may activate animals, or may, as by Caliban and once by Miranda (I. ii. 406–8), be confused with human beings; or each may function alone. The general conception, widely understood, may, despite what is due to artifice and plot fabrication, be allowed to give us a sense of spiritual reality behind or within phenomena; a reality, or essence, that makes phenomena live. So it is not strange to find that what is true of Caliban's nature poetry is true also of his spiritual poetry. His words have the same immediacy of style.

Before I approach Caliban's lines on music, it is as well to make an apology. I am working now, as not before, at what is called 'literary criticism'. As a critic rather than an interpreter, I have what may seem some strange, though tentative, judgements. I myself have always a hankering for facts. I tend to respect Byron's statement, thinking of *Marino Faliero,* in his letter to John Murray of 2 April 1817, that 'pure invention is but the talent of a liar'. I have for long been critical of *Macbeth* for subjecting its protagonist to an unfair treatment of the sources, and have often suggested that the stage record of ill luck attending performances may accordingly be due to the activity of inimical spirit-powers. My own books have been strongly factual, as were *Atlantic Crossing, The Dynasty of Stowe,* my poems *Gold-Dust,* and still more the biography of Jackson Knight, my brother (*Jackson Knight: A Biography* (Alden Press, Oxford, 1975)). True, imagination has given them a colouring, and factual report in the biography included, necessarily, spiritualistic experience. Faithfulness to the factual, if honest, will include much that is strange. I certainly never regard the 'factual' as excluding the 'supernatural', or things beyond ordinary sense-perception.

This emphasis on the factual, or on 'reality', accounts for my high rating of Shakespeare's accomplishment in Shylock. The poetic conception and treatment is used to present to us a Jew as a well-known figure with an aura of racial attributes; yet, as misfortune closes in on him, he has the thrust and realism of great tragedy. The coalescence of actuality and imagination is perfect. Beside him it is easy to see Macbeth and Lear as extravagances. Othello covers a racial problem, like Shylock, with a personality well realised, the all-important and dramatically dominating handkerchief being so dissolved into his personal aura that its semi-superstitious nature is discounted; but the plotting is arbitrary, as Shylock's story is not. Shylock is so well done that he is, like Falstaff, in danger of ruining the drama in which he occurs.

These are personal studies, and it may be because Macbeth and Lear are more dissolved into their separate poetic universes that they are less acceptable as persons; and that may be part of a yet greater task. I do not know. All I emphasise is that, as rounded *persons,* Shylock, Falstaff and possibly Othello stand out. For a whole play, *Timon of Athens,* discussed fully in my *Shakespeare's Dramatic Challenge* (1977), has, as a whole, something of the impact I am trying to describe, exerting the pressure of reality: Hazlitt well says that of all his plays Shakespeare was here most 'in earnest'. It has no extrinsic supernatural machinery though a kind of supernature is in the action: Timon as Promethean semi-superman, his 'god'-given gold and his Nirvana ending. Timon's nature contacts and critique of society correspond, point by point, to the Red Men's culture. The play has faults, of course, presumably being in an unrevised state; and Timon, as a person, is not without looseness of delineation. In both *The Merchant of Venice* and *Timon of Athens* riches, the central concern of the European world, are a primary concern.

If all, or some, of this be allowed, then Caliban with his rich earth contacts, which correspond so closely with those of aboriginal natives, and especially the Red Men of North America, undoubtedly qualifies as an outstanding Shakespearian delineation in the realistic mode. His nature contacts enclose a whole range of animals. They may be blended with spirits in his curses and his thought of Prospero's use of them to torment him, or he may feel them directly. But what I would point to is the way they affect us, whatever the reference: the 'raven's feather' of his curses, the 'tumbling hedgehogs' of his torment, the 'nimble marmozet' and 'blind mole' of direct apprehension, all are equally living and vivid presences verbally conveyed. I hazard again the suggestion that they hold a reality beyond any others in Shakespeare; the rest are more 'literary', at the best more 'imaginative'. With Caliban, as Lear says of Edgar, we have 'the thing itself' (*King Lear,* III. iv. 109)

Now as the Red Indians, whom John Cowper Powys calls, in his *Autobiography* (London, 1934), XI, 548, 'this most original and formidable race among all the children of men', had wonderful spiritual apprehensions, so also does Caliban. The Red Men lived in a richly peopled universe beyond normal sense-perception. They believed in spirits within animals and men; they had superlative visionary experiences; they heard atmospheric voices, songs and music, and, above all, they dreamed; honoured dreams were a large part of their life. The record is clear in *Black Elk Speaks* and elsewhere.

When Caliban and his companions hear Ariel's song, the Europeans are afraid of this invisible, ghostly music. Not so Caliban. It is to him part of his normal, clairvoyant, apprehension, and he speaks lines on the intimations around us which do not relate merely to Ariel's song, but have a purely general implication:

> Be not afeard. The isle is full of noises,
> Sounds, and sweet airs, that give delight, and hurt not.
> Sometimes a thousand twangling instruments
> Will hum about mine ears; and sometime voices
> That, if I then had wak'd after long sleep,
> Will make me sleep again; and then,' in dreaming,
> The clouds methought would open and show riches
> Ready to drop upon me, that, when I wak'd,
> I cried to dream again.
>   (III. ii. 147–55)

The riches of Caliban's vision contrast with the 'trash' of the glistening robes set to entrap them as the two aspects of riches contrast in *The Merchant of Venice* and *Timon of Athens.*

These were the lines at which my brother murmured with subdued intensity during a performance of *The Tempest* by Charles Doran's Company which we attended together at Oxford in 1922, 'What does it mean?' – thereby prompting, perhaps inaugurating, my life's work in Shakespearian interpretation. With all the critical confidence I can muster, I assert that these few marvellous lines, like Caliban's nature poetry, and for the same deep reason, transfix us with a direct, convincing and unique report of the powers surrounding us. Our perceptions are normally constricted to an arbitrary selection of phenomena. Were they not, we might, as Alexander Pope has it (*An Essay on Man*, I, 200) 'die of a rose in aromatic pain'. The absurdity of our normal supposition that the nature of the surrounding universe is limited to our normal sense-perception has been admirably discussed in Arthur Ford, *The Life Beyond Death*, assisted by Jerome Ellison (London, 1974 (1st edn 1972), I, 38–41, also V. 114.) Abnormal children who have difficulties of communication may none the less have experience of voices and music unknown to normality. As with a radio, we may not know how to turn on the switch; but the music in the atmosphere and the voices are there for when the switch is on, none the less. For Caliban the switch is always on; he makes no distinction between man and spirit, the natural and the supernatural, and sees and hears what to us is wonderful; his every accent is there to prove it. We forget the occasion. We are, for the moment, outside *The Tempest*, but inside the universe; a spiritualistic universe. The universe of the Red Men.

In *Black Elk Speaks* we have a true and mainly autobiographical account of how Black Elk as a youth was caught up into a heavenly vision which fertilised his life, laying on him commands to serve his people. He had extrasensory experience, travelling back to America in spirit when he was in Europe with a circus. He practised spiritual healing. The story is interthreaded with animals. At his central visionary experience we are told:

All the universe was silent, listening; and then the great black stallion raised his voice and sang... His voice was not loud, but it went all over the universe and filled it. There was nothing that did not hear, and it was more beautiful than anything can be. It was so beautiful that nothing anywhere could keep from dancing. (III. 39)

We are reminded of Caliban's 'thousand twangling instruments'; it is a similar, vast music, travelling the universe. 'Voices', like Caliban's, of all kinds are on page after page of Black Elk's story.

> In a sacred manner they have sent voices.
> Half the universe has sent voices.
> In a sacred manner they have sent voices to you.
> (XVI. 137)

Voices are everywhere. There are dreams too, as in Caliban's speech. Dreams are universally respected by primitive cultures, but were probably rated more highly, and were more habitually experienced and used, by the Red Men than by any other culture on record. Indian medicines or charms, we are told in *The Oregon Trail*, 'are usually communicated in dreams' (XV. 212). Of a healer in *Black Elk Speaks* we hear that he performed 'after he had sung a certain sacred song that he had heard in a dream' (II, 21). Dreams are the opening to the higher, visionary consciousness. There was 'a dreamer religion', to whose devotees dreams were 'the sole source of supernatural power' (Mc Luhan, *Touch the Earth*, 56, 178n).

Finally, when Black Elk tries to recapture his early transcendent experience while his people are wilting under European oppression and injustice, recalling his lost vision and the failure of his life's work, at the book's heart-rending end, he cries to the Great Spirits:

Again, and may be the last time on this earth, I recall the great vision you sent me. It may be that some little root of the sacred tree still lives. Nourish it then, that it may leaf and bloom and fill with singing birds. Hear me, not for myself, but for my people; I am old. Hear me that they may once more go back into the sacred hoop, and find the good red road, the shielding tree!

(For the importance of hoops in Red Indian culture, see the Catalogue of 'Sacred Circles', noted above; also McLuhan, 178.)

In tears, 'the old man raised his voice to a thin high wail, and chanted':

In sorrow I am sending a feeble voice, O Six Powers of the world. Hear me in my sorrow, for I may never call again. O make my people live!

For some minutes 'the old man stood silent, with face uplifted, weeping in the drizzling rain' (*Black Elk Speaks,* Postscript, 190–1). So too Caliban weeps for the riches he had envisaged: 'I cried to dream again' (III. ii. 155).

For Caliban, nature and spirits are one; and what is true of his nature-poetry is true of his spiritual apprehensions. I see them outspacing all Shakespeare's other spiritual adventures, great as they may be. The most dramatically exciting are composed of the traditional, and to that extent factual, elements: the black magic of *Macbeth,* folklore; the Ghost in *Hamlet,* a blend of folklore and theology; the vision of Jupiter in *Cymbeline,* Roman mythology; the angels in *Henry VIII,* Christian. Though great as drama, and often the greater for their use of tradition, they remain artefacts. For equivalents to Caliban's lines, where the extrasensory is so cogently, yet simply, experienced, bearing every impress of actuality, we can point to Joan's defence in *I Henry VI* (V. v. 36–53); to Glendower's spirit-music in *I Henry IV* (III. i. 226–8, 233–5); to the healing scene in *All's Well that Ends Well* (discussed in my *The Sovereign Flower* (London, 1958), II. 148–54); and to the resurrection of Hermione in *The Winter's Tale,* which comes from the will to place esoteric possibilities within a normal plot. These do not, however, so wonderfully compact the whole truth as Caliban's lines, which, indeed, in their statement of the mysteries beyond ordinary preception, may be allowed to make good sense of Shakespeare's symbolic powers elsewhere. They might even be seen as an introduction to the Shakespearian universe; and perhaps this has something to do with *The Tempest's* being placed first in the Folio. Caliban's lines are comprehensive and unique. This may be, as with his nature-poetry, a question of style, though its style is necessarily slightly different. It does not, as psychic descriptions so often do, lack vigour, but is fully and imagistically alive, to be experienced by the reader or listener as an immediacy.

If, as Dr Johnson said ('Preface', 16, *Johnson on Shakespeare,* see p. 127n. below), 'there is always an appeal open from criticism to nature', then the quality of Caliban's poetry, in both its natural and supernatural contacts, becomes apparent. In it, Shakespeare forecasts what may be the future of world literature, concerned less with the fictional than the factual, but with a factuality that encompasses the supernatural.

In the story, Caliban realises his foolishness in thinking Stephano a god, and seeks for 'grace' (v.i. 295). That is a reasonable ending, which we might set beside the conclusion to *Hiawatha,* where the Red Men are to be converted to Christianity; which again, given the period of composition, we may regard as a normal conclusion. What is important, however, is not the end, but the events that form the main substance.

Something, but far from all, of Caliban's natural kinship and its higher extensions is given by Robert Browning's *Caliban upon Setebos,* so admirably studied in Thomas Blackburn's *Robert Browning* (London, 1967, IV, 155–61). There is more in Beerbohm Tree's approach, in costume, make-up and general sympathy, as recorded in his illustrated souvenir edition of *The Tempest* (London, 1904). Tree's sensitivity to Shakespeare's poetry is evident from his bird-song interlude in his production of *Much Ado about Nothing,* long before Caroline Spurgeon's researches into Shakespeare's imagery, and his Weird Women actually seen floating in 'fog and filthy air' in *Macbeth* (I. i. 12); as well as in his own vocal recordings from *Richard II, Julius Caesar* and *Hamlet.* But never was his status in poetic understanding more evident than in his electing to act Caliban himself, and his building up of the part even at the cost of some overbalance. I am thinking of his conclusion, as pictorially illustrated in the souvenir, showing Caliban alone on the island rocks, and looking out sadly, according to the stage direction, on the departing ship. A copy is shown in my *Shakespearian Production* (London, 1964).

Here our analogy collapses. The Red Men would have been glad enough to see the last of the Europeans.

Postscript, October 1977

Since writing this paper, my attention has been drawn by Professor Gamini Salgado to Leslie A. Fiedler's *The Stranger in Shakespeare,* which contains a careful study of *The Tempest* in relation to its forecast of colonisation, paying exact regard to Caliban. Some of my own points are made: see especially the reference to European 'Technology' (IV. 238). Mr Fiedler observes throughout 'a kind of music' and 'natural rhythm' in Caliban's talk (235). I should point also to the brilliant analyses in D.G. James's *The Dream of Prospero* (Oxford, 1967, 81, 106, 111–14).

I have concluded certain recent performances of my dramatic recital, 'Shakespeare's Dramatic Challenge', with a short delineation of Caliban in Red Indian guise.

Note

[1] Mark van Doren, *Shakespeare* (New York, 1939), 325–6. In his notes on *The Tempest,* Dr Johnson quotes Warburton as follows: 'It was a tradition, it seems, that Lord Falkland, Lord C.J. Vaughan, and Mr Seldon concurred in observing, that Shakespeare had not only found out a new character in his Caliban, but had also devised and adapted a *new manner of language* for that character' (*Johnson on Shakespeare,* ed. Walter Raleigh (London, 1908, repr. 1929), 66).

IX Vergil, Shakespeare and the Seraphic

(Jackson Knight Memorial Lecture, University of Exeter, 1976).[1]

Sunt lacrimae rerum et mentem mortalia tangunt.

(*Aeneid*, I. 462)

My first thought today must be one of gratitude to the Classical Society of the University for having established these Memorial Lectures, and to the Classical Staff for their consistent support. After hearing speakers so far beyond my range in classical learning, I count myself highly favoured by being asked for a contribution of my own to honour the memory of Jackson Knight.

My brother, in the introduction to his translation, said that the *Aeneid* had, 'from Roman days to ours', a fame beyond all rivals, and that one might contend that it was the best of all poems. Shakespeare now has a worldwide eminence, some would say pre-eminence. It may accordingly be important to show what these two supreme poets have in common.

Vergil started his great poem with the claim that he was going to write of 'arms and the man'; and yet no great poet had a greater detestation of war. His early *Eclogues* are poems of rusticity, love and peace. 'It was in his Arcady, the pastoral world of his memories and of his fancy', writes E. V. Rieu in his Introduction to *Vergil: the Pastoral Poems* (Penguin; I shall quote from this translation) that Vergil 'sensed the spirit that pulsates in everything that is, and makes a harmony of man, tree, beast and rock'. Nature is 'at one with man, though towns and politics and war' obscure the truth. Here he expresses 'his vision and his very self most clearly'. Rieu regards the *Eclogues* as 'symphonic variations on this elusive theme'.

Some of them are love-poems. In *Eclogue* II Corydon is distraught by love of the boy Alexis. Male love of this kind is at its best in elegy, where spiritual connotations exert authority, as in Byron's *Thyrza* poems and Tennyson's *In Memoriam:* so here, *Eclogue* V celebrates the death of Daphnis, who 'shed grace' on all around. Now he is dead, all nature is kind, and even wolves are harmless to their prey: 'good Daphnis stands for peace':

Clothed in new glory, Daphnis stands at Heaven's Gate, where all is wonderful, watching the clouds and stars below his feet.

The seraphic intuition is superb. In what is called the 'Messianic' *Eclogue* (IV), we have an address to a baby soon to be born, heralding a new, Saturnian, golden age: 'With him, the Iron Race shall end and Golden Man inherit all the world.' All is to be peace. The ox will no longer fear the lion. We are reminded of Shakespeare's Sonnet 107:

Not mine own fears, nor the prophetic soul
Of the wide world, dreaming on things to come...

and its prophecy that

Incertainties now crown themselves assur'd
And peace proclaims olives of endless age.

We may compare the place of the *Eclogues* within Vergil's total work with that of the Sonnets within Shakespeare's; and with the rustic elements in *Venus and Adonis*.

In the *Georgics*, a poem on farming, Vergil's approach is different. He writes of agriculture, trees and animals with more practicality and detail, but less inwardness, than in the *Eclogues*. There nature was as a companion to man; here man uses nature. There is a greater realism. Animals fight: bulls in Book III (220–41), bees in Book IV (67–87). They suffer from disease (III. 440–530; IV. 251–80). Love is not idyllic, it drives horses half mad (III. 242–83). Ugly incidents are recorded: a calf is beaten to death (IV. 299–304). A storm is terrific in description (I. 311–37). What Vergil is doing is trying to face the facts of nature, which has to be controlled with labour and skill, or it regresses:

> For a law of nature
> Makes all things go to the bad, lose ground and fall away...
> (trans. C. Day-Lewis; I. 199–200)

Except perhaps only for the bees, which have a wonderfully organised state, meticulously described (IV. 149–96); as too in Shakespeare's *Henry V* (I. ii. 187–204).

Man's place within a hard nature is defined; many passages accumulate great power, on storms and horses especially. There are also deeper meanings. Some say that the bees are semi-divine (IV. 219–27). We have in Book IV a lengthy description of Aristaeus's loss of his bees and his search for more. Colin Hardie in his 1970 Jackson Knight Memorial Lecture entitled *The Georgics: a Transitional Poem* (1971; 2nd edn, The University of Exeter, 1980), regards Aristaeus and his lost bees as signifying Vergil's dissatisfaction with his own poetry, and through the story of Orpheus's descent to the Underworld which follows, he sees a precursor of Aeneas's descent in the *Aeneid*. The *Georgics* is thus a 'transitional poem'. It contains a number of passages on human warring, but more important is the dark realism of its whole treatment of man's wrestling with nature, which serves as an approach to Vergil's later wrestling with the ultimate horror of human warfare.

Before passing to the *Aeneid,* I shall consider some of Shakespeare's views on war. War as war is seldom his primary concern, apart from *Henry VI* and the later *Henry V, Troilus and Cressida* and *Coriolanus*. In *Henry VI* it is vividly handled. The saintly King, in a long soliloquy, ponders on the civil war and envies the simple country shepherd, to whom 'the hawthorn bush' gives 'a sweeter shade' than any royal canopy (*3 Henry VI,* II. v. 1–54). The country's internal warring in this period is known as the Wars of the Roses, a neat compacting of war's horrors with nature's beauty. The King watches a 'Son that hath killed his Father' followed by a 'Father that hath killed his Son', and comments:

> Woe above woe! grief more than common grief!
> O, that my death would stay these ruthful deeds.

> O, pity, pity; gentle Heaven, pity.
> The red rose and the white are on his face...
> *(3 Henry VI*, II. v. 94–7)

War's horror is best studied in a civil war, which drives to an extreme, and isolates the heart of the matter. Wilfred Owen's well-known pronouncement on his war poetry, that 'the poetry is in the pity' does not perhaps do justice to his own poetry, and is a doubtful comment on poetry elsewhere; but it fits much of *Henry VI*.

Especially we are aware of young life being hideously slaughtered. Here is a passage on the death of young Rutland:

> Revoke that doom of mercy, for 'tis Clifford;
> Who not contented that he lopp'd the branch
> In hewing Rutland when his leaves put forth,
> But set his murdering knife into the root
> From whence that tender spray did sweetly spring.
> *(3 Henry VI,* II. vi. 46–50)

The fierce Queen Margaret can be as pathetic as anyone. Here she is bewailing the death of Prince Edward:

> Butchers and villains! Bloody cannibals!
> How sweet a plant have you untimely cropp'd!
> You have no children, butchers! If you had
> The thought of them would have stirr'd up remorse.
> But if you ever chance to have a child,
> Look in his youth to have him so cut off
> As, deathsmen, you have rid this sweet young prince!
> *(3 Henry VI,* V. v. 60–6)

'Sweet' again; and again the young life is compared with a severed 'spray' or 'plant'. Perhaps the most moving of all, however, concerns an older man, but even here the comparison involves young life:

> And as the butcher takes away the calf,
> And binds the wretch, and beats it when it strays,
> Bearing it to the bloody slaughter-house,
> Even so remorseless have they borne him hence;
> And as the dam runs lowing up and down,
> Looking the way her harmless young one went,

> And can do naught but wail her darling's loss,
> Even so myself bewails good Gloucester's case.
>   (*2 Henry VI*, III. i. 210–17)

'Darling': the emotions roused are in large part maternal, as again in Constance's lament in *King John* that 'never must I behold my pretty Arthur more', thinking how her grief supplies his place and 'puts on his pretty looks, repeats his words' (III. iv. 89, 95). 'Pretty' is widely used in Shakespeare. It is more than visual in application; as in 'You are full of pretty answers' (*As You Like It*, III. ii. 288); it is used too for female figures; but its most striking and repeated use is for children or youths, as in 'Steep'd in the faultless blood of pretty Rutland' (*Richard III*, I. iii. 178) or 'pretty York' (*Richard III*, twice, II. iv. 26 and 31). The princes murdered in the Tower are pathetically beautiful:

> Their lips were four red roses on a stalk,
> Which in their summer beauty kiss'd each other.
>   (IV. iii. 12–13)

They were 'the most replenished sweet work of nature' ever framed since the start of creation. More happy is 'This pretty lad will prove our country's bliss' in *3 Henry VI* (IV. vi. 70), spoken of Richmond.

We know from the Sonnets how responsive Shakespeare was to male beauty, so often in literature the theme of elegies. In the Sonnets the loved one does not die, but similar intuitions make poetry from these slaughtered youths in *Henry VI*; we might add young Talbot in *I Henry VI* (IV. iii). Their deaths turn hearts to stone. In a vicious circle, blood leads to blood, and there seems no end to it. Men become ruthless, driven by avenging Furies.

Pastoral life is associated in Shakespeare with peace. After his early work (for most of *Henry VI* must be early, though since it was not published till the Folio in 1623 we cannot be sure of every word) the pastoral element persists: in *A Midsummer Night's Dream*, *As You Like It*, and *The Winter's Tale*. Shakespeare plays less on pity, though the associated effect of nature's loveliness being despoiled by war is strong in *Richard II* (III. ii. 4–26; III. iii. 93–100); it contains a fine image of peace,

> which in our country's cradle
> Draws the sweet infant breath of gentle sleep.
> (I. iii. 132–3)

In *Henry V* we have Burgundy's long speech on the ravages of war despoiling the crops and countryside (V. ii. 23–67). Everything possible is done in *Henry V* to counter the at first sight 'jingoistic' theme; as in Henry's address before Harfleur, the words of Williams to him the night before Agincourt, his long soliloquy comparing, as did Henry VI, the simple pastoral life with the responsibilities of kingship, his conscience-stricken prayer, and finally, and significantly, the French killing of the baggage-boys that so rouses his wrath (III. iii. 1–43; IV. i. 130–55; IV. i. 250–304; 309–25; IV. vii. 1–11 and 59).

Shakespeare's poetry surmounts pity, as Nietzsche said that it should, at the last, but only at the last, be surmounted (*Thus Spake Zarathustra*, IV. 20; see my *Christ and Nietzsche*, 171–2). It is the more virile for this surmounting, but the pitiful tones reverberate within. Children suffer cruelly: Arthur in *King John*, Mamillius in *The Winter's Tale*, Young Macduff in *Macbeth:*

> What, all my pretty chickens and their dam
> At one fell swoop?
> (*Macbeth*, IV. iii. 218–19)

In *Troilus and Cressida* and *Timon of Athens* war's absurdity is satirised; in *Timon of Athens* the desecration of motherhood and children by 'contumelious, beastly, mad-brain'd war' is, among much else, remembered (IV. iii. 125; V. i. 179). In *Coriolanus*, when the opposing iron and military values are given an extended and in part sympathetic treatment – as in the description and words of Coriolanus' young son (*Coriolanus*, I. iii. 60–73, V. iii. 127) – the hero finally submits to his mother's supplication; once again the softer, more Christian values are one with a maternal emphasis. Peace at the conclusion to *Cymbeline* is given a noble poetry, and finally celebrated in Cranmer's prophecy at the end of *Henry VIII*.

We could almost say that, though he faces and fulfils the demands of the greater, more virile compulsion, Shakespeare's total action is always liable to be viewed through the eyes of the pitying King in *Henry VI*.

That is what happened, perhaps even more vividly, in Vergil. When Aeneas sees in Carthage a pictorial representation of the Trojan war, tears come to his eyes. Here and elsewhere I quote from my brother W.F. Jackson Knight's translation of the *Aeneid* (Penguin).

Agamemnon and Menelaus were there, and Priam; there, too, was Achilles, merciless alike to all three. Aeneas stood still, the tears came, and he said: 'O Achates, where in the world is there a country, or any place in it, unreached by our suffering? Look; there is Priam. Even here high merit has its due; there is pity for a world's distress, and a sympathy for short-lived humanity...' So he spoke. It was only a picture, but sighing deeply he let his thoughts feed on it, and his face was wet with a stream of tears. For he seemed to see again the antagonists warring around the defences of Troy, on one side the Greeks in flight before the charge of Troy's manhood, and on another the Trojans in retreat, and the crested and chariot-borne Achilles in pursuit. Still in tears he recognised in another scene the snow-white tents of Rhesus' encampment, betrayed to Diomede during the early hours of sleep and wrecked by him; and Diomede himself, bloody from the great massacre, was shown driving the fiery horses away to the Greek camp before they could taste the grass of Troyland and drink the water of Xanthus. Elsewhere poor young Troilus was pictured in ill-matched combat with Achilles and in flight before him; he had lost his weapons and his horses had bolted; he was on his back trailing from his empty chariot, but still grasping his reins, with his neck and hair dragging over the ground, and his lance pointing back and tracing lines in the dust. (I. 458)

'Poor young Troilus': the pathos of slaughtered youth is strongly evident, as in Shakespeare. When Aeneas is persuaded to tell Dido the story of Troy's fall, the same piteous note recurs:

Majesty, too terrible for speech is the pain which you ask me to revive, if I am to tell how the Greeks erased the greatness which was Troy and the Trojan Empire ever to be mourned. I witnessed that tragedy myself, and I took a great part in those events. No one could tell the tale and refrain from tears, not even if he were a Myrmidon or a Dolopian, or some soldier of the unpitying Ulysses. Besides, the moist air of late night falls swiftly from the sky. The stars are setting and they remind us that we too must rest. Still, if you are truly anxious to learn what befell us and to hear a short account of Troy's last agony, even though I shudder at the memory and can hardly face its bitterness, I shall begin. (II.3)

During the account we watch the pitiless slaughter of King Priam and Aeneas's subsequent sight of Helen and his first thought of executing vengeance on her, only to be prevented by his goddess-mother, Venus, who removes the clouds from his mortal vision, enabling him to see the gods themselves labouring at Troy's destruction. Human agency is discounted; she commands him to reject vengeful thoughts and submit to the divine will.

Before the war in Italy, guided by the Sibyl of Cumae, Aeneas goes to the Underworld, by way of 'Tartarean Acheron' (VI. 295); the Sibyl is ruled by the goddess Hecate. The surrounds are dark, but we move on to a happier realm, called Elysium. Here Aeneas meets his dead father, Anchises, and receives prophecies concerning the future of Rome, seeing figures of futurity; he has, that is, a sight of what he is to fight for, his task in the poem being to lay the foundations of Rome's greatness. At the culmination of these prophecies we have, characteristically of Vergil, a youth walking beside the great conqueror Marcellus. He is 'young, very handsome and clad in shining armour, but with face and eyes downcast and little joy on his brow' (VI. 860). He would have been a great man himself, had he not died young:

No other boy of our Ilian clan shall uplift the hopes of his Latin ancestors so high, and in none of her sons shall the future land of Romulus take such pride. O righteousness, and old-time faithfulness, O hand unconquerable in war! None could have safely encountered him in arms, whether marching on foot against the foe or mounted and pricking spurs into a foam-flecked charger's flanks. Piteous boy, if somehow you can break through your harsh destiny, you also shall be a Marcellus. (VI. 875)

An interesting retrospective prophecy in which the boy's future fate is left uncertain, though he did in fact die. This 'piteous boy' is as a culmination to the various prophecies. His old-world graces may be compared with those attributed in Shakespeare's Sonnets to the youth there honoured (Sonnets, 68, 106; see my *The Mutual Flame*, 82–5).

Aeneas leaves by a gate where spirits send visions 'which are false in the light of day' (VI. 896). This may mean that they belong to a dream-world; but dreams have their own truth. Anyway, Aeneas had received forecasts that were to come true, and as for the rest, it has been necessarily all highly imaginative, and all that matters is what has been delivered through that imagination.

Vergil in mid-career has a descent to the Underworld; and so does Shakespeare, in *Macbeth*. In the Cauldron scene Macbeth visits, like Vergil, 'the pit of Acheron' (III. v. 15). The Witches, who correspond to the Sibyl, are, like her, ruled by Hecate (III. v.; for Hecate, see also II. i. 52; III. ii. 41). The surrounding atmosphere is more evilly toned than in Vergil, but its opposite is also strong. We have an emphasis on young life. There are two Child-apparitions, following the Armed Head, childhood as against iron: the Bloody Child and the Child Crowned with a Tree in his Hand, signifying a victory for true kingship and nature (IV. i. 68–89). Macbeth's crimes have culminated in his attempt to cut off the creative process. He tries to murder Fleance and actually murders Macduff's family. The Child-apparitions and show of future kings that follows, descendants of Banquo and Fleance, stretching 'to the crack of doom' (IV. i. 117), and so symbolising the creative process, are the positive elements of the Cauldron scene. All carry truth and wisdom. Moreover Shakespeare, like Vergil, is speaking as a national prophet. The show of future kings, with sight of 'two-fold balls and treble sceptres' (IV. i. 121), denotes the union of realms under James I; just as Aeneas has sight of Rome's futurity, Macbeth has sight of Great Britain's. As in Vergil, we have, at the end, an implicit suggestion that the whole has been a subjective, dream-like experience, since the Witches or Weird Sisters have vanished without being seen by Lennox (IV. i. 136).

In the early books of the *Aeneid* we have noticed the pathos of Vergil's war descriptions; but pity alone cannot make the poetry of war, despite Wilfred Owen's remark. Vergil has to face stern compulsions; but, as with Shakespeare, the softer valuations are never for long forgotten. Here too they attain their greatest intensity when young life is involved, as with the death of 'young Troilus' in the pictorial scene. Throughout the war in the *Aeneid* the feeling for young life and the pathos of its destruction is keen. In the *Aeneid* Vergil describes battling at its most ruthless. Aeneas has a duty laid on him by divine ordinance to lay the foundations of Rome. The war starts after Aenēas has made a compact with King Latinus, whose oracles have told him of the arrival of a stranger who would come to found a city; and it was arranged that he should wed Lavinia, the King's daughter, previously betrothed, or all but betrothed, to Turnus. Juno, ever hostile to the Trojans, sends the Fury, Allecto, to arouse resentful passion in Turnus and Amata, Lavinia's mother, so that they become ferocious. Amata inspires other women with Bacchic frenzy, and they become half-mad. It is important to see that the war has a supernatural origin, female in tone: in Juno, Allecto, Amata and her women companions. We have already seen the gods active in the Trojan war. We may point to the supernatural causes of human disruption as defined in Ulysses' 'order' speech in *Troilus and Cressida* (I. iii. 94–101), and also to the female causations in *Macbeth*. A dark feminine evil is strongly present in both.

Turnus is young, the 'down' of youth 'on his cheeks' (XII. 221); his 'attractive grace and his youth' appeal to his followers (VII. 473). He is a fine warrior and leader of a people who are to be King Latinus's main allies. He is henceforth committed to the war. Beside the supernatural prompting, he has every reason for resentment. Aeneas is an interloper, called more than once a pirate (*praedo*, X. 774; XI. 484), demanding land in foreign parts, and in addition claiming a princess as bride who was expected to have been the bride of Turnus. Aeneas has no right on his side at all, except that divine ordinance has chosen him to be the originator of Rome's future greatness.

The war contains incidents of heart-rending horror and pathos. Nisus and Euryalus are young inseparables who engage together in a heroic exploit in the traditional Spartan style. Euryalus is the younger. They are discovered behind the enemy lines. Euryalus is captured and slain. Nisus tries to save him:

But even as he spoke the sword, forced strongly home, pressed through the ribs of Euryalus and burst his white breast; he rolled writhing in death, the blood spread over the lovely limbs, and his neck, relaxing, sank on his shoulder. He was like a bright flower shorn by the plough, languishing and dying, or poppies, weighted by a sudden shower of rain, drooping their heads on tired necks. (IX. 431)

Like Shakespeare, only with a more beautifully expanded treatment, the boy's death is given a nature comparison. The same happens with the death of Pallas. Pallas, who comes with the Arcadian allies of Aeneas, assumes an especial emphasis; he is, in fact, as we shall see, most important. He is slain in battle by the mighty Turnus, and is given a pastoral funeral by his Arcadian followers:

Others, with nimble hands, made a bier of flexible wickerwork plaited with wild-strawberry shoots and oak-twigs, building the couch on it high and shading it with a canopy of leafy branches. Here they laid their young hero down, to lie in state on this rustic bed. He was like a flower nipped between the finger and thumb of some young maiden, a soft violet or a drooping hyacinth, languishing, with no glow of life in it now, though its natural shape has not left it yet; but earth, its mother, feeds it no longer, and renews its vigour no more (XI. 64)

Twice he is called 'piteous'. He is the type and symbol of all pastoral beauty, like Daphnis in the *Eclogues*. Though a warrior, he somehow symbolises peace.

So, too, is it with Lausus, the youth who is killed by Aeneas in attempt to save his wicked father, Mezentius. Even Aeneas, not usually a courteous slayer, is kindly:

O piteous boy, what shall Aeneas the True give to you to match your high feat of arms and your great goodness? Keep for yourself the arms which gave you so much joy... (X. 825)

As in Shakespeare, the emotions roused are parental. The grief of Euryalus' mother is reported at length, till her weeping spreads throughout the army (IX. 474–502). Pallas's father, Evander, is pitied by Aeneas: 'Oh, that poor father, fated to look on at the harrowing funeral of his boy!' (XI. 53); and his subsequent lament is moving. At Lausus' death Aeneas's sword drives through 'the tunic which his mother had woven for him from threads of gold; and his blood streamed into the fold of it' (X. 818).

These incidents are so emphatic that a psychological comment may be in place. In *Roman Vergil* my brother writes that of the people in the *Aeneid* who are made 'excitingly attractive', most meet 'with a sad and violent end'. Dido is foremost of them; of the rest nearly all are young warriors:

The *Aeneid* confirms the report of Donatus, that Vergil was principally liable to this sort of affection. The same is reported of Sophocles. This characteristic in Vergil indicates the femininity of mind, and the impression made by early association. He was emotionally awake during his education. Like many great poets, he retained what is misleadingly called an adolescent psychology. Some feminine characters are, however, also presented affectionally by Vergil. Camilla, the fighting maiden, is made attractive; but she, like the disguised Venus who met Aeneas near Carthage, is attractive with a certain athletic boyishness. Camilla has a sad end too. Less sad is the destiny of the truly feminine characters, Creusa, first wife of Aeneas, who is given peace in death on the last night of Troy, and Andromache, wife of Hector, found by Aeneas in Chaonia married now to Helenus, and living in a soft quiet sadness not far from peace. Anchises, father of Aeneas, Iulus, his son, and Lavinia, whom Aeneas married dutifully at the end, have comparatively happy destinies. The divine mother of Aeneas is a voice and a presence of heavenly loveliness and blessing. A conclusion is possible. For Vergil, passionate attachments have associations of tragic failure. The calmer, deeply moral affections of the family and the home are creative, and endure. Love demands abnegation, before it comes into its rightful power. (Peregrine edn, IV. 146)

The conclusion is just and true to life; but we may, remembering our many elegies, say that these more poignant engagements of what I call the 'seraphic' are simply too good to last and are best when crowned by death, their true home.

We may call Vergil's poetic temperament 'bisexual', like Shakespeare's, whose feminine intuitions were as authentic as Vergil's were when treating of Dido; both see women as *from within*. Shakespeare's women may often have been more appealing to him in that they were performed by boys, and his frequent use of boy-disguise may be compared with Venus in huntress's disguise, or Camilla the warrior-maid, in part male. Another thought. Shakespeare in his weightier works has no finely realised boys of full-length treatment, except possibly for Mamillius, but here Vergil scores. Ascanius or Iulus, Aeneas's son, is finely depicted:

And see! In the thick of them was the young Dardan prince himself, fit indeed for Venus' especial love. His handsome head was uncovered, and he glittered like a jewel set against dark gold to be an ornament for neck or head, or like gleaming ivory skilfully inlaid in boxwood or in terebinth from Oricum; his hair was clasped by a circlet of pliant gold, and streamed down from it over his milk-white neck. (X. 132)

That is comparatively easy stuff for Vergil; but what is more important is the general treatment throughout, where, in a number of contexts, we feel his presence as a real boy, as in his beautifully characterised excitement during a hunt (IV. 156–9), or in his talk when the Trojans eat the cereal platters in which they had previously placed food: 'Hullo,' said Iulus, jokingly, 'we are even munching our tables!' (VII. 116), thereby fulfilling a prophecy. When he first draws blood with his bow, he says, again with a boy's accents: 'There! Now go and make fun of bravery, you boastful man!' (IX. 634). He can also talk sedately, as with a prince's responsibilities on his young shoulders (IX. 257 ff.).

Aeneas himself is strangely presented as a warrior. Though he is given descriptions asserting the terror of his warring, these are comparatively few; fewer, that is, than those given to Turnus. Diomede, it is true, recalls his fighting in the Trojan war: 'I have faced his vicious javelins and closed with him hand to hand; trust my experience when I tell how mightily he springs up behind his high-held shield, and what is the cyclone-force of his spinning spear' (IX. 282). In the present war his power depends in part on the divine arms that Venus has got Vulcan to make for him. For the rest, he is far from attractively presented. He is always getting angry; not with the legitimate fury of a warrior, but just in an unhealthy rage. Pallas's death makes him a cruel slaughterer. He captures four young men to be sacrificed as offerings to Pallas's ghost (X. 517–20). He is callous to those he slays. One he decapitates, and 'kicked the warm trunk rolling, and spoke over it from his vindictive heart':

Lie where you are, who expected us to fear you! Your mother shall never lay you fondly in the earth, or consign your remains to any stately family tomb. For you shall be left to the wild birds of prey, or plunged in waters where the wave shall toss you and hungry fishes mouth your wounds. (X. 557)

He is simultaneously awe-inspiring and ugly. Horses are frightened by him 'pacing onwards with his long strides and roaring terror' (X. 572). He seems gigantic. He taunts those he vanquishes. A wounded man is flung from his chariot. Aeneas taunts, saying that the horses were not cowardly, but 'it is you who have decided to desert your team'. The man has a brother. One pleads, and Aeneas answers: 'That is not how you were talking of late. Let brother forsake not brother. Now die' (X. 599). Only after slaying Lausus does he show any pity. He is in addition rendered on occasion rather absurd. He is wounded, and has to withdraw from the battle: 'Savagely growling, Aeneas stood there leaning on his long spear, with a throng of his warriors around him, and Iulus among them in great distress' (XII. 398). When he is healed by Venus's divine aid, he is almost comically impatient as they arm him, brandishing his spear; and next, rather egotistically, tells Iulus to watch him fight in order to learn from his example, and gain inspiration from such a father and uncle as he himself and Hector. It is all a trifle off-centre. Even allowing for heroic valuations, it jars.

Why does Vergil do this? How does it agree with Aeneas's early accounts of the horrors of warfare? Well, here too, Aeneas is in no doubt as to the horror. We hear of 'his whole heart distracted by the horror of the war' (VIII. 29). He is distraught by pity:

Oh, piteous, that such fearful massacre hangs over the poor Laurentine people! Terrible, Turnus, is the penalty which you shall pay to me! (VIII. 537)

He has a case:

Ah, Latins, how unjustly and unhappily you have been involved in this terrible war which leads you to shrink from friendship with us! So you beg from me indulgence for the lifeless who perished by the chance of Mars? Why, for myself, I should as willingly have granted it to the living! I only came hither because Fate has here allotted to me a place to be my home. (XI. 108)

He does not, he says, fight against a whole nation, but only King Latinus, who broke the treaty, and especially against Turnus, on whose strength Latinus relies; it would have been better if the dispute could have been settled by single combat. So he gives permission to burn the bodies of 'your piteous countrymen'. King Latinus himself admits that he 'wickedly went to war', ignoring the oracles (XII. 31). Later Aeneas wishes to tear up and burn King Latinus's capital, source of a 'wicked war', if it does not surrender (XII. 567–9). He loudly accuses Latinus, 'calling the Gods to witness that once again he was being forced into battle, that twice over the Italians had become his enemies, and that this was the second violation of a truce' (XII. 581). When Allecto first infected Turnus with fury, we hear that 'in him there rioted the bloodthirsty lust of the blade, the accursed lunacy of war...' (VII. 461). Vergil, and Aeneas too, is in as little doubt about the 'lunacy' as was Shakespeare's Timon.

We may suggest that it is just because Aeneas so loathes war that, once engaged, he becomes brutal; he cannot fight naturally and by instinct, as does Turnus; he is a pacific idealist forced into violence against his will. Or we may suppose that it was the death of Pallas, whom Aeneas must, despite his short acquaintance, have deeply loved, that caused those ugly incidents we have reported. Or we may say that he is not a consistent character at all, but a composite, an artefact made to enact a hero who has to fulfil a destiny. His arms are divine; perhaps that is why they come first at the opening of the *Aeneid*: 'This is a tale of arms and of a man' (I. 1). With them, he fights not as one person, but as many:

Like Aegaeon, said to have had a hundred arms and a hundred hands, and to have blazed forth fire out of fifty breasts through fifty mouths, clashing fifty similar shields and drawing fifty swords to face the thunder-strokes of Jupiter; even so Aeneas wreaked his victorious savagery over all the field when once his sword-point warmed. (X. 565)

He fights less as a man than as a communal destiny, able to oppose gods, like Aegaeon. He fights too for Pallas, the Arcadian, who comes from the future site of Rome, where we are told that Saturn once governed with a reign famed as a golden age, because 'so gentle and peaceful was his rule, until gradually an inferior and tarnished age succeeded, mad for war and lusting to possess' (VIII. 325). King Latinus, when making his treaty, also says that he is of 'Saturn's kin' (VII. 49, 203). Saturn overstands the conflict, and Aeneas fights as progenitor of Augustus as 'founder of golden centuries once more in Latium, in those same lands where once Saturn reigned' (VI. 794). That may be why Aeneas is compared here with Aegaeon as an enemy of Jupiter, who overthrew Saturn and introduced war. Aeneas is, paradoxically, fighting pitilessly in the cause of peace.

These are difficult matters. For elucidation we may turn to Shakespeare. In *Henry IV*, Prince Hal is less a person than a composite, synthetic in the bad sense. Rationally, there may be no inconsistency, but emotionally there is not the unity that there is in Hotspur and Falstaff. He is constructed as Henry V in embryo, as a Christian warrior in the making. His central activities are bounded by his early soliloquy and his final rejection of Falstaff; and the fitting together is arbitrary. As Henry V he is more convincing, and much is done, as we have seen, to humanise his warring; he is like Aeneas in his fury at the slaughter of the baggage-boys and his ruthlessness in response. He feels God is on his side (IV. vii. 91; 113–28), like Aeneas.

We may say that the creation of Prince Hal is dictated from above rather than from below. As a man, Hotspur is far more convincing. In the same way Aeneas is synthetic, and for the same reason. The Christian warrior is a contradiction in terms, and yet Shakespeare must try to make one, just as we, in our time, have to try to make sense of Christian warring. Now Vergil, though not a Christian, was near enough to one to hit at least upon this contradiction in terms. His whole problem is this: war is hateful and cruel; it destroys all I love, all that is covered by the early pastoral *Eclogues* and, in the *Aeneid*, Pallas, from Evander's pastoral, Arcadian land. But if God's purposes are to be fulfilled, it is necessary. What then? We must have righteous war in cause of a nation-to-be, powerful, yet pacific, as in Cranmer's prophecy at the conclusion to *Henry VIII*. Both poets are too honest to shirk one jot of war's cruelty; both knew that 'contumelious, beastly, mad-brain'd war' (*Timon of Athens*, V. i. 179) is the ultimate, or all but the ultimate, obscenity; and yet Cranmer includes 'terror' among the attributes of Elizabeth's reign: 'peace, plenty, love, truth, terror' (*Henry VIII*, V. v. 48). Perhaps Vergil is rather *resentful* at having to make a hero-warrior, and for this reason piles on him all the denigrations his art can, within reason and without spoiling his poem, compass.

In Milton's *Paradise Lose* the same contrast is raised to gigantic proportions. Satan is heroic in Books I and II and arouses our response; he is also a perfect unit at first. He has the power-content of the poem. Later on, this power-content is transferred to the Messiah as victor; but the Messiah is scarcely a person. His chariot with its sound as 'of a numerous host' and its multitudinous death-dealing eyes is as a community, and may be indirectly referred to the people of Britain, as I have argued in *Chariot of Wrath* (reprinted in *Poets of Action* (1967), 156–62). The heroic Talbot in *I Henry VI* says that what people see of him is only a 'shadow', but that were his 'whole frame' seen it would appear titanic; and he proceeds to show that his 'substance, sinews, arms and strength' are in his supporters (II. iii. 50–63). So too Hal is in a way a communal figure, as king-to-be; and Aeneas certainly is, with his divine arms and national destiny; especially, as we have seen, when he fights not as a man, but, like Aegaeon, as a multitude.

The case is clear when we study Turnus, who corresponds in our Shakespearian comparison to Hotspur. Humanly speaking, and divine ordinance discounted, all is in his favour. He has every right to regard himself as wronged. He is young, 'splendid to see' (VII. 783), and a magnificent warrior. His warring is superb, and superbly described. He rallies his followers when they fail. Again and again we thrill to his prowess. At one point (IX. 727–816) he fights alone within the enemy camp, like Shakespeare's Coriolanus: 'At once the vision of Turnus became a thing of unearthly terror as it blazed on Trojan eyes. Horrifying to them was the clashing of his arms; blood-red quivered the plumes on his crest, and lightning flashed and flared from his shield' (IX. 731).

He is a born leader, efficient and practical: 'But nothing

could delay Turnus, cramp him, or hold him back. Vigorous and quick-acting, he moved the whole of his battle-front against the Trojans and posted men to meet them on the shore' (X. 308). When he slays Pallas, he is chivalrous (X. 493), quite belying Aeneas's complaint that in doing it he neglected 'all courtesies of war' (X. 532). He is compared variously to a wolf, eagle, tiger, lion in brilliant and gripping similes. He is like a stallion breaking free to the open plains to bathe in a river, 'and afterwards leaps ahead, lifts his neck, and neighs in delight, his mane dancing over withers and shoulders' (XI. 492). Aeneas is given nothing like that. The comparisons applied to Aeneas are fewer and less attractive. He is like baleful Sirius burning 'with sinister glare (X. 273); or like a storm-cloud which makes farm folk 'shudder in foreboding' (XII. 451). Pursuing Turnus he is like a hound after a stag, but that is a man-controlled beast and not wild: 'The untiring Umbrian hound hangs on to him, mouth wide open, and at every moment about to grip, snapping his jaws as if he already had him, but biting nothing and eluded still' (XII. 749). A hound would not so well suit Turnus, who is as a force of nature, with nature's wild energies; besides, the description is rather cruel, as those for Turnus never are.

To Turnus, Aeneas is an effeminate eastern foreigner: 'Grant me to bring him low, that half-man of a Phrygian, and with main strength to rend and rip his corslet from him. Let me foul in the dust that hair crimped with curling-tongs and oiled with myrrh!' (XII. 95). We are to accept this as, in part, true, and toning with his general characteristics.

Aeneas is complex. He loves Pallas with a love which contrasts with his ill-fortuned, heterosexual relationship with Dido. He consults a medium, the Sibyl, and has communion with the dead. He is dominated by his mother, Venus, and through her enjoys supernatural aid, so that he becomes a terror in war, while hating it. He is in turn sentimental and brutal. Above all, he is dedicated, under divine ordinance, to the future of Rome and pacific empire. He appears to embody much of Vergil himself; many of his characteristics are such as are often found in men of genius. His qualities are abnormal; some, like Turnus, may react sharply in dis-approval; yet much is in line with the New Testament.

Against this baffling composite, we have the forthright, heroic and male Turnus. He is a brave and efficient warrior, as one born for war. He is utterly normal; for to men as at present constituted, war is normal. Sexually he fights for his rights to a normal marriage, with Lavinia. To him Aeneas appears despicable.

Great tension is built in us, wondering when and where Turnus and Aeneas will meet. At a time when single combat is being arranged between them and ritualistic observances are prepared, Turnus is modest and lovable:

The sight of Turnus himself increased their anxiety yet further when he stepped out in front without a word, and in humble piety paid reverence at the altar with downcast eyes and the down of young manhood showing on his cheeks, where the youthful colour had paled. (XII. 219)

The combat does not come off. General fighting starts and Turnus continues in fearful deeds, finely depicted:

He was like blood-red Mars himself when, aroused near the cold streams of Hebrus, he clashes his shield and gives rein to his battle-mad horses to herald war.... Like Mars, and as vital as he, Turnus lashed his horses, steaming, sweating, through the battle's throng. (XII. 331)

Again:

And as when the blast of north winds from Edonia roars across the dark Aegean driving the rollers to the shore, and the storm-clouds flee from sky before the winds' assault, so did the ranks before Turnus wherever he carved his way. (XII. 365)

His powers are evident.

His semi-divine sister Juturna takes over Turnus's chariot, Aeneas following. Turnus senses afar off the danger of the Latins' city, being attacked by the Trojans. Though now weary, he returns to the city:

'Sister,' he said, 'at this very moment Fate is prevailing over us. Think not to cause delay. Let us follow where God and our own hard fortune call. I am resolved to meet Aeneas hand to hand, and bear whatever bitterness death may hold for me. Sister, never again shall you see me forget my honour. But first, I entreat you, let me do this one mad deed before I die.' Having spoken he leapt from his chariot to the ground, left his sister sorrowing, and darted on through the missiles of the foe. With one violent rush he burst through the battle's centre. He came like a rock crashing headlong down from a mountain-crest, wrenched out perhaps by a wind after floods of rain have washed it free or else time has crept beneath it with the years and worked it loose; sheer downwards the great crag charges with a mighty impulse, self-willed, bounding upwards off the ground, and rolling before it in its path forests, and herds, and men; so Turnus charged to the city's wall through shattered ranks where the ground was soaked deepest in streams of blood and the air whistled with the shafts of spears. He made a gesture with his hand and as he did so he shouted: 'Rutulians, now desist. Latins, restrain your spears. Whatever fortune holds in store, it is for me. Right requires none but me to atone for the truce on your behalf and find decision by the sword.' All drew apart and left a space in the midst. (XII. 676)

The following contest is determined by Aeneas' supernatural arms and allies. Turnus's sword has been good enough for ordinary contests,

but as soon as he faced instead divine weapons forged by Vulcan himself, the mortal blade as it struck flew in splinters like brittle ice, and now its fragments gleamed back at him from the yellow sand.
(XII. 739)

When Aeneas cannot release his spear from a tree where it is enfixed his mother Venus does it for him. And there is worse. Now that the issue is to be determined, Jupiter himself takes charge. He sends a female demon, called 'Daughter of Night', to harry Turnus:

When she saw the Trojan lines and the army of Turnus, at once she shrank to the form of that small bird which in the night-time perches on tomb-stones or deserted roof-tops and eerily sings her late song among the shadows. Changed into this shape, the demon noisily passing and passing again flew into the face of Turnus and beat his shield aside with her wings. Every limb of Turnus went limp, numbed by a strange dread. His hair stiffened in horror; his voice was clogged in his throat.
(XII. 861)

Aeneas, from 'his relentless heart', taunts him. Turnus answers:

Arrogant foe, it is not your heated words which affright me. I fear only Gods, and especially the hostility of Jove.
(XII. 894)

He seizes a great boulder, but his limbs are helpless and his blood frozen. Whatever he attempts, the demon prevents it. Aeneas's spear is cast and Turnus falls. At the last, he asks mercy for his father's sake; either his life, or his dead body. Aeneas is at first in doubt, but he then sees slung over his shoulder a baldric Turnus had taken from Pallas, which arouses his 'vengeful bitterness'.

This baldric, we have been told, had a design depicting a number of murdered bridegrooms (X. 497–9). We need to offer an interpretation, as my brother interpreted the maze design on the temple gate at Cumae: such elements in a great poem are not likely to be meaningless. Why should Pallas carry it? As a necessary obverse, perhaps, of the seraphic beauty: a negative must appear, if only indirectly. Perhaps, since Pallas symbolises an esoteric, platonic love, this baldric the more fittingly depicts a desecration of normal marriage. Anyway, sight of it in Turnus's possession arouses Aeneas's wrath:

'Are you to be stolen hence out of my grasp, you who wear spoils taken from one whom I loved? It is Pallas, only Pallas, who by this wound which I now deal makes sacrifice of you; he exacts this retribution, you criminal, from your blood.' Saying this and boiling with rage he buried his blade full in Turnus' breast. His limbs relaxed and chilled; and the life fled, moaning, resentful, to the Shades.
                    (XII. 947)

There the *Aeneid* ends.

Following the principle of the *Henry VI* plays, we have another example of a piteous death – Pallas's – turning Aeneas's heart to stone. But there must be more in it, if Vergil meant, and we must presume that he did, though the poem was left unrevised, to end like this. We have to think poetically and by association. Pallas, like Daphnis, is associated with idyllic pastoral and young male beauty. Asserting the necessity of war to support what is idyllic and peace loving, Aeneas slays the slayer, as we, in our time, have had to do. Such is the nature of war. That Vergil is not happy about it, and does not regard the solution as satisfactory, may be supposed: as we have seen, he goes to extreme pains to denigrate Aeneas and build up Turnus. To call Turnus 'you criminal' (*sceleratus*) is unforgivable; Turnus is pretty nearly the most guiltless person of consequence in the poem. For this reason, I object to Byron's grouping him, in a letter to Francis Hodgson of 12 May 1821, with villains – his only villainy is his being the enemy of the divinely ordained hero – though I would applaud the general tenor of Byron's meaning:

I must also ask you, is Achilles a *good* character? Or is even Aeneas anything but a successful runaway? It is for Turnus men feel, and not for the Trojan. Who is the hero of *Paradise Lost*? Why, Satan – and Macbeth, and Richard, and Othello, Pierre, and Lothario, and Zanga?

Besides Shakespeare, Byron is referring to plays by Thomas Otway, Nicholas Rowe, and Edward Young.

Well, I have given my explanations, so far as I have any; but, as a final comment, I cannot see Aeneas as following the prediction of Rome's characterising greatness as defined in Anchises' prophecy:

But you, Roman, must remember that you have to guide the nations by your authority, for this is to be your skill, to graft tradition onto peace, to shew mercy to the conquered, and to wage war until the haughty are brought low.
(VI. 851)

In the prophecy of peace under Elizabeth at the conclusion to *Henry VIII*, Shakespeare's last word to his countrymen, 'terror' is included; perhaps something like this was close to Vergil's meaning. We may not like it, but today we are still living with this problem.

Between Vergil and Shakespeare is Dante: he is the voice of the Christian scheme, formulated and organised, in which this particular problem, which generates the works of Vergil and Shakespeare, cannot exist. At the two ends – just before the creation and just after the dissolution – of this overruling system in which Christianity was, or was supposed to be, supreme, the great voices we are discussing speak. Perhaps the intervening centuries account for Shakespeare's ability in *Antony and Cleopatra* (IV. xii. 51) to reverse Vergil's love-tragedy and its unhappy continuation in the Underworld into a love-victory beyond death:

Where souls do couch on flowers, we'll hand in hand,
And with our sprightly port make the ghosts gaze.
Dido and her Aeneas shall want troops,
And all the haunt be ours.[2]

Perhaps that death-vanquishing accent could not have been
naturally sounded in Vergil's day.

It seems that in their treatment of war Vergil and
Shakespeare both bring to light a yet unsettled problem
which really existed too in Dante's world, though it was not
recognised. Had the medieval system solved it in action, it
would, presumably, not have collapsed.

Notes

[1] This lecture is an amplified version of one I gave many years ago at
Exmouth, an outline of which was included in a booklet *The Great
Tradition*, edited by W.F. Jackson Knight, Exmouth 1945.
Acknowledgements are due to Messrs. Faber and Faber Ltd. for my
quotation from *Roman Vergil* and to Messrs. Penguin Books Ltd. for
quotations from E.V. Rieu's translation of the *Eclogues* and my brother's
translation of the *Aeneid*.

[2] In his visit to the Underworld, Aeneas is sternly rejected by Dido. The
strange emphasis on 'Widow Dido' in *The Tempest* (II. i) is discussed by
Colin Still in *Shakespeare's Mystery Play: a study of The Tempest* (1921;
reissued as *The Timeless Theme*, 1936). Throughout, Still makes continual reference to *Aeneid VI*. See also Northrop Frye, Introduction to
The Tempest (Baltimore, Penguin Books).

PART TWO

There follow discussions of three outstanding contemporaries which should assist our response to the Shakespearian enigma.

X   Lyly as Shakespearian Precursor

(from *The Review of English Studies*, XV, 58, April 1939)

Elizabethan thought was more linguistically alive than ours. Perhaps the reputation of puns and word-play varies according to an age's literary strength (and is indeed rising today): you find them in Hebrew literature and Greek drama. Word-play sees similarity in opposites. Metaphor is a sort of pun; and Elizabethan conversation may have held, weakly, the metaphoric and allusive quality of Bacon's prose. That Elizabethan tragedy depended on a verbal joy now lost is generally allowed; that *Ralph Roister Doister* is a word farce only slightly dependent on situation and action has not been, I think, noticed: hence its surges of doggerel absurdity rising at high moments to nonsensical word-makings of a rough syllabic music. Lyly's verbal and allusive extravagances, and their contemporary popularity, must not be too sharply dismissed: his dramatic work relates significantly to his euphuism. Before turning to the plays I would make two points concerning *Euphues* itself.

The style is neatly balanced and heavily antithetical in word, phrase, sentence, paragraph. Complex cross-antitheses are usual. Consider this one:

What is he, Euphues, that, knowing thy wit and seeing thy folly, but will rather punish thy lewdness than pity thy heaviness? (*Euphues,* Bond, vol. I, 208)[1]

Observe that the technical essence can be characterised – and if it can be it must be – as substance. This sentence expresses a lively awareness of opposites. Now Lyly's style plays constantly round psychological contradictions. In *Euphues* soliloquy, letters, dramatic argument regularly express mental conflict. Lyly's 'Ay, but...' connections in fictional self-communing serve continually to introduce battalions of opposing reasons to what precedes. Implicit in his method – which is also his matter – there is therefore dramatic conflict. The antithetic style of *Euphues* reflects that balancing of contradictions that is also the core of Elizabethan drama. However luxuriant and leisurely the book as a whole may seem, it has thus a dramatic immediacy and tension faintly analogous to the very different, yet also epistolary, manner of Richardson. A certain wisdom of accepted uncertainty is always at the back of the opposing parties or principles rooted in the nature of drama: this wisdom is Lyly's pre-eminently.

Second, we have a mass of pseudo-scientific, natural and classical comparisons. Though there is gross exaggeration, the thing exaggerated is of vital poetic importance. Lyly continually refers human and psychological issues to the natural universe. True morality must be in some sense truth to nature: it is Hooker's problem in Book I of his *Ecclesiastical Polity*. It is everybody's problem, rooted in the very structure of poetic expression. Consider this typical passage:

> The similitude you rehearse of the wax, argueth your waxing and melting brain, and your example of the hot and hard iron showeth in you but cold and weak disposition. Do you not know that which all men do affirm and know, that black will take no other colour? That the stone Asbeston being once made hot will never be made cold? That fire cannot be forced downward? That nature will have course after kind? That everything will dispose itself according to nature? Can the Aethiope change or alter his skin? or the leopard his hue? Is it possible to gather grapes of thorns or figs of thistles? or to cause anything to strive against nature? (*Works*, ed. Bond, vol. I, 191)

The explicit human – natural reference here is implicit throughout the multitudinous, crazy similitudes of *Euphues*: a desire at once to read the human mind in terms of the living physical universe and see that universe and its properties – including inorganic matter (remember the rock in *Love's Metamorphosis*) – as a vital extension of the human mind. In Wordsworth you have the philosophy of it; in all poets the practice of it. Certainly Lyly's references smell overstrong of medieval bestiaries and alchemy: but the Renaissance mind in wording a new consciousness of nature is often driven to expression in medieval terms – as we shall find too in Marlowe. The generalised and intentional force of Lyly's comparisons blends easily into his use of a well-known proverb near the end of my quotation, followed by the transcription, similar in both substance and direction, of a famous New Testament passage. The fundamentally serious quality and profound intention is thus clear.

Lyly's numerous mythological – especially Greek – references tone with the upsurge of Renaissance Hellenism generally: and this too relates to my last argument, since Greek mythology is continually for Renaissance and Romantic poets the natural grammar for a consciousness that has broken the man-nature opacity. In *Euphues* the stress falls mostly on pseudo-scientific learning: in the plays, on Greek mythology.

The neat antitheses of *Euphues* recur in the balanced parties and general symmetry of design in the plays. These show vital conflicts though no powerful train of action: they are static and spatialised rather than narrative, yet their vivid immediacy never lacks excitement. The conclusions to the first two scenes of *Endimion* will illustrate this technical mastery. Scene beginnings also consistently rivet the eye. Though the action is slow to advance, its very static unrest is so emphasised at a re-entry that suspense is strong:

No rest, Endimion? Still uncertain how to settle thy steps by day, or thy thoughts by night? (*Endimion*, II. iii. I)

A trick Shakespeare assimilated thoroughly: soliloquy often exquisitely expands the dualised personality of a central figure, whetting your attention to the outcome. As you read, you see:

Yonder I espy Endimion. I will seem to suspect nothing, but soothe him, that seeing I cannot obtain the depth of his love, I may learn the height of his dissembling. (*Endimion*, II. i. 47)

You are jerked into a stage-awareness and your anxiety sharpened. All that tires in *Euphues* under strict compression ignites. Instead of listening, you see; instead of knowing, experience. Dramatic suspense adds a dimension to your receptivity: and Lyly's progress from *Euphues* to the plays miniatures neatly the movement from *The Faery Queen* to Shakespeare. Effects are narrowed and intensified under a tight dramatic technique. There is far less pseudo-science but new vital personifications of Hellenic myth.

As in Spenser, different sorts of allegory or symbolism jostle each other. Lyly, like Spenser, is a Court poet: the title-page to *Euphues* says: 'Very pleasant for all gentlemen to read, and most necessary to remember.' He is even closer to Court life than Spenser. He transmits the electric touch of contemporary social eroticism, somewhat like Pope. In all poetry we expect a particular event or person to be at one with a generalised significance: but in Spenser and Lyly there is the additional complication of masked contemporary meanings. If these are too organic something may be lost for future ages: the work is too closely bedded in its own birth. With Spenser I feel this, but less with Lyly. Most of his drama can, like Shakespeare's, be read without searching too exactly for such origins: and when, as in *Endimion*, such independence in reading is not possible, there is somehow a pleasing necessity about our very mystification. Lyly's plays more precisely that any others reflect the Court of Elizabeth; our interest is closely involved in this; his pregnant love analyses come hot, as it were, from knowledge of Court flirtations; and we rather like to feel there are points in the dialogue and sometimes the whole structure to which we cannot respond as directly as his first audience. The very flavour of the plays would be different were he always transmuting, instead of reflecting, his day. Lyly is not, and is not wanted to be, Shakespeare. The conventional choice of *Endimion* as Lyly's most representative play is probably fortunate enough: it distils and intensifies his general qualities. Its various allegories are of shifting importance. There is Cynthia = Elizabeth, Tellus = Mary Queen of Scots, and the otherwise-to-be-interpreted other persons; parallel with this, and of changing importance, is Cynthia = the

Moon, and Tellus = the Earth, without further correspondences; and last, the more generalised sense that we receive of
a hero set between a high and divine love and earthy
and unscrupulous passions. Cynthia rules the action from the
start and statuesquely takes charge at the close. That
Cynthia – Elizabeth should so dominate Lyly's most dense
and weighty single play is apt, since the queen is necessarily
the focal point of all that courtly eroticism at the back of his
work. The imaginative and factual coalesce. The Queen is
close-involved in the mysterious dream allegories at the
play's heart; so that Lyly's most deeply imaginative, even
mystic, apprehension is appropriately locked, as by a navel
string, to the age of its birth. Cynthia's particularity as
Elizabeth becomes itself a universal.

Often, however, his persons and plots, and continually
isolated exquisite movements of dialogue, have symbolic or
poetic force of the most normal kind. There is a new strength
in advance of the Moralities. Those started with a rigid
abstraction: poverty, good deeds or such like, and set it
walking in human form. The resulting personality either
outgrows the conception and general plan, or stays severely
limited. The Elizabethan recognises the complexity and
contradictions and dramatic oppositions *within* the single
personality and the baffling indecisiveness of all moral
categories. So he starts with a concrete, often mythical or
pseudo-historical, figure and lets his abstract thinking play
round and into its growth. The ideas within his human
delineation will be many and paradoxical. Where there is a
seeming figure of the medieval sort, it will shadow some vast
and universal idea such as Cupid = Love: itself, in Lyly, one
tissue of contradictions. The weakness of the Moralities is
suggested by their name. Moral categories are on a plane
below that of poetic creation (which is not therefore
independent of them), and, if allowed to direct autonomous-
ly the plan, tend to impose a seeming simplicity on a real
complexity. 'Death' or 'Love' are realities so ultimate that
they hold power beyond the shifting concepts of the moral
order, and can safely be personified in any age. The
communist or pacifist propagandist art of today might study
this problem with profit. Of course, a Christian propaganda

does not exactly incur this limitation, Christianity being itself
a complex poetry first and an ethic, if at all, afterwards. It is
significant that when Lyly uses a medieval touch in *The
Woman in the Moon* his personified qualities are vast and
non-ethical: Nature, Concord, Discord – the two last, under
their own names or in symbols of Music and Tempest being
the rooted dualism throughout Shakespeare. But generally
Lyly lets his plays grow from, and form about, some
concretely conceived story.

I pass to consider Lyly's more direct content, what the
plays say to us. Love, as in *Euphues*, is his whole theme. He is
as aware as Spenser of its complexities: he is more aware than
Spenser of its inward contradictions. His understanding is at
once purer and more realistic. He can refer to crude, and in a
sense healthy, lust but seems to have little or no sense, as
have Spenser, Marlowe and Milton, of the sexual nature in
subtle mental disease: in this he is with Shakespeare.

Campaspe dramatises a typical Renaissance conflict, of
soldiership and love. The whole play is redolently Elizabethan. The choice of an Alexander story is apt; since
Alexander and Caesar have here an almost Messianic
authority. The Elizabethan ideal must be a soldier, yet a
Christian gentleman. Shakespeare's Theseus and Lyly's
Alexander are correspondent, precisely: strong and master-
ful, yet gentle:

Alexander as he tendereth virtue, so he will you; he drinketh not blood,
but thirsteth after honour, he is greedy of victory, but never satisfied with
mercy. In fight terrible, as becometh a captain; in conquest mild, as
beseemeth a king. In all things, than which nothing can be greater, he is
Alexander. (I. i. 48)

As in *A Midsummer Night's Dream* the poet shows his hero
returning from conquests, not actually seen at any bloody
work: so exploiting the positive while not the negative aspect
of valour. Alexander is anxious to

have as great care to govern in peace, as conquer in war: that whilst arms
cease, arts may flourish, and, joining letters with lances, we endeavour to
be as good philosophers as soldiers, knowing it no less praise to be wise
than commendable to be valiant. (I. i. 80)

Which is answered by Hephaestion's:

Needs must that commonwealth be fortunate, whose Captain is a Philosopher and whose Philosopher is a Captain. (I. i. 85)

The typically Elizabethan conception shows how close we are in this (earlier) play to the equation of Cynthia with Elizabeth in *Endimion*. The play's central problem is the age's problem, intrinsic to such a book as Castiglione's *Courtier*. What is the perfect courtly, humanistic existence? Notice Alexander's courteous and delightful conversation with Apelles: and how exquisitely the warrior-king is balanced against the artist. The Elizabethan aims at the paradox of a Christ-like warrior: Alexander and Theseus. And when his foes are vanquished, how must he act? What is left to do? The solution is, dramatically at least, obvious: he must fall in love. Which Alexander does, shocking his soldier retainer, Hephaestion:

What! is the son of Philip, king of Macedon, become the subject of Campaspe, the captive of Thebes? Is that mind, whose greatness the world could not contain, drawn within the compass of an idle alluring eye? (II. ii. 31)

He reminds Alexander of Campaspe's mortality. This is Lyly's recurrent problem – if love is divine, why so brittle and so sternly to be controlled? Yet, if it be not, then what is? Alexander is given a typically neat defence:

My case were light, Hephaestion, and not worthy to be called love, if reason were a remedy, or sentences could salve, that [which] sense cannot conceive. (II. ii. 77)

Being a king, he says, his passions are greater than others'. Hephaestion must cease

with arguments to seek to refel that which with their deity the gods cannot resist. (II. ii. 89)

Again, a typical thought of Lyly's: love's superb strength. Moreover, says Alexander, is it not likely and reasonable that the captive Campaspe should return an Alexander's love? But note the exquisite reply:

You say that in love there is no reason, and therefore there can be no likelihood. (II. ii. 110)

The light dialogue plays over psychological profundities. Alexander's arguments are turned against himself. Lyly's persons are often so tangled in the mysterious contradictions and irrationalities of their own love. Hephaestion turns out to be right. Campaspe loves Apelles, the painter:

I perceive Alexander cannot subdue the affections of men, though he conquer their countries. Love falleth like dew as well upon the low grass, as upon the high cedar. (V. iv. 127)

Which holds a lucid and lovely truth comparable to its New Testament original. Alexander ends the fine, generous-hearted hero, as little subdued by a selfish passion as Theseus is taken in by the seething imaginations of lunatic, lover, or poet. He leaves love to 'seamsters and scholars' and 'fancies out of books', like Theseus, while Apelles takes Campaspe. This is not strange. The king, the soldier, man of action, is often greater than poet or philosopher to the Elizabethan, as Christ is a greater, apart from all theology, than a Dante or a Shakespeare – the man who lives, not writes, his record. So:

Hephaestion: The conquering of Thebes was not so honourable as the
                subduing of these thoughts.
Alexander: It were a shame Alexander should desire to command the
                world, if he could not command himself.
                                                    (V. iv. 148)

This touches, for an instant, something beyond both love and warriorship. But – and it is a big one – the play ends on a delightfully pregnant remark:

And, good Hephaestion, when all the world is won, and every country is thine and mine, either find me out another to subdue, or, of my word, I will fall in love. (V. iv. 153)

If we thought Love dethroned, we are wrong: so often a seeming conclusion in Lyly turns into its opposite. Every separate statement is, by itself, a shadow only of the profound movement of his dialogue, something bigger, heavier than his delicate phrases at first suggest. So here the problem of an ultimate good remains. The love that rules these plays is definitely sexual and romantic. Yet Lyly distinguishes between a high and low variety in *Endimion*. Cynthia seems to inspire a somewhat Platonic fervour:

O fair Cynthia! O unfortunate Endimion! Why was not thy birth as high as thy thoughts, or her beauty less than heavenly? (II. i. 1)

But it induces the usual lover's 'sad and melancholy moods of perplexed minds, the not to be expressed torments of racked thoughts' (II. i. 9): the unrest and perplexity to which Lyly so often refers. Eumenides is entrapped in the fairly usual Elizabethan conflict of love and friendship. First we have:

Ay, let him sleep ever, so I slumber but one minute with Semele. Love knoweth neither friendship nor kindred. (III. iv. 109)

But soon after:

The love of men to women is a thing common and of course: the friendship of man to man infinite and immortal. (III. iv. 114)

Geron advises him that

Love is but an eye-worm, which only tickleth the head with hopes and wishes: friendship the image of eternity, in which there is nothing movable, nothing mischievous. (III. iv. 123)

Whatever precisely 'friendship' may mean here – and to an Elizabethan it meant more than to us – the issue is fairly clear. Lyly often thus, provisionally, criticises the uncertainty and insubstantiality of purely sexual attraction, as in *Love's Metamorphosis*:

I do not think Love hath any spark of Divinity in him; since the end of his being is earthly. In the blood he is begot by the frail fires of the eye, and quenched by the frailer shadows of thought. What reason have we then to soothe his humour with such zeal, and follow his fading delights with such passion? (I. i. 9)

The central reality is turned round and round for continual inspection. One moment we are told that 'liking, a curtsy, a smile, a beck, and such like, are the very quintessence of love' (*Sapho and Phao*, I. iv. 16). But Eumenides in *Endimion* considers his approach to Semele in words (almost exactly repeated by Shakespeare's Troilus) that do deep intellectual justice to the riches of desire:

I pray thee, fortune, when I shall first meet with fair Semele, dash my delight with some light disgrace, lest embracing sweetness beyond measure, I take a surfeit without recure: let her practice her accustomed coyness, that I may diet myself upon my desires: otherwise the fulness of my joys will diminish the sweetness, and I shall perish by them before I possess them. (III. iv. 96)

That is, in the very preliminary tension something is known which in satisfaction is lost. The full possession with full enjoyment is an impossibility. As though in love there is a necessary fiction not to be actualised, or if actualised, fatal, or maybe enjoyed in death: perfect love on earth being a self-annihilating paradox. So exquisitely is the delicate, bright agony in all its mystery analysed, criticised, defined at every turn. And with what Shakespearian ease the problem of Spenser's 'Bower of Bliss', that of the essentially mental twist in human desire, is not ignored, but assimilated from a higher plane of reference. Love is shown as compact of contradictions and paradoxes. It is

a heat full of coldness, a sweet full of bitterness, a pain full of pleasantness; which maketh thoughts have eyes and hearts ears.... (*Gallathea*, I. ii. 16)

As in Biron's long love-defence in *Love's Labour's Lost* this heightened awareness adds new powers to the senses, a thought insistently recalling certain passages from the Gospels. The impossibility-working aspect of love is reflected' by the miraculous love-changes arranged by Cupid and Venus in the plays: the fanciful plot, as in *A Midsummer Night's Dream*, mirroring a psychological truth. The mysteries of love are divine mysteries:

O divine Love, which art therefore called divine because thou over-reachest the wisest, conquerest the chastest, and dost all things both unlikely and impossible, because thou art Love. Thou makest the bashful impudent, the wise fond, the chaste wanton, and workest contraries to our reach, because thyself is beyond reason. (*Gallathea*, III. i. 102)

Again:

Madam, if love were not a thing beyond reason, we might then give a reason of our doings, but so divine is his force, that it worketh effects as contrary to that we wish, as unreasonable against that we ought. (*Gallathea*, III. iv. 54)

There is no hope of a logical consistency. Constancy is highly valued here; yet at *Love's Metamorphosis*, III. i. 90, we have Niobe remarking that 'the oak findeth no fault with the dew, because it also falleth on the bramble', and 'the only way to be mad is to be constant.' Infinite are the twisting mazes and contradictions. So in the same play Silvestris speaks of

Jealousy, without which love is dotage, and with which love is madness; without the which love is lust, and with which love is folly. (IV. i. 22)

What other writer has so honestly put down the baffling fact? And when we are convinced of love's whimsical and perverse extravagances, Cupid himself (who should know) is found saying:

Why, Ceres, do you think that lust followeth love? Ceres, lovers are chaste: for what is love, divine love, but the quintessence of chastity, and affections binding by heavenly motions, that cannot be undone by earthly means, and must not be controlled by any man. (*Love's Metamorphosis*, II. i. 122.)

Where chastity does not mean, of course, physical renunciation. This passage, but for the style, might have come from the marriage service. 'Such is the tying of two in wedlock as is the tuning of two lutes in one key...' (*Sapho and Phao*, IV. iii. 75). And indeed Lyly continually suggests, delicately, a Christian cast of thought, except that his main god is Cupid.

All these passages should be studied in their contexts. I merely point to the range and subtlety of the analysis. From it all Cupid emerges as a great and irrational god, 'no more to be suppressed than comprehended' (*Sapho and Phao*, II. iv. 17). *Love's Metamorphosis*, which most explicitly of all points by action and symbolism Lyly's philosophy, shows Cupid's victory over the would-be cold nymphs of Ceres. 'Dare they blaspheme my godhead,' asks Cupid, 'which Jove doth worship, Neptune reverence, and all the gods tremble at?' (IV. i. 60). That is, love is the greatest of cosmic forces. Lyly knows its cauterising pain, its fantastic and frail joys, its god-like strength. It may be set beside some more commonsense, prosaic and rational essence: friendship in Eumenides, warrior-government in Alexander. But its unreasoned para-doxes are never subdued to moral categories. If Alexander and Cynthia are above love, that is because they are conceived as semi-divine already and play central parts similar to Venus or Cupid elsewhere. Apart from this, each play is a bridal symphony in measured prose.

Lyly's love apprehension is new and striking. His faith in the naked impulse of sexual attraction is exceptionally pure and independent of all moralisings. He is more interested in studying and projecting the impulse than in judging its results. The eros-perception is dramatically best consum-mated in marriage: but his analyses concern the thing itself, in which positive and negative impressions are inseparable. His conflicts are subtle and intricate with no easy black-and-white solutions. The Bower of Bliss, which is parasitic on a sin-consciousness, is to him an unknown field. The stream of romantic love welling from Provence and fertilising mediev-al allegory is locked now in the tight reservoirs of Lyly's dramatic work, forming new depths. Love has become, for the first time, dramatic, challenging the religious conscious-ness which through the centuries preceding held a monopoly over drama. This forces the creation, or borrowing, of a new, non-Christian theology. Hellenic myth obviously fits his need. Cupid – variously projected – is his main god. In this he follows medieval allegory, yet with a certain Hellenic kinship rather than an Ovidian latinity. Also Venus, Ceres, 'Sacred Neptune', all have their rights. Observe that Ceres in *Love's Metamorphosis,* stands for chastity, for marriage–fertility as opposed to love naked and unrelated, Cupid himself not being precisely a marriage god. Lyly's use of divine beings is a sincere mythology. The movement is intensely significant. Drama is close by its very nature to religion in that both hold an extra degree of shared, communal and immediate realism over secondary sorts of literature. Both are ritualistic and involve a temporary living of the action concerned. The Puritan consciousness has always recognised this threat, and consequently opposed the stage. Lyly's work rivals Christian dogma and is itself coloured with many traditional religious tonings. Asked what he thinks of love, Diogenes, a typical sex-opposing ascetic of an extreme and unrealistic sort recalling Thersites and Apemantus, answers: 'A little worser than I can of hate' (*Campaspe*, V. iv. 58). And observe such a movement as this from *Sapho and Phao:*

> *Sybil:* Why, do you love, and cannot obtain?
> *Phao:* No, I may obtain, but cannot love.
> *Sybil:* Take heed of that, my child!
> *Phao:* I cannot choose, good madam.
> *Sybil:* Then hearken to my tale, which I hope shall be as a straight thread to lead you out of those crooked conceits and place you in the plain path of love.
> (II. i. 33)

Note the similarity to a Christian confession – Lyly is using old implements for a new task; the theological supremacy of the god of love; and the treatment of a psychological case such as might interest the science of today.

Which leads to another thought. The erotic adventure of Renaissance drama and literature generally is, fundamentally, the propulsive centre of the more generally observed scientific quest of the modern world, its attempt to face actuality afresh and interpret faithfully, without preconceived critical formulae. Observe this scientific literary awareness finding place in the movement from the medieval moralities to the dramatic *Interlude of the Four Elements:* as also in Lyly's *Euphues* itself. So, after the rigid certainties of moral theology, Lyly faces instead the mystery of human personality most intensely known in eros-perception in all its paradox and irrationality. Hence one of his plays, *The Woman in the Moon*, is concerned entirely with the creation of woman. The recognition of woman as equal to yet diverse from man is at the back of the whole sex-cult of the modern world. So this genesis myth shows the infusing into Pandora by various gods of all wayward passions. She is the prototype of Shakespeare's Cleopatra. The limitation of medieval theology is that it does not allow for a Cleopatra. So, breaking away from moral absolutes, Lyly writes from an original and challenging perception of the life-fire comparable not to medieval theology, but rather to the New Testament itself. He crowns Cupid, or Eros, for the first time in England as lord of dramatic ritual: a place held by him – a jealous little god - ever since, with new cinematograph realms added recently by that very science he also, if the truth were known, inspires.

It may be said I read too deadly a seriousness into a fantastic maker of pretty phrases. Certainly, Lyly can make them - no one better: 'My thoughts, Eumenides, are stitched to the stars'. (*Endimion,* I. i. 4). Or again,

Eurota: How did it take you first, Telusa?
Telusa: By the eyes, my wanton eyes, which conceived the picture of
           his face, and hang'd it on the very strings of my heart.
                                             (*Gallathea,* III. i. 55)

These are everywhere. But to point his more philosophic profundity, I shall note a few exquisite miniatures of compressed dialogue of a sort all his own. Here is one:

Alexander: Is love a vice?
Hephaestion: It is no virtue.
                                      (*Campaspe,* II. ii. 15)

Was ever intellectual richness so compacted? Love is more ultimate than the moral order, like the rain or sun, beyond praise or blame and careless of both. Yet the moral order is not indicted, far from it. Neither vice nor virtue. Is that a compliment or criticism? We are left uncertain, but supremely aware. Here is another, less pregnant but delightful:

Parmenides: Madam, you need not doubt it, it is Alexander that is the
               conqueror.

Timoclea:	Alexander hath overcome, not conquered.
Parmenides:	To bring all under his subjection is to conquer.
Timoclea:	He cannot subdue that which is divine.
Parmenides:	Thebes was not.
Timoclea:	Virtue is.
	(*Campaspe*, I. i. 41)

Alexander's talk with Apelles, the painter, is crammed with suggested depths. I point to two:

Alexander:	When will you finish Campaspe?
Apelles:	Never finish: for always in absolute beauty there is somewhat above art.
	(*Campaspe*, III. iv. 80)

Alexander tries his hand at painting:

Alexander:	But how have I done here?
Apelles:	Like a king.
Alexander:	I think so: but nothing more unlike a painter.
	(*Campaspe*, III. iv. 110)

What perfection lies in Apelles' tiny answer, what courtly, humorous and, finally, philosophic depths! The relative importance of art and learning to soldiership and kingship, the passive and the active life, was a vital Renaissance dualism. So, too, Diogenes' criticisms of kingship go deep:

Alexander:	Why then, dost thou owe no reverence to kings?
Diogenes:	No.
Alexander:	Why so?
Diogenes:	Because they be no gods.
Alexander:	They be gods of the earth.
Diogenes:	Yea, gods of earth.
	(*Campaspe*, II. ii. 125)

Campaspe is uniquely strong in this sort, partly because its plot gives less scope for more concrete symbolisms. But you find them elsewhere. In *Endimion* the problem of eternal value and temporal mortality is given completely, and almost answered, in six short phrases ('immortal' is a favourite love-association in Lyly – *Endimion*, I. ii. 34; II. i. 43):

Tellus: She shall have an end.
Endimion: So shall the world [*i.e. that which so argues is itself no less mortal
            than what it presumes to criticise; observe that Endimion addresses
            Tellus, the Earth*].
Tellus: Is not her beauty subject to time?
Endimion: No more than time is to standing still. [*i.e. it is as much
            beauty's nature to exist somehow in its own changeless and eternal
            right as it is for time to move.*]
Tellus: Wilt thou make her immortal?
Endimion: No, but incomparable.
                                    (II. i. 83)

It is utterly honest, value is left facing mortality. But, where
the terms are 'incomparable', is reference involving comparison possible? See the two senses subtly held by 'incomparable': excessively beautiful, and not to be compared with any
mortal reasonings. Strange as it sounds, Lyly's excellences in
this kind hold something of the quality of Christ's replies in
the Gospels: simple and devastating at once because the
speaker's mind moves above the irrelevance of the question.
Here is my last example, and a very pretty one:

Silvestris: Sweet Niobe, let us sing, that I may die with the swan.
Niobe: It will make you sigh the more, and live with the salamich
              [*salamander*].
Silvestris: Are thy tunes fire?
Niobe: Are yours death?
                              (*Love's Metamorphosis*, III. i. 128)

With which I close my list. Note that they are by nature
dramatic, not so much proving or disproving a point, but
balancing one way of thinking against another.

   Lyly's mind is essentially philosophic; but it is no less
essentially poetical. I offer an example of his use of gentle
surprise, his way of revealing unexpected depths of exquisite
symbolic artistry. The three lovers in *Love's Metamorphosis*
have been rejected; and in revenge persuaded Cupid to turn
their ladies respectively into a rock, a rose and a bird.
(Observe: mineral, vegetable and animal recalling the 'scientific' universe of *Euphues*.) As the play draws to its close and
other complications are smoothed out, the lovers ask Cupid
to reverse his miracle. There are only a few pages left and you
expect an easy conventional agreement. But the ladies still

refuse: if need be, they will be metamorphosed again; but love they will not. One is at a loss as to Cupid's answer: it is perfect. If they will not love normally he will turn them next into life forms thoroughly loathsome. Observe how the symbolism – as so often – offers opportunity for a profound psychological interpretation. Next, see Lyly ring the changes on his symbols. The men are penitent and excuse their original action thus: one only wished to end his life on the rock; the next to spend his existence gazing on the rose and so die; the third, that his love might fly for ever from him, to cause his own death. The girls melt – but it is not quite over. One stipulates that her husband attributes any coldness or hardness in her to her rocky experience; the next, that if she is shrewish her husband remember roses have thorns; the third, that if she is not always at home, it is to be remembered her lover first gave her wings. Again, deep meanings are softly shadowed, meanings that involve the reciprocal antagonisms and rights of the sexes: remember Pandora. Notice, too, how the central symbols remain fixed while the author and his persons play with them, extract meanings from them. This is the way of the purest symbolism as opposed to allegory: a true symbol does not properly stand instead of something else. Meanings can be found in it: it is not conditioned by any meaning.

Each play has a controlled and variably significant design. *Campaspe* is human and simple. *Endimion* is the most imaginatively compressed and involved, thick with close-enwoven suggestions, perhaps even too dense and opaque in contemporary meaning. *Love's Metamorphosis* is probably the most intellectually profound, with a beautifully transparent symbolism. The Neptune-sacrifice of a maiden in *Gallathea* is interesting, 'sacred Neptune', it may be, representing floods of violent passion to be contrasted with the love-god who sets the difficulties to rights, since love in Lyly is more aesthetic than sensual: Lyly is in his way a moralist, though under Cupid's ensign; never exactly a sensuous writer. He is 'intellectual' compared with Spenser, or even such a work as Drayton's *Endimion*. Beneath his English pastoralism and Hellenic mythology – note the woods of Lincolnshire delightfully and characteristically made the home of a Neptune cult in *Gallathea* – there is continually meaning, though it would be unwise to pluck at it too fiercely. Behind the miraculous changes arranged by Cupid in more than one play are possible psychological significances as I have already noticed. Sometimes there are dark, almost tragic essences: the passion of Tellus in *Endimion;* the money-greedy Erisichthon's cutting of the tree sacred to Ceres and its consequent pain – a fine opportunity for symbolic interpretation – in *Love's Metamorphosis;* satire on greed again in *Midas,* with again the obvious contrast of metallic and natural values. But mainly such poisonous evils are avoided, and analysis and plot both confined to the infinite complexities of love, with a steady movement towards a ceremonious conclusion.

Shakespeare's debt to Lyly has been often emphasised; though it is as much a natural kinship as a debt. Thought parallels bristle on page after page. I would stress a wider parallel of design, a measured and purposive working out of complications unfurling to a satisfying, often somewhat ritualistic close. This, so beautifully executed in Lyly, is part of the Shakespearian art always. And I do not mean only Shakespeare's lighter work. Lyly's thought points the mind as much to the metaphysic of love in *Troilus and Cressida* and *Antony and Cleopatra* as to *Love's Labour's Lost* and the Sonnets. So too the central dream in *Endimion* and its recapitulation at the end forecast Posthumus's dream and description in *Cymbeline:* note the part played by the eagle in both plays. And the conclusions, and indeed the whole designs, are so ceremoniously satisfying through use especially of two sorts of *centrality,* both throwing forward to Shakespeare.

First, there are central dominating figures: Cynthia, Venus, Cupid, Alexander. All the plays reflect Elizabethan royalism in that they possess some dominant and central figure of worldly or divine authority or, as in *Endimion,* of both; persons of power on whom everything depends, and who yet do not steal the whole action like Marlowe's protagonists. This reflects, of course, the queen-centred Court life of the play's origin. And we see how Lyly and Shakespeare constructed admirable art forms (remember

Shakespeare always has his king or duke) partly because the
queen-centred life around Elizabeth was itself of art-form
quality: they had a hub on which to revolve. Moreover, a
hub that could inspire a belief—however transient – like this:

Gyptes: They are thrice fortunate that live in your palace, where Truth
is not in colours, but life, virtues not in imagination, but
execution.

Cynthia: I have always studied to have rather living virtues than painted
Gods; the body of Truth, than the tomb. (*Endimion*, IV. iii. 48)

Which shows how an earthly paradise was, or seemed, at
hand to the Elizabethan imagination. The actual was
eros-impregnated on a grand scale, and Elizabethan literature
is one of the results. The synthesis of loyalty and eroticism in
Endimion's adoration for Cynthia points ahead to the twin
positive forces of Shakespeare's work; the romantic and
kingly ideals, not so distinct then as now. Kindred dual
feelings are blended into Shakespeare's Sonnets, neither
flattery nor sexual emotion quite, but something to us
slightly alien made of both.

There are, secondly, central symbols, the impregnating of
some object with a central significance, such as the Well, or
the sleeping figure of the hero himself, in *Endimion*, or the
Tree in both *Gallathea* and *Love's Metamorphosis*. Such a
symbol taking, as it were, the stage-centre of the play's
massed area (and often it will therefore be an object central on
the actual stage) lends concreteness and focal length to the
action round it; serves as a heart to the organism, as the
central person is its spine and head, and the ceremonial
conclusion its crown. Time and again art-forms of
Shakespearian texture, whether in poem, play or novel,
show such central symbolisms: something both created by
and reacting on the dominant conflicts concerned; the body's
heart.

Lyly's formalised and ceremonious designs enclose acts of
sacrifice or other ritual and devotion to one or other of his
gods. A fervent piety breathes in all these, especially in the
sublimation and victory of Cupid over the chastity of Ceres'
nymphs in *Love's Metamorphosis*, and the friendly exchange of
sacrifices between the two divinities, Cupid and Ceres;

reflecting a synthesis of naked desire and marriage fertility, perhaps of all Lyly's most significant symbolic stroke of art. Sacrifice and piety are intrinsic to Lyly's conception of love; a humble, rich, sweetly human thing. Campaspe and Apelles talk of Venus who can, of course, almost be equated with Cupid:

> Campaspe: How is she hired: by prayer, by sacrifice, or bribes?
> Apelles: By prayer, sacrifice, and bribes.
> Campaspe: What prayer?
> Apelles: Vows irrevocable.
> Campaspe: What sacrifice?
> Apelles: Hearts ever sighing, never dissembling.
> Campaspe: What bribes?
> Apelles: Roses and kisses: but were you never in love?
> Campaspe: No, nor love in me. (*Campaspe*, III. iii. 34)

Notice the religious tonings. Lyly's religious feeling in the plays may recall his more specifically Christian and Biblical moralisings in *Euphues*. He was saturated in all that first before becoming an artistic devotee of his eros-cult. This is correspondingly sweetened and ennobled. It is his essential humility and purity before direct human experience that brings Lyly closest to Shakespeare and makes his humour sympathetic and kindly, the antithesis of Jonson's: compare his satire on alchemists (in *Gallathea*) with Jonson's. Lyly's comedy there with the Astronomer who falls into a ditch whilst studying the stars is, characteristically, a humour playing around the philosophic. Such humour (of Shakespearian sort) is, like his dialogue, dependent often on a sudden awareness of a big simplicity breaking through a slight complexity. Remember his delightful fun with Latin tags in *Endimion;* with Sir Tophas as 'three-quarters of a noun-substantive' (III. iii. 16); and remember he is a schoolmaster, producing with his boys as players. A deeper wisdom puts learning in its place: yet surely no Elizabethan used learning to better purpose; nor any literary genius of the first order in English literature was more fit to be, as well, a teacher of children.

For this is, in short, his humanistic message:

There is no man so savage in whom resteth not this divine particle, that there is an omnipotent, eternal, and divine mover, which may be called God. (*Campaspe*, I. iii. 35))

And, yet, paradoxically – and to be true to him we must preserve a paradox –

I cannot see, Montanus, why it is feigned by the poets that love sat upon the chaos and created the world; since in the world there is so little love. (*Love's Metamorphosis*, I. i. 1)

That may be. But it is not the fault of Lyly's plays.

Note

[1] The references follow R. Warwick Bond's fine and indispensable edition of Lyly's works, Oxford University Press, 1902. Spelling, and in some instances punctuation, have, however, been modernised.

Additional Note, 1984
    My reading of Spenser's 'Bower of Bliss' on pp. 162 and 164 follows that of C.S. Lewis in *The Allegory of Love*.

XI   Webster's *Duchess of Malfi*

(from *The Malahat Review*, Victoria, IV, October 1967;
composed 1937-9)

I

I have often written of the Shakespearian play as 'set spatially
as well as temporally' in the mind, noting its area of imagistic
and symbolic appeal. *The Duchess of Malfi* shows an even
thicker clustering of such impressions than Shakespeare. A
brake is applied to the action by it, as with the stickiness of
Hardy's prose, like a wet, ploughed field, organically
retarding the clogged and fettered progress of his unhappy
people. Numerous, often conflicting, colours interthread
Shakespeare's carpets: in *The Duchess of Malfi*, though there
are certain tableaux of colour, the toning of thought and
image is more level: black, brown, grey, a spurt of flame
occasionally, but for the rest hardly a purple.

Many ordinary and rather uninteresting man-made objects
are mentioned, as a group nearly, and yet not precisely, fitted
by the term 'mechanical'. These contribute to the dun tonings
generally: such as 'touch-wood', 'rough-cast', 'spectacles',
'shoeing-horn', 'glass-house', 'dirty stirrup riveted', a 'false
key', 'rusty watch', a 'heavy lump of lead', breasts 'hoop'd
with adamant', 'three fair medals cast in one figure'. The
work of artisans is often suggested, sometimes their trades
named: 'tradesmen', 'rope-maker', 'soap-boiler', 'picture-
maker', a 'curious artist' taking a watch to pieces in order to
mend it, a 'curious master' in the 'quality' of making wax
figures, a 'strong-thigh'd bargeman', the 'galley-slave' at his
oar. Often we touch the specifically scientific or mechanical:
that 'fantastic glass invented by Galileo', safety 'runs upon

enginous wheels', death's door goes on 'strange geometrical hinges'. 'Mathematics', 'geometry', 'corrosive', 'perspective', 'curious engine' come in naturally. Here is a more extended example: 'I would have a mathematical instrument made for her face, that she might not laugh out of compass'; or

> When Fortune's wheel is over-charg'd with princes,
> The weight makes it move swift.
> (III. v. 112)

An age-old image given a more scientific twist. Webster, like many seventeenth-century poets, often uses the mathematical, geometrical, or scientific drive in an abstract judgement: 'as if he were ballass'd with quicksilver' is typical. The list is unShakespearian in its comparative emphasis, and is only slightly foreshadowed in Marlowe. It reflects town rather than country life; is homely, realistic, and a little depressing. Sometimes there is a predominant cast of cynicism, often something of a hard, dry humour.

Nor is war here romantic: rather its modern engines come in for unpicturesque stress; no flashing shields or knightly armour. There is talk of 'great battles', 'towns of garrison', 'a new fortification', a 'fort-bridge'. Servants speak of a switzer 'with a pistol in his great cod-piece', the 'moulds' of whose buttons were 'leaden bullets'; 'paper bullets' are used in the Shakespearian sense of 'witticisms'; the Duchess imagines herself 'shot to death with pearls'; Bosola compares the Cardinal and Ferdinand to 'two chain'd bullets'. Fire may be suggested: 'a hollow bullet filled with unquenchable wild-fire'. Pistols play a part in the action. Impressions of gunpowder and cannon occur. Though Count Malateste 'has worn gunpowder in his hollow tooth for the toothache', he is afraid the smell of gunpowder will spoil the perfume of his mistress's scarf. There is a powdery, sulphurous smell over the play:

> *Pescara:*   The Lord Ferdinand laughs.
> *Delio:*   Like a deadly cannon
>   That lightens ere it smokes.
> (III. iii. 65)

The Duchess imagines herself as standing on a mine about to blow up; and again

> O misery: like to a rusty o'ercharg'd cannon
> Shall I never fly in pieces?
> (III. v. 121)

A good instance of the unromantic yet sulphurous threat of this play's impressions. The action moves in a world of 'touch-holes' and 'fire-locks', there is a background of human enmity and smouldering danger. It is part of Webster's stock-in-trade: you get as much, or more, in *The White Devil*. Talk of war is frequent: some of the chief persons are, or have been, at the wars; and at a central point, the Cardinal, chief villain of the piece, is installed as a soldier. Renaissance war here is realistic, mechanical and sulphurous, blending with other hell-tonings to be observed later: there is little or none of Shakespeare's 'pride, pomp and circumstance of glorious war'.

From this realistic and often drab toning certain references to rich stones unhappily and ineffectually shine out. There is satire on gold as in the Apothecary scene of *Romeo and Juliet*. The Duchess dreams of the diamonds on her coronet of state being changed to pearls, forecasting tears. Riches are thus, in one way or another, toned evilly as when Julia talks of 'stealing a diamond'. They are, as it were, smothered by the palling smoke and muffled thunder of the impregnating condemnation that constricts our world. Asked by Bosola if the cords of execution do not terrify, the Duchess answers:

> What would it pleasure me, to have my throat cut
> With diamonds? or to be smothered
> With cassia? or to be shot to death with pearls?
> (IV. ii. 222)

The ultimate worthlessness of riches is intrinsic to the thought: such references in their contexts intensify the gloom.

I pass from such man-warm objects or implements to observe nature references, seeing how they blend in with our other impressions. There are, as in *King Lear,* many animals, usually unpicturesque. Often they are felt in a semi-human way: the 'politic dormouse', 'irregular crab', 'abortive hedge-hog', 'impudent snake', 'old fox', 'tame elephant'. We have flatterers compared to 'lice', foxes carrying fire among crops, servants as 'vipers', children as 'young wolves'. Suffering is often in some fashion suggested: a 'bear in a ring', a leveret dying 'without any resistance', a mouse uncomfortably housed 'in a cat's ear' (a typical macabre stroke of humour), English mastiffs grown fierce with being tied up, a bird's wings clipped, birds entrapped, a spider's 'black web'. Subtle torture is in this:

> the bee
> When he hath shot his sting into your hand
> May then play with your eye-lid.
> (IV. i. 92)

There is mad Ferdinand's self-inflicted penance of driving 'six snails' before him to Moscow as a trial of patience, a ludicrous touch recalling Lear's madness. Most of the animals are ugly or fearsome either directly or through superstitious associations: the mule, the mole, 'dogs and monkeys', paraqueto, scorpions, porcupines, crows, jackdaws, starlings, magpies, caterpillars, glow-worms, worms (especially in association with death), wolves and owls (both frequent). A man lifts his nose like 'a foul porpoise before a storm'. The madmen's dirge concerns 'ravens, screech-owls, bulls and bears'. The frequent man – animal association in varied guise is important. 'This mole does undermine me' is pure Webster. In a strange speech at II. i. 47–60 animals are used to suggest disease ('the most ulcerous wolf and swinish meazle') and harmless quiet beasts are mentioned in contrast to human 'deformity'. Ferdinand ends up digging graves, a man's leg on his shoulder, howls and says he is a wolf. Aptly in such a play where man's nature is so ruthless the chief villain descends to this wolvish horror. *King Lear* is often suggested, and Swift continually forecast.

There are, however, some happier bird-images. Innocence is compared to a 'turtle', the soul to a lark in a cage. Again,

> The robin redbreast and the nightingale
> Never live long in cages.
> (IV. ii. 15)

or,

> The birds that live i' the field
> On the wild benefit of nature, live
> Happier than we; for they may choose their mates
> And carol their sweet pleasures to the spring.
> (III. v. 25)

Webster's mind is occasionally Shakespearian in its feeling for wild nature's innate beneficence. Such touches come on the ear plaintive and distant, a far fluting as from a distant world.

Direct nature-reference apart from animal life is slight, and fairly obvious, mostly Shakespearian but with little or no evidence of first-hand observation: winds, showers, heaven's thunder, destroying tempests, 'foul weather'. These are used normally. There is little sunlight. The eyes of a forward prostitute 'carry a quiver of darts' which are 'sharper than sun-beams': but it is a lonely reminiscence of Spenser or Lyly in a significant context. This is a sunless world: 'Let not the sun shine on him till he's dead', says Ferdinand of Antonio. The Duchess curses the stars and all unwintry seasons. Winter and darkness are our stage. Much of the action is enveloped by night. Bosola enters 'with a dark lanthorn' talking of that 'melancholy bird' the owl, Antonio 'with a candle', on the mysterious night of childbirth: a characteristic association, setting more fit for a Duncan's murder. In pitch darkness, with no 'torch' or 'taper' burning, Ferdinand presents the Duchess with Antonio's supposed hand. He is himself found at 'dead of night' carrying a man's leg. This is our world:

> In what a shadow or deep pit of darkness
> Doth womanish and fearful mankind live!
> (V. v. 125)

But, as with other nature-references darkness is not so much recreated from any direct particularised experience – for example, Shakespeare's 'dead vast and middle of the night' – as expressed through traditional associations. Webster's

animal and natural impressionism seems to be summed in
Ferdinand's phrase after the murder: 'I'll go hunt the badger
by owl-light'.

Once the 'spheres' are mentioned, but the universal nature
is mostly shut out, dimmed by pressing agonies, distorted by
wolvish actions, the best smeared and overlaid by human and
pessimistic thinking and superstition. There are more nature-
references of the *Euphues* sort used with a sense of legendary
belief: such as the cedar tree made firm by shaking; or we
may have, once, reminiscence of Greek myth, persons
transformed to pleasant natural objects. These have only a
secondary, literary reality, similar to the salamanders,
basilisks, and cockatrices elsewhere. 'I have this night digged
up a mandrake' is a good Websterian scene opening. But
never, or seldom, is nature directly seen or felt in and for
itself as a preliminary to its use for a more general poetic
purpose. Our animals are mostly thick-coated with superstition, or used mainly, more evidently than in Shakespeare, as
man comparisons. They have less rights on their own as
animals; that is not normally relevant here. Much of
Webster's impressionism is rooted in medieval pseudo-
science. Always, as it were, to quote Tennyson's *In
Memoriam,* a 'web is woven across the sky' of direct sight.
Exact analysis and weighing of his imagistic quality leads to
this important result: Webster's world is a mind-world; his
nature, a studied nature; his horrors, mind-horrors, saturated
in conventional superstition. The saturation is part of the
horror. Each touch is pondered and weighty, the superstition
heavy with accumulated centuries of fear.

Astrology plays an important part. There is talk about
'setting a figure' for the nativity of the Duchess's child.
Bosola reads out in detail the calculations: 'The lord of the
first house, being combust in the ascendant, signifies short
life...', and so on. Elsewhere, told that some hold that all
things are written in the stars, Bosola characteristically
replies: 'Yes, if we could find spectacles to read them'. We
hear of a soldier who fights by the almanack shunning
'critical' days. Stars are naturally here impregnated with such
pseudo-scientific superstitions, their native glory unfelt:

> We are merely the stars' tennis-balls, strook and bandied
> Which way please them.
> (V. iv. 63)

The air is heavy with superstition. Sometimes it is criticised, as when Ferdinand wonders if love potions are more than the fraud of mountebanks, or the Duchess calls Cariola a 'superstitious fool' for disliking the irreverence of a pretended pilgrimage. But there is, too, the Duchess's dream of pearls and Antonio's grim interpretation. Superstition is felt powerfully, whatever is said. Here is the quality distilled:

> How superstitiously we mind our evils!
> The throwing down salt, or crossing of a hare;
> Bleeding at nose, the stumbling of a horse,
> Or singing of a cricket, are of power
> To daunt whole man in us.
> (II. ii. 80)

How quiet, yet how ominously weighted the simple, limping accents fall: this is a philosophic, inactive world, paralysed by fears of all sorts. Witches are often referred to. They give the Devil suck, convey man through the air on whirlwinds, whisper charms in a 'deformed' silence, stick needles into wax figures: the normal and traditional beliefs.

An orthodox belief in Hell is therefore natural. All the chief persons express a dim faith in an after-existence, though the phrases are mostly cheerless. Hell-tonings are to be expected. Fire is here evil. I have already noticed the cannon references. There is violent fire observed in Ferdinand's villainous eye; the Cardinal, talking to Bosola, considers their evil scheme as a fire well burning; Ferdinand would have the Duchess and Antonio burned in a stopped-up coal pit, so that their smoke might not rise to Heaven, or wrapped in their own sheets saturated in 'pitch or sulphur', then lighted. Fire is evilly impregnated:

> I have this Cardinal in the forge already,
> Now I'll bring him to the hammer.
> (V. iv. 92)

Notice the mechanic workshop suggestion: the whole play is something of a devil's smithy. The world is a hell:

> Th' heaven o'er my head seems made of molten brass,
> The earth of flaming sulphur, yet I am not mad...
> (IV. ii. 27)

The Cardinal at the end is puzzled concerning the 'material fire' of Hell; and soon after sees a figure 'armed with a rake', recalling Dante. Nearly all the fire images are hellish, as the stars are threatening: fire or light as a cosmic and optimistic force is almost unknown. Hell and the Devil are on everyone's lips: 'Those houses that are haunted are most still till the Devil be up.' 'Deep groans and terrible ghastly looks' are usual impressions. One of the few classical touches in this medieval horror is that of Charon's boat conveying dead souls 'o'er the dismal lake'. And even the more sanctified religious colourings, outwardly Christian and orthodox, are likely to be fateful.

We hear of 'Doom's-day', a 'solemn vow', a 'sacrament o' the church'. The Cardinal is a central figure; and the shrine of Our Lady of Loretto an important scene, with the entrance of pilgrims. Ferdinand is met 'behind St Mark's church', come from digging up bodies in the graveyard. There is the Echo scene among ancient ruins of an abbey and talk of its long past, and the men buried there. Religion here often suggests an eternity of tomb-like death: traditional Christianity is as much a matter of death as Lyly's Hellenic piety of life. Often a dark religion is ranged against simple love. The Cardinal and the Duchess are the final human antagonists. Bosola suggests the Duchess be given 'a penitential garment' with 'beads and a prayer-book' for having married Antonio: the opposition is imaginatively explicit. She herself asks why she should be 'cas'd up like a holy relic' since she has 'youth and a little beauty': notice how the understatement of her claim reflects the stifling of the grimly religious gloom.

And yet the religious tonings have here their own sombre, grave-like magic. The persons' words, their questions and plaintive half-worded hopes, linger wanderingly as about the vaults of some vast, ruined cathedral of a

universe, echoing, self-answered, no more. Or maybe it is
rather the 'suburbs of hell' we are in – delightful phrase! Once
a sweeter Christianity is shadowed, as when Bosola, told by
the Duchess of her marriage for love to a simple steward,
calls her bed a 'fair seminary of peace', says how 'unbe-
nefic'd' scholars will pray for her, Turks and Moors turn
Christian; a strange, tangled, but of course mainly hypocri-
tical speech (III. 2. 324–41) associating Christianity with
simple love. Even so, it is in its context ironic. Religion is
usually a matter of wicked cardinals, stone ruins or tombs;
or, if blessed, an other-worldly eternity:

> In the eternal church, sir,
> I do hope we shall not part thus.
> (III. v. 84)

Webster's ghostly phrase strikes like a chill and a doubt even
when it would seem most to comfort.

It is a world of disease: no impression is more powerful
than that of disease. Physicians and midwives, poisons and
medicines, hospitals – medical terms of all sorts pile up
amazingly from a close inspection. Here are some of the
ailments: smallpox, leprosy, ague, apoplexy, frenzy, melancholy (considered as a physical ailment), palsy; and here some
medicines (or poisons): a deadly honey-dew, 'Balsamum',
'desperate physic', poisoned apricots, poisoned pills, 'possets
to procure sleep', lemon pills, 'lenitive poisons', a 'lingering
poison', 'rhubarb' to purge 'choler'. We hear of a 'sick man's
urine', a 'sick liver', 'one in physic', galls overflowing livers,
mad folk 'from the common hospital', 'broken sleeps'. The
plague is especially frequent: 'one sick of the plague', 'give
out she died o' the plague', cities 'plagued with plagues',
plagues that 'make lanes through largest families'. Princes'
images are made 'as if they died of the tooth-ache', death is a
'mandragora' to make the Duchess sleep, Ferdinand suffers
from a 'very pestilent disease' called lycanthropia. Seeing
Julia of whom he is tired the Cardinal remarks prettily,
'Yond's my lingering consumption' and later makes her kiss
a poisoned Bible. Pain, we are told, is removed by fear of

worse, as tooth-ache by sight of the operating 'barber'. Wisdom is a 'foul tetter' running over the body. Places at Court are like beds at a 'hospital', one man's head at another's foot. We hear how physicians applying horse-leeches to a swelling cut off their tails to led the blood run through. A great physician cured the Pope by making him laugh so that the 'imposthume' broke. Childbirth is inverted to a sickness: the Duchess 'is sick a days, she pukes, her stomach seethes...'. Notice with what sickly cynicism or fatalism these impressions and the way they are used soak our play's texture: it positively drips with diseases. This is how people talk of anger:

Ferdinand:	Have not you
	My palsy?
Cardinal:	Yes – I can be angry
	Without this rupture – there is not in nature
	A thing, that makes man so deform'd, so beastly,
	As doth intemperate anger.
	(II. v. 71)

Webster seems to feel man as by nature deformed:

Man stands amaz'd to see his deformity
In any other creature but himself.
But in our own flesh, though we bear diseases,
Which have their true names only ta'en from beasts,
As the most ulcerous wolf, and swinish meazle;
Though we are eaten up of lice and worms,
And though continually we bear about us
A rotten and dead body, we delight
To hide it in rich tissue.
(II. i. 52)

A revealing, Swiftian, speech. Death and disease go hand in hand. Told by Bosola he is come to make her tomb, the Duchess asks, 'Dost thou perceive me sick?' Almost her last words are that her little boy be given 'some syrop for his cold', a touch losing something of the pathos a less disease-ridden context might give out; and she forgives her executioners since human actions of cruelty are only bubbles on that vast sea of world disease which the play reveals: 'the apoplexy, catarrh, or cough o' the lungs would do as much as they do.' When someone says

> Come: I'll be out of this ague;
> For to live thus, is not indeed to live
> (V. iii. 59)

we tend to endorse the statement; and one of the last impressions to linger is

> Pleasure of life, what is't? Only the good hours
> Of an ague...
> (V. iv. 78)

Life is a living death.

So the play is weighty with death. As the climax of the Duchess's murder approaches there is insistence on every detail. Bosola is come to make her 'tomb'; has with him a coffin, cords and bell; acts the part of the fatal bellman. Webster depicts not a murder but a careful explicated dramatisation of the hideous quality of death. Bosola, high priest of the occasion, so often a voice to the play's movement, speaks the moral of it all:

Thou art a box of worm-seed, at best but a salvatory of green mummy. What's this flesh? A little curded milk, fantastical puff-paste. Our bodies are weaker than those paper prisons boys use to keep flies in: more contemptible: since ours is to preserve earth-worms. (IV. ii. 123)

Though he may talk of the soul in the body as a caged lark the stress is far heavier on the body's death than the soul's life. Indeed, it scarcely exists, the body – soul dualism being to a Renaissance poet a thought, but not a lived and felt actuality. Death here is a 'hideous storm of terror'. Men suffering from lycanthropia 'steal forth to churchyards in the dead of night and dig dead bodies up'. Asked to take up Julia's body Bosola remarks

> I think I shall
> Shortly grow the common bier for church-yards:
> (V. ii. 344)

The Duchess and Bosola play with the idea of tombs, of what stuff will he make hers?

> Bosola: Nay, resolve me first of what fashion?
> Duchess: Why, do we grow fantastical in our death-bed?
>   Do we affect fashion in the grave?
>   (IV. ii. 150)

Tombs are usual: 'And wherefore should you lay fair marble colours upon your rotten purposes to me?' and 'Think you your bosom will be a grave dark and obscure enough for such a secret?' and –

> You have a pair of hearts are hollow graves
> Rotten, and rotting others.
>   (IV. ii. 345)

This all blends into images of ruin. The Duchess is like 'some reverend monument whose ruins are even pitied', a phrase strangely feeling the pathos of the inanimate in decay. In his last speech Bosola says

> We are only like dead walls, or vaulted graves,
> That ruin'd, yields no echo.
>   (V. v. 121)

The whole tragic action of the play – indeed almost the play itself – is once referred to as a 'noble ruin'. But best of all is the fine description earlier of the 'ruins of an ancient abbey' now, significantly, a 'fortification':

> I do love these ancient ruins.
> We never tread upon them but we set
> Our foot upon some reverend history.
> And questionless, here in this open court
> (Which now lies naked to the injuries
> Of stormy weather), some men lie interr'd
> Lov'd the Church so well, and gave so largely to it,
> They thought it should have canopied their bones
> Till Doom's-day. But all things have their end.
> Churches and cities (which have diseases like to men)
> Must have like death that we have.
>   (V. iii. 10)

Webster's impressionism feels the Renaissance as the ruins of a past age, not the birth – and we can remember Webster's sickly view of birth – of a new one. His poetry points consistently back, as Shakespeare's does not. The Shakespearian phrase has an immediate sap in it that keeps it taut, erect, whatever its explicit content; whereas Webster's limping rhythms only add to the nerveless horror or pathos of his meaning. His death-horrors are the traditional ones: graves, worms, mouldering flesh, ruins and decay. It is an intellectual horror at certain sense-impressions, totally negative, and in its way conventional, an inborn convention, that is, of the human mind in general: it is not necessarily rational. Although orthodox tonings suit well here – and the inevitability of the association is of almost terrifying significance – yet none of it is Christian in the Gospel sense: 'Let the dead bury their dead.' The Gospel feeling for immediate and forward-thrusting life is a positive for which we must go to Shakespeare or the Hellenists, Lyly, Elizabethan lyric and the Romantics; or, as I shall show, certain aspects of Webster's human understanding as distinguished from his close net of sickly-traditional impressions, sweet only with the sweetness of death.

There is no warmth of human joy here; instead, a freezing cold:

> 'Tis even like him that in a winter night
> Takes a long slumber o'er a dying fire
> As loth to part from it: yet parts thence as cold
> As when he first sat down.
> (III. ii. 237)

A lovely instance of the recurrent Websterian movement: a few lines succeeded by a limping half-line close. Cold dominates, in association with negations, in opposition to love; as when Ferdinand's tears of pity were 'frozen up' by his evil nature whilst the Duchess lived, or the single life is compared to Anaxarete, 'frozen into marble'. 'I'll not freeze i' the business' is a more general, obvious phrase; and so, too, this fine miniature:

> I must look to my footing;
> In such slippery ice-pavements, men had need
> To be frost-nail'd well...
>   (V. ii. 367)

But in both cold is hostile. There is a cold horror often. The very incidents build it. Holding the dead hand (supposedly Antonio's) in the dark the Duchess says: 'You are very cold.' Icy, corpse-like horror. Again, seeing the supposed dead bodies of Antonio and his children, she would join the frozen group:

> If they would bind me to that lifeless trunk
> And let me freeze to death.
>   (IV. i. 79)

'A cold tomb-stone o'er his bones' is the most anyone here can wish for. There are 'anatomies' set by doctors 'i' th' cold yonder in barber chirurgeon's hall'. Russia to the writers of this period a word of wintry suggestion (we may remember its use in *The Winter's Tale*) occurs three times. There is mention of a 'slave-born Russian'; there is Ferdinand's driving his team of snails to Moscow; and the Duchess cursing

> those three smiling seasons of the year
> Into a Russian winter: nay, the world
> To its first chaos.
>   (IV. i. 117)

Winter, chaos, death. A certain stillness freezes Webster's stage: it is paralysed by a horror till horror itself shakes paralysis to a keener agony. Flames give no warmth here: both its sulphurous and icy tonings derive from medieval, Dantesque, hells such as those in Claudio's fearful death-speech. We 'seem to sweat in ice and freeze in fire,' says Bosola. 'A cold sweat' is a phrase occurring more than once. So the cold has nothing of Marlowe's Swiss holiday imagery of scintillating, sun-flashing crystals. The play significantly closes with the sun coming out to dispel the snowed-up recollections of our wintry horror. But during the action there is only cold of a corpse-like pallor, a frozen horror, and thoughts of an eternity icy as the stony vaultings of a ruin'd church. Here it is all summed up:

> that speech
> Came from a dying father: your kiss is colder
> Than thát I have seen an holy anchorite
> Give to a dead man's skull.
> (III. v. 102)

On the one side, human love; on the other, holiness, orthodox religious colourings, a skull, icy death. Again, the associations, and still more their compact and organically satisfying result, are of insistent significance.

For Webster's associative technique is of an unswerving precision. If a man stuffs up his ears here, it is with black cotton wool. His area of choice may be limited but the variations within that area are subtle, coherent and organic. There is nothing like Marlowe's jarring imaginative inconsequences and arbitrary oppositions. Whatever Webster's references to artisans and mechanic trades or objects, there is no mechanical journeyman work in his artistic structure. *The Duchess of Malfi* has as perfect an organic life as anything in our literature, every tissue is in its place. And therefore finally it delivers negatively the exact message which Lyly delivers positively: their statements, necessarily, converge. (See pp. 164–6). His substance may be different, but his art obeys the same inevitable logic of associative law. Marlowe, whose *Faustus* presents a conflict of the erotic and the medieval, gives you neither in clarity; his work expresses neither (nor therefore their conflict) satisfactorily. But also there is always a close philosophy within Webster's imaginative precisions. We see how the newly human is impressionistically smothered by the traditional and medieval: by orthodox tonings of all sorts, age-old superstitions, mouldering ruins of the mind of man. And this blends into his harsh, bitter realism concerning the present: as though the past was now a revolting corpse; and the present merely a hideous, insentient intruder, desecrating with its own disease the ruins of the past. In this world is set the action and its conflict; in this world the Duchess placed to champion the trust in humanity, especially woman, that beats in Lyly's Pandora and Shakespeare's Cleopatra.

II

To pass now to Webster's more specifically human exposition. I have noticed references to trades and artisans. What might be called middle-class professions come in for far more notice than in Shakespeare, the general effect tending to satire. Lawyers are not heavily attacked, but legal terms occur in association with Antonio's stewardship. The law is associated with prisons and suitors, and called a 'foul black cobweb', and we hear of a 'lawyer's mule' and a vicar going to law for a tithe-pig to 'undo' his neighbours; though judge and jury and the ceremonial of a law court once receive respectful notice. Besides the vicar just noticed, ecclesiastical reference is varied and thick: the Cardinal, as a pillar of the Church, exists as a bitter comment. Astrology and physic are suggested continually and often critically. These more learned professions are those represented by the four speaking madmen, according to F. L. Lucas's identification, in the ghoulish masque. From which we see how close is the organic coherence of the whole. This masque is at the play's heart, summing or tying up many elsewhere dominant strands into a significant symbolism: the madmen are not just a means to torment the heroine, but are themselves important. They indicate a world gone mad in study, recalling Swift's 'projectors' at Lagado. There is the astrologer drawing doom's-day close with a 'perspective'; the lawyer and his vision of Hell, though I cannot see in his first remark a direct professional reference; the priest and his parish amours, his talk of damnation, his play with 'wenches' in the midst of 'tombs', a significant opposition; and the doctor whose making of a 'soap-boiler' 'costive' was his 'masterpiece'. Doctors are elsewhere satirised, especially in the ludicrous play between the over-confident doctor and mad Ferdinand. Both come off poorly: 'Are you out of your princely wits?' says the doctor. The 'forty urinals filled with rose-water', the 'anatomies' in 'barber-chirurgeon's hall' are satirically toned, and the doctor is knocked down for his pains. All this points ahead to Swift and Shaw. Webster's scientific interest is all along clear from his imagery, but he does not seem very fond of scientists. Academic literary learning gets a lash. We hear of 'fantastical' scholars who study to know

> how many knots
> Was in Hercules' club, of what colour Achilles' beard was,
> Or whether Hector were not troubled with the tooth-ache.
> (III. iii. 51)

all to gain the reputation of a 'speculative man'. The satire touches that of certain passages in Pope's *Dunciad*. Webster's satiric by-products of his vast and properly non-satiric whole have often a modern application.

Soldiership is unromantically presented. Bosola can, to serve his purpose, describe an ideal soldier-courtier, but more characteristic is the mockery of Malateste wearing gun powder in a hollow tooth, keeping paintings to express 'battles in model', fighting 'by the almanack', running from battle to save his taffeta scarf. The reward of a soldier's hazardous calling is ironically described in the mathematical imagery of Bosola as 'a kind of geometry';

> *Delio:*   Geometry?
> *Bosola:*   Ay, to hang in a fair pair of slings, take his latter swing in the world upon an honourable pair of crutches from hospital to hospital.
> (I. i. 63)

Webster's penetration goes deep, his play being more modern than you might think.

The princely ideal is similarly reversed. Princes are shown as rotten to the core, patronage as uncertain, advancement an evil and deceiving incentive. Princes' images on their tombs are carved as if their eyes were 'wholly bent upon the world', not looking to Heaven. The Duchess before her death opposes 'Heaven's gates' to 'princes' palaces'. Princes are greedy and remorseless materialists ready to 'spoil a whole province and batter down goodly cities with the cannon' for their own ambition. Factions among 'great men' lead to wanton destruction; 'great men' may be warned that the unfortunate are sometimes more valuable than they. 'Politicians' and especially 'intelligencers' are mean creatures, selling their souls for nothing. 'Off, my painted honour!' cries sin-struck Bosola; it is a danger to 'receive a prince's secrets'; the 'favour' of princes is 'changeable'; a politician is 'the devil's quilted anvil', a good example of Webster's compressed macabre wit. Society is rotten with selfish greed:

> Oh, this base quality
> Of intelligencer! Why, every quality in the world
> Prefers but gain or commendation.
>   (III. ii. 375)

Princes pay 'flatterers' in their own false coin, places at Court are like 'beds' in a 'hospital'; and so on.

These prevailing thoughts relate to the main human figures of our drama and the main conflict. Satire on place and supposed 'honour' blends with the family pride of the Cardinal and Ferdinand, which is the originating spring of hostile and evil action. Love is opposed by a rotten social code. Her family resent the Duchess's marriage both, it is suggested, for greed of gold and because Antonio is a commoner. Their jealousy is a complex of antipathies. It is not a worn-out problem: there is, perhaps must be, an eternal opposition between the familial and the sexual, often taking the shape of social objection, and here in addition incurring an accusation of lust.[1] 'The Duchess's love is smirched by unjust suggestions: to wed twice is 'luxurious', a matter of 'lustful pleasures', though 'honour' in her husband might excuse it. It is all totally irrational, but not out-of-date. Hamlet himself was guilty of a similar non-sequitur. Antonio is called the Duchess's 'lecher' to be shut in a cell such as 'anchorites' put to 'holier use': again observe the opposition. Bosola suggests the Duchess's 'delicate skin' be tormented by a 'penitential garment'. The body is a 'prison', 'sin' is in man's 'conception': can bodily pleasure be pure? The Duchess asks why marriage is forbidden her, ironically observing that she is starting 'no new custom'. Against her is her brothers' puritanical disgust, like that of Mr Barrett in *The Barretts of Wimpole Street*. A false idealism based on greed and outward 'place' gives birth to a perverted puritanism. Webster presents a crucial family condensation of the disease of the modern western world, aptly remarking how 'kindred' commonly agree worse than strangers. Sex here is often crudely and puritanically phrased: courtesans, strumpets, whores are often mentioned. The princely Cardinal himself, centre of the play's social structure, inconsistently keeps a mistress. It is all there, the usual insincerities, the usual desecrations. Secondary values crush primary ones, it is a decadent social and family system desecrating a wholesome love. In this diseased society a puritanical religion, greed for wealth, and social respectability are all ranged against the Duchess's choice.

Though the impression is so often medievalist and supernatural, the main persons themselves, as distinguished from any general attitude to society, are conceived with a Renaissance realism and insight. Webster is, in his own fashion, inside his persons. They are all individuals with a certain stage dignity, at least to start with, and a strange static sort of direction, pointing if not progressing. They are conceived, especially the three villains, with a Shakespearian sense of force, together with a certain warmth of sympathy. No one is wholly evil. The fiery and haughty Ferdinand repents after the Duchess's death. His eyes 'dazzle'; he slinks off to hunt badgers by owl-light; and goes mad. There is nothing quite like Iago's perfect and baffling unity. These villains, as in the Cardinal's phantasma of a 'thing arm'd with a rake', tend to condemn themselves, like Richard III after seeing ghosts and Lady Macbeth in sleep. But, like Richard III and Macbeth himself, Ferdinand dies with a super-confidence not readily to be analysed:

> I will vault credit and affect high pleasures
> Beyond death.
>   (V. v. 86)

His words recall the similar, even stronger, human confidence in *The White Devil*. It is a trust in the individual's native human force, irrespective of morality. We find it pre-

eminently in Shakespeare and *The White Devil;* it is here less
vividly in *The Duchess of Malfi.*
Webster's two great plays revolve round the central
women. Whatever puritanical essences appear in his work,
his human creation is planted firmly in the positive love-trust
celebrated so differently in Lyly. He has a wholesome,
unromantic faith, far from the eye-lust and aestheticism of
Marlowe. Webster's own mind starts with no innate sex
conflict at all: the terrific figure of Vittoria Corrombona, her
womanly power and attraction, the irrelevance of moral
categories in our judgement of her, indicate this. Webster's
negations are not finally sexual. I deduce this most important
result: having got straight, as it were, on the matter of sex, he
is in a position to attack the next great problem, death, with
its subsidiaries of evil and suffering, as Marlowe or Milton
could never have done.
    The play must be given a Renaissance understanding. The
motorforce of evil in action comes at first sight mostly from a
person or persons, more evidently than in *King Lear* where
Edmund dissolves into the universalised suffering of the
whole, yet not so precisely as in *Othello,* where Iago is so
humanly particularised and evidently responsible. I used to
wonder how Webster's universal poetry on fate and death
could blend as it does with so human and exceptional an evil:
the Duchess seemed to be unlucky in her brothers, that was
all. But to the Renaissance mind a traditionally supernatural
evil may often be humanised: the divine is seen in human
terms, as in Shakespeare's Desdemona, Cleopatra and
Hermione; the Devil may take the shape of Iago, or be split
into a trinity of villains in *The Duchess of Malfi.* In *Macbeth,*
however, evil is supernatural. In *The Duchess of Malfi,* though
the impressionism recalls *Macbeth* and is full of religious
colourings, mouldy superstitions and hauntings, no single
supernatural figure or event, no witches, no ghost, here takes
the stage; and, though there was certainly a ghost in *The
White Devil,* it would somehow be strange if one did. This
massive play, more than any one work of Shakespeare, splits
its universal negations of suffering, evil and death into a
close-inwoven variety of medieval colourings and Renaissance psychology that contains all that a poet of his day

knows or feels about them. Shakespeare takes different directions in turn: this one play contains, or at least suggests, all. Responsibility cannot be definitely located; rather it pervades the whole. We are not invited to allot blame.

The movement from a medieval to a humanist conception, the Devil becoming Iago, is here compacted in the opposition of a supernatural impressionism and a wholly naturalistic humanism.

Ferdinand is a straight human study: aristocratic, fiery, unprincipled. The Cardinal is more mysterious. He is 'able to possess the greatest devil and make him worse'; again, 'He is a melancholy churchman. The spring in his face is nothing but the engendering of toads'; yet – and coming as it does curtly at the end of a speech on his 'dark and devilish nature' it is a truly Shakespearian touch – 'some good he hath done'. He stands icily cold, a background figure, setting the action, though himself, like the Duchess's passivity against which the action is directed, rather motionless. There is in him a semblance to the Church he represents as seen by Webster, but he cannot be wholly so equated. A central piece of stage pageantry shows his installation as a soldier, which may be related to the Echo scene in an ancient disused abbey, now turned into a 'fortification'. Both incidents reflect that smouldering Renaissance war-threat Webster feels to be rising among the ruins of a dead or dying faith.

Bosola is our most complex person. Often he is a choric voice to the action, which he directs and comments on throughout, both criminal and avenger in one. He is a born moralist, though a professional murderer. His blend of pity with a scientific interest in another's suffering and stern conscience saddled to an unmoral nature reflect Webster's own artistic and creative, almost scientific, psychology and that in the Renaissance mind that gives us the dispassionate human analyses of Machiavelli and Bacon. He is unfailingly honest with himself. He knows that an intelligencer is a 'quaint invisible devil', that 'place and riches' are 'bribes of shame'. At first he refuses Ferdinand's offer, then accepts. He can wholeheartedly pursue the evil which he also paradoxically hates.

He is a cynic and his cynicism, like Iago's, takes a

Manichean form. His conversation with the old lady strangely parallels Hamlet's with Ophelia: her 'painting' is to him a 'scurvy face-physic'. He continues with two speeches loaded with physical nausea (smallpox, ordure, spittle, plague) and pronounces a formal, Swiftian denunciation of man's 'deformity'. His attitude to the Duchess's pregnancy is coarse. But he can speak profoundly of the limitations of wisdom and counsel 'simple honesty'. He easily recognises goodness, without following it: he speaks with religious fervour of the Duchess's love, then meditates on his own duplicity. His satire on princes and flatterers is continual and sincere. Those flatterers who now insult Antonio at his fall are 'lice'. Above all, he is a student of humanity. He talks to the Duchess of Antonio's low birth in order to observe her reaction, his short phrases winning each an interesting and expected speech in reply. He describes with sensitivity the Duchess's state in imprisonment to Ferdinand, her resignation to death, nobility in adversity and loveliness in tears appealing strongly to him: 'She will muse four hours together...' Ferdinand, as usual impatient, prefers to study no longer 'in the book of another's heart'. Bosola can enjoy showing the Duchess the supposedly dead Antonio, ironically stimulating her grief with 'Come, you must live', and 'O fie! Despair? Remember you are a Christian'. He may be partly sincere. He is giving religious counsel. When he says that he pities her we are baffled: it may be so. He asks Ferdinand *why* he torments her – again so interested – and suggests that he go no farther. He himself will not visit her again in his own shape, but goes disguised readily enough, talking of the body's corruption, bringing bell, coffin and cords of execution, leading her 'by degrees to mortification'. Again, he is giving ghostly counsel. Her courage amazes him:

> Yet, methinks,
> The manner of your death should much afflict you.
> This cord should terrify you?
> (IV. ii. 219)

It is a laboratory of suffering, Bosola the vivisecting scientist. On Ferdinand's entry he turns his attention on him, asking

how the children have offended, telling him to fix his eye
steadily on their and the Duchess's dead bodies, transferring
his former technique to his master, this time with more
success. Denied his reward for crime he repents explicitly and
irrevocably. We now feel that he all along hated his evil
course: maybe he did; but he found it fascinatingly interesting. More phrases now pour from him: conscience, innocence, hell and so on. He becomes the avenger.

> The weakest arm is strong enough that strikes
> With the sword of justice.
> (V. ii. 379)

During the final scene of violent murders Bosola acts as
high-priest of the occasion still, chorus and chief actor in one.
He is almost a projection of the author involved in his own
play: at once pathologist, criminal, avenger and penitent. An
impersonal voice following all the twists and turns of the
action, he yet remains a convincing person. He is a most
striking conception, more complex than Iago, and with
many touches of Hamlet. No other period could have made
him.

In Bosola many of the play's dominant themes converge.
He is its philosophy in action. The paradoxes of his nature
can be best resolved by study of his Manichean strain fusing
a semi-religious fervour with a life-denying negation. At the
climax, just before the Duchess's death he, the criminal, rings
his bell and pronounces, or chants, the religious moral of his
crime:

> Of what is't fools make such vain keeping?
> Sin their conception, their birth, weeping:
> Their life, a general mist of error,
> Their death, a hideous storm of terror.
> (IV. ii. 188)

Here, and in the murders that directly follow, is twisted and
finally knotted together the recurrent association of religion
and death. The association is dramatised as murder, the
imaginative logic exquisite.

Among these adverse forces is set to shine out as some rich

jewel from a funeral velvet, the love of the Duchess and
Antonio. This is presented without idealisations. Antonio is
an accountant, the widow proposes to him. She can talk quite
broadly of bed pleasures, with a certain honest lack of
reticence. She has no sense of sin, and seems untouched by
that strong sense in the others. She approaches Shakespeare's
sunlight heroines in her wit, especially during the death scene:
she is, despite differences, in the tradition of Lyly's girls,
Rosalind, Portia, and certain strains in Cleopatra, a tradition
seeing woman as a sweet force of humour, gentleness,
strength and common-sense; and perhaps it is this more than
anything else which the literature of the modern world adds
to medieval Christianity. There is here a poor stage for her
gifts, which are muffled and clouded by the dark forces. Yet
marriage is beautifully felt: the 'sacrament of marriage' is the
'first good deed begun in the world' after the creation, says
Antonio; it knows no purgatory, but contains either heaven
or hell. Like everyone else here, he can however speak
critically:

> Say a man never marry, nor have children,
> What takes that from him? Only the bare name
> Of being a father, or the weak delight
> To see the little wanton ride a cock-horse
> Upon a painted stick, or hear him chatter
> Like a taught starling.
>   (I. i. 456)

Even so, an uncritical simplicity and warmth burns through
the idle phrases. The exquisite presentment of Giovanni in
The White Devil witnesses Webster's love and understanding
of children: and this quality is one with that proud unmoral
faith which he gave to the creation of Vittoria Corrombona
in *The White Devil*, like Shakespeare's to his Cleopatra, an
erotic and feminine and non-moral trust without which love
of children alone is, it may be, sentimentality. We find both
in Webster. Less forceful than in *The White Devil*, they are
yet fundamental in *The Duchess of Malfi*. The Duchess,
Antonio, and the children are a passive group, defined more
by what happens to them than by what they do; the Duchess
is often a tragic voice only; but they, the Duchess especially,

alone form the one side of our central conflict. They stand for human, especially feminine, love; for common-sense, for family peace, against a world and its society diseased and sick to death.

III

Webster's world is socially rotten, the very impulse of family instinct conflicting cruelly with family tradition; and all professions and grades in the community are satirically condemned. But the play is more than a social document. Love is here inherently luckless, the body of man itself a walking disease; and finally, there is death and its twin attendants, mouldering graves and icy-dark eternity. This death is perhaps neither good nor bad, but it is fearful, dark, and cold. What then, we may ask, is the final purpose of all this – the phrase is Webster's – 'talk fit for a charnel'? What is the author doing? He is trying to express in warm action the freezing horror of a corpse; to give outward dramatic manifestation to what the play calls 'not-being'; to express the quality of death in a sequence. That is why the Duchess must be 'brought by degrees to mortification'; why we have the icy hand, the group of plaster corpses, the showing her of cords and coffin. Webster artificially loads on us and her all possible traditional elaborations of the horror of death. His people live death. The greatest torture of those in hell is that they 'must live and cannot die'; to 'live thus is not indeed to live'; the play is all 'a sensible hell'. Webster would make 'not-being' live before our eyes. He refuses any supernatural action with a masterly reserve. But there is little positive sense-perception of bodies in health: the people are all ghosts, they have no proper bodies till they becomes corpses: they act in a sort of frozen stillness, are dead before the play starts. It is amazing that the thing is done at all. Webster's play is written from a ruling perception of death comparable to, but subtler than, that presented in Donne's sermons, Burton and Browne.

The Duchess remains unshaken by all attempts to fright her with her own death, asking how a more picturesque implement would benefit her, serenely and rationally facing the fact, unmoved by sense-horrors. Yet she is horrified at the hand and supposed group of corpses. Death is more fearful in those she loves than for herself. There is, moreover, a pervading stoical and resigned feeling that suffering may have a purpose. The fish's price is not known till it is near the fire; men are valued highest in misery; only 'Heaven's scourge-stick' makes men go right; lovers are parted as a 'curious artist' takes a clock or watch to pieces in order to mend it; men bruised like cassia to get their perfume; we shall find excellent company in the other world. Is this the truth? Or this:

> all our wit
> And reading brings us to a truer sense
> Of sorrow.
> (III. v. 82)

Is man's best fate to be the 'tann'd galley-slave' resigned to torment? To be the plaything 'tennis-ball' of fateful stars? The answer is indecisive. The massed tonings suggest that death has the final say. But may death itself be kind? All the people, good or ill, feel some faint, strangled and religious sense of a beyond, though these touches often seem no more than necessary constituents among so many others to the packed and varied exposition of traditional thinking on death. Julia dies with: 'I go, I know not whither'; haughty Ferdinand will affect 'high pleasures' beyond death; there is Bosola's bitter 'mine is another voyage'. Asked by the Duchess if we shall know one another in the next world, Cariola answers 'Yes, out of question', the incident recalling Tess's question to Angel Clare on Stonehenge. The Duchess's death has religious direction: those who strangle will pull 'heaven' down on her, she 'kneels' for her entry. Maybe 'in the eternal church' lovers part no more. This play's meticulous analysis of death in action, death in the tomb, death in the soul – for Ferdinand's and the Cardinal's hearts are 'hollow graves rotten and rotting others' – is an attempt at death penetration. It probes the question, hoping therein to find its own answer: 'O that it were possible', says the Duchess, 'to hold some two days' conference with the dead', for that would teach us something we 'never shall know here'. This play is such a conference. It is a communing with death. The play elucidates its own problem, it contains its own answer.

It implicitly asserts the final unreality of death, by speaking almost wholly in deathly terms. This forces both a phraseology and imagery of mouldering quality. I have shown how most of its associations, certainly all that refer to death, are traditional and conventional, often superstitious, expressing stock reactions, worn by centuries of use: owls, wolves, graveyards, bones; or an eternity dark and inhumanly, icily, holy. The play's vast area presents a massive ruin scattered with mental débris. All the worst in folklore and orthodoxy is used and emphasised. But there is little direct and vital nature contact: natural images of trees and birds tend either to be generalised or to smell of medieval oil, and the stars are thoroughly astrologised. There are no minute exactitudes of observation of the Shakespearian or Tennysonian sort; still less are there any vast natural or cosmic positives, such as the sea throughout Shakespeare, or the mountains in Goethe's *Faust* and Ibsen. Webster's world is too narrowly and inwardly human to be real; its infinities are the vast and accumulated poisons of fear, agony and evil in the human mind. It would appear that to talk of death well we must avoid actuality, that it is best defined in terms of the unreal. The play implicitly says this. The strange healthiness of *King Lear* is one with its avoidance of traditional eternity thoughts and conventionalised horrors. *Macbeth* relates its superstitions directly to a moral and perverted evil, and they are dispelled in the end, as much by Macbeth as by Malcolm. Macbeth breaks free. Webster's action drives home the truth that evil, which is an aspect of death, contradicts itself. There is a perverse irony towards the end, almost a macabre humour. Bosola repents after the murder, the Duchess recovers, he is at the foot of heaven's mercy-seat, she dies. In error he kills Antonio, the one man he in his new repentance would give his life for. He, the implement of death, is a living contradiction: so are his actions and his fortunes alike. His very existence is a grim irony, and he knows it. The Cardinal, who arranged not to be interrupted while he disposed of a corpse, is not interrupted, through his own plan, while he becomes one. As for **Ferdinand**, his madness, horrible as it is, is almost as comic as horrible. The human forces of death contradict their own humanity, they tend to become de-individualised, paradoxical, comic. Their disintegration reflects Webster's human faith.

This thought applies to the whole play. The arrangement of action is heavily artificial. Unreal horrors are, if not central, yet approaches to the central horror: there is the supposed dead hand, the supposed group of corpses. What if the Duchess's own death, succeeding these, were equally a delusion? Certainly it causes her less suffering. Webster's horrors are aesthetic horrors, his imagery, so literary and backward in pedigree, 'smells of mortality', to transpose a Shakespearian phrase; it is the result of a blackened thinking. The serene reason of life finds no home here: 'for the subtlest folly proceeds from the subtlest wisdom'. Is death itself such a folly? The Echo scene compresses that thought imaginative-ly. From these ancient ruins come back the grim words 'like death that we have', 'deadly accent', a 'thing of sorrow', 'thou art a dead thing'. This scene is a miniature of Webster's universe. Every word is spoken first by Antonio and Delio. If you will walk among such ruins, you must expect an echo to interrupt your talk; and if you will end all your sentences with death, don't blame the echo. This is an interesting example of how imaginative architectonic may itself shadow an answer posed but insoluble, or at least left unsolved, on the plane of the author's explicit thought; just as Webster's creative human understanding is to be distinguished from his poetic impressionism.

The 'problem' of death is, therefore, not to be answered in its own terms which continually dissolve as smoke under analysis, but rather by a concentration on forces of life; on those forces which flame with fitful violence in *The White Devil* and burn steadily, if dimly, in Webster's Duchess here.

The Duchess of Malfi has a harmony all its own. Its metaphysical contradictions are its imaginative truth, all false balances being redressed in the act of statement. Its horrors are sweetened by the author's fearless acceptance, his resigned artistic enjoyment: there is no *Macbeth* intensity, no Marlovian shiver of fear, but rather a passive relaxation. The negations have, more than in most dark works, a positive, harmonious quality. There is no violent conflict: if the Duchess were more vital, death horrors would be unthroned from their centrality. The action unrolls with a pleasing inevitability and, twice, something of a colourful pomp. Both war and the Church are given incidents of pageantry, the Cardinal's ceremonial installation as a soldier, the pilgrims at the Shrine of Our Lady of Loretto. These contrast with the dun tone of the drama's thought and imagery; and still more with the more horrible events that follow; but there is a certain aesthetic richness about the horrible as well as the more obviously picturesque scenes, recalling that phrase in Flecker's *Hassan:* 'Agony is a fine colour'. The organic structure, the massed piling of event on event, though wanting occasionally in narrative logic, has a precise, if rough, imaginative coherence. On the picturesque is reared, mountainously, the pictorially gruesome: the tableau of death shown to the Duchess, the murder. The heart of the whole play is the Masque of Madmen and Bosola's entry with bell and coffin. The masque builds a grotesque harmony of dance and music into the central horror. Bosola rings his bell and chants

> Of what is't fools make such vain keeping?
> Sin their conception, their birth weeping...
>   (IV. ii. 188)

There is a measured and ceremonial purpose, it is a controlled *ritual* of murder, with a certain ghoulish placidity to be distinguished from the middle scenes of conflict in *Macbeth* and *King Lear*. It is all strangely harmonious. After the Duchess's death the action descends. There is the disintegration of Ferdinand and the Cardinal, and the final murders. Except for the great Echo scene, perhaps the finest example of concentrated 'atmosphere' in our drama, the movement might seem to droop. The drama follows the normal Shakespearian structure, the climax central, though with no sense of the Shakespearian ceremonial at the end; I think necessarily, considering the nature of its statement. Moreover drooping is not here inorganic: disease is a dominating impression, and the very blank-verse, yet colloquial, rhythms of its speech tend continually to limp. Finally we can, if we please, see another use in the falling action. The Duchess has been buried deep in her own play, which next closes over her, her grave is heaped not with earth but with more death. Webster has thus his own consistent if funereal harmonies; his play expands and balances in the mind like a massive and a weighty dream; perhaps the most beautiful and profound creation of a mood in our literature.

Note

[1]For a discussion of the question as to whether Ferdinand's charges are prompted by an incestuous love for his sister, see Clifford Leech, *John Webster*, London, 1951, 99–106.

XII   John Ford: Dramatist of the Heart

(Presidential Address to The Devonshire Association, *Report and Transactions,* CIII; Exeter, 1971) I follow the Mermaid edition, printing unvoiced syllables in full.

In the heroic adventures of Elizabethan seamanship Devonshire has cause for pride. New ways were being opened across the globe by Spain, by England: a new expansion, attended by national rivalries and war, was being won. Adventures may be either external or internal. There are within man's psyche oceans no less dangerous than was the Atlantic to an Elizabethan ship; and here, at this Renaissance period of the western world, England especially was active. Shakespeare and his fellow dramatists were exploring the human heart, or soul. This more difficult exploration is not yet finished; we are still part of it today. It too may be heroic and need courage. If we look back for guidance to these dramatic precursors, we shall all think first of Shakespeare; and some of us will do well to think also, and perhaps next, of John Ford, his heir in spiritual perception. John Ford came from Ilsington, in Devon.

In drama man explores and analyses his earthly condition. The medieval Mystery Cycles relied on the Christian tradition, placing human destiny within the great process from Eden at one end to the great Judgement at the other. At the Renaissance, man, thrown back on himself, makes separate dramas, with recurring stories of violence and revenge working up to a miniature 'Judgement Day', often of ceremonial tone; as at the conclusions of *Hamlet* and *King Lear.*

This great age of our drama started under Elizabeth, gathered strength and volume under James I, and continued into the reign of Charles I. There was variety, tragic and comedic, but the central strain was revolutionary and volcanic. Man's instincts and ambitions were revealed, unleashed; as in Marlowe's *Tamburlaine* and *Faustus*. Dramas concentrated on blood and lust and hideous revenge, as in Kyd's *Spanish Tragedy,* in Marston, Webster, Tourneur, Middleton; and there are Jonson's sulphurous Roman dramas, *Sejanus* and *Catiline.* What, we may ask, is all this for? The aim is to reveal, assimilate and contain these dark powers. Not all dramas are successful: some leave us in disquiet, or cynicism; the best attain what the Greeks called a *katharsis,* or 'purification'. No one will deny the health-giving powers of Shakespeare, who worked through the terrors of tragedy to the mystic intimations of his last plays. Towards the end of our period there was a general shift in tone towards a more optimistic drama; as in the work of Beaumont and Fletcher and Massinger. Many external conditions in staging and in society favoured such a change; the Court encouraged themes of Platonic love. Such was the setting for the works of Ford.

Little is known about him: he was admitted to the Middle Temple in 1602; he took to writing; his best plays are of classic standing.

Before noticing these we may glance at a lesser work, *The Lover's Melancholy* (published 1629).[1] The plot, set at Famagusta in Cyprus, is mainly interesting for one person, Parthenophil, a youth of magical excellence and beauty, who turns out, like Shakespeare's Rosalind and Viola, to be a girl in disguise, so putting everything to rights for a happy conclusion. Such figures recur in this period, from the plays of Lyly onwards. They may be variously boys or girls-in-boy-disguise. They may be called 'bisexual', symbolising strength with grace. We think naturally of Plato, especially the *Phaedrus*, the boy angels of medieval pageantry, and of Shakespeare's Sonnets. In Massinger and Dekker's *The Virgin Martyr* (1622) such a boy turns out actually to *be* an angel. These persons indicate perfection in human form; they are usually associated with love; we may call them 'seraphic'.

To such idealism Ford was instinctively attuned. Parthenophil is said to be a youth of 'an excellence more high' than 'mere creations' (I. i).[2] He is, like so many of our own time, a musical youth. He is found in a Greek poetic 'paradise', Tempe:

> A sound of music touched mine ears, or rather
> Indeed entranced my soul. As I stole nearer,
> Invited by the melody, I saw
> This youth, this fair-faced youth, upon his lute,
> With strains of strange variety and harmony,
> Proclaiming, as it seemed, so bold a challenge
> To the clear quiristers of the woods, the birds,
> That, as they flocked about him, all stood silent,
> Wondering at what they heard. I wondered too.
>
> (I. i)

Parthenophil has 'beauty, youth, carriage and direction' such as to 'ravish admiration' from anyone 'endued with reason' (I. i). His qualities are more than aesthetic. He, or she, has been wandering in Greece and visiting Athens for its wisdom:

> If earthly treasures
> Are poured in plenty down from Heaven on mortals,
> They rain amongst those oracles that flow
> In schools of sacred knowledge: such is Athens.
>
> (V. 1)

'Sacred': Athens, we may almost say, is Ford's 'Jerusalem'. When she turns out to be Meleander's daughter, Eroclea, the father's phrases recall Shakespeare's *Pericles*.

The desired end of Renaissance drama is to entune man's fearful instincts to the seraphic perfection. To this end Ford is deliberately devoted. *The Lover's Melancholy* has some relevant lines:

> As there is by nature
> In everything created contrariety,
> So likewise is there unity and league
> Between them in their kind: but man, the abstract
> Of all perfection, which the workmanship
> Of Heaven hath modelled, in himself contains
> Passions of several qualities.
>
> (IV. iii)

Ford's greater plays will the adjustment of 'passions' to 'perfection'. It is not easy; it demands utter sincerity and also courage, the courage of Blake's 'mental fight' in *Milton* or Nietzsche's 'saint of knowledge' in *Thus Spake Zarathustra* ('The Wizard', IV. v).

It is because his aim is single and simple that the first plays we shall discuss are only in part satisfactory. He has to fill out a five act drama with sub-plots that scarcely interest us and humour of doubtful appeal. These hold significance as back-ground and contrast to his main theme, and may to that extent be intellectually, though perhaps not theatrically, justified.[3] Our attention is, however, only transfixed by the central story, which attains at high moments a nobility and an incandescence of supreme quality, the more impressive for his level style. Ford's diction is choice but never ostentatious; he eschews metaphor and imagery; no literary skills are allowed to fog his statements. Despite these refusals he can give us passages of sustained and rising emotion that compare favourably with the best dramatic rhetoric of his day.[4]

The transmutation of passions to perfection, Nietzsche's 'transvaluation of values', involves facing and using these passions.[5] It is for this reason that all new ethical doctrine will be, or anyway seem, immoral. Herein lies the importance of drama: it can reveal sympathetically an anti-social instinct while accepting society's condemnation. Drama is as a step towards the perfection; it hints directions without solving all our problems.

Ford's best known drama is called, not very happily, *'Tis Pity She's a Whore* (published 1633). 'Whore' means simply 'sexually immoral'. The title suggests, perhaps for reasons of policy, a total repudiation untrue to the drama.

The subject is incest. The young Giovanni and his sister Annabella love each other and indulge their love. Being with child, she submits to a marriage with Soranzo, who discovers the truth, and plans revenge. Ford covers all the usual violences of the period; his sub-plot has its crimes and cruelties. But what he is mainly concerned with is the more ambiguous and indeterminate theme of the young lovers' passion. He deliberately, perhaps to ensure our sympathy, patterns it on the analogy of *Romeo and Juliet* with a Friar closely based on Shakespeare's, and Annabella's 'tutoress', Putana, playing the Nurse. The lovers' youth is stressed.

Giovanni's love is firmly contrasted with religion: the Friar calls it a 'leprosy of lust' rotting his 'soul', and urges him to resist with prayer and contrition (I. i). He tries and fails. He could wish 'it were not in religion sin to make our love a god'; prayers, tears, fasting have availed nothing. Religious counsels are to him mere 'dreams' and 'old men's tales' concocted 'to fright unsteady youth'. His whole self is behind his love and leaves no option:

> 'Tis not, I know,
> My lust, but 'tis my fate that leads me on.
> Keep fear and low faint-hearted shame with slaves!
>
> (I. iii)

There is throughout an emphasis on youth, integrity and courage.

His sister has confessed a corresponding passion: they kneel to each other, each saying 'Love me or kill me.' The moment is one of mystical insight, a 'music' beyond 'dream', a perfection of being: 'I would not change this minute for Elysium' (I. iii).

Giovanni calls on the ancients for support, reminding the Friar what he has himself taught regarding the correspond-ence of body and mind; beauty and reason surely involve each other and virtue is 'reason but refined'. The Friar's reply demands exact attention:

> Indeed, if we were sure there were no Deity,
> Nor Heaven nor Hell, then to be led alone
> By Nature's light – as were philosophers
> Of elder times – might instance some defence.
> But 'tis not so: then, madman, thou wilt find
> That Nature is in Heaven's positions blind.
>
> (II. v)

The lines hint an insecurity: all depends on the possibility of a deity whose fiat is arbitrary and irrational, in opposition to 'Nature's light' and the wisdom of ancient Greece. The rhymed couplet lacks conviction. Giovanni, as did Romeo with *his* Friar (*Romeo and Juliet*, III. iii), takes his stand on youth. Were the Friar young he would understand (II. v). To Annabella the Friar urges the horrors of Hell and its multifarious torments, but even here he is near giving away his case:

> Sigh not; I know the baits of sin
> Are hard to leave: O, 'tis a death to do't.
> Remember what must come. Are you content?
>   (III. vi)

He admits that his counsel is as an emotional 'death'; only fear supports it.

The rash engagement drives inevitably towards violence. When her newly-married husband, Soranzo, discovers that Annabella is with child by another his ferocity is matched by her scorn, and neither is lacking in vocabulary. She tells him that he is honoured to father a child got by so 'angel-like' a man as her lover, but he shall never know who it is:

> *Soranzo:* Not know it, strumpet! I'll rip up thy heart,
>   And find it there.
> *Annabella:* Do, do.
> *Soranzo:*   And with my teeth
>   Tear the prodigious lecher joint by joint.
> *Annabella:* Ha, ha, ha! the man's merry.
>   (IV. iii)

He pulls her up and down by her hair while she sings of love.

Annabella, imprisoned in her room, is next tormented by conscience. Giovanni, still in his 'Elysium' and calling 'hell' merely a 'slavish and fond superstitious fear', hears that they are discovered (V. iii).

The action rises to the usual climax of blood and vengeance. Soranzo has, very conveniently, a birthday party coming, exactly the kind of occasion our revenge dramas delight in. On receiving his invitation Giovanni, despite the Friar's warning, is ready for what must follow:

> Not go! stood Death
> Threatening his armies of confounding plagues,

> With hosts of dangers hot as blazing stars,
> I would be there: not go! yes, and resolve
> To strike as deep in slaughter as they all;
> For I will go.
> (V. iii)

He is now determined:

> Be all a man, my soul; let not the curse
> Of old prescription rend from me the gall
> Of courage, which enrols a glorious death.
> (V. iii)

Our emphasis regularly falls on courage.

Giovanni and Annabella meet. Death is near. As so often in Shakespeare there is, before the end, an interim of wistful and meditative calm. The great mystery approaches:

Giovanni:	The schoolmen teach that all this globe of earth Shall be consumed to ashes in a minute.
Annabella:	So I have read too.
Giovanni:	But 'twere somewhat strange To see the waters burn: could I believe This might be true, I could believe as well There might be Hell or Heaven.
Annabella:	That's most certain.
Giovanni:	A dream, a dream! else in this other world We should know one another.
Annabella:	So we shall.
Giovanni:	Have you heard so?
Annabella:	For certain.
Giovanni:	But d'ye think That I shall see you there? – You look on me – May we kiss one another, prate or laugh, Or do as we do here?
Annabella:	I know not that.

(V. v)

And yet Giovanni has his own spiritual reliances. He calls on 'all the spirits of the air' and the whole universe as his witnesses:

> Never till now did Nature do her best
> To show a matchless beauty to the world,
> Which in an instant, ere it scarce was seen,

The jealous Destinies required again.
Pray, Annabella, pray! Since we must part,
Go thou, white in thy soul, to fill a throne
Of innocence and sanctity in Heaven.
Pray, pray, my sister!
(V. v)

Annabella calls on 'blessed angels' to guard her. Giovanni now admits that 'perhaps the laws of conscience and of civil use' may 'justly blame' them, yet he remains sure that their love has been such as to except them from a normal judgement. He kisses her, asks forgiveness, and stabs her. It is done to 'save' her 'fame'; for 'honour doth love command'; the act is one to 'glory in'. The scene ends with a ringing couplet:

Shrink not, courageous hand, stand up, my heart,
And boldly act my last and greater part!
(V. v)

Heart, the seat of both love and courage, is to Ford an empowered concept, or symbol.[6]

The thought sequence of this dialogue is interesting: from Giovanni's scepticism in regard to orthodox eschatology, through near acceptance of belief in an after-life, to full reliance on 'spirits of the air'; and then a return, with a difference, since now purified of conventional morality, to the orthodox phraseology of 'white in thy soul', 'innocence', 'sanctity', and 'Heaven'. And now, too, the one essential good assured, Giovanni can admit, in general, the wrongness of incest, especially in regard to the necessary conventions of 'civil use'.

The conclusion follows. Giovanni comes to the feast with Annabella's heart on his dagger:

The glory of my deed
Darkened the mid-day sun, made noon as night.
You came to feast, my lords, with dainty fare:
I came to feast too; but I digged for food
In a much richer mine than gold or stone
Of any value balanced; 'tis a heart,
A heart, my lords, in which is mine entombed:
Look well upon't; d'ye know it?
(V. vi)

The 'heart' here becomes a visible dramatic entity. Though the one heart is now as the 'tomb' of the other, yet the moment is one less of sorrow than of 'glory'. This end is positively, even joyfully, apprehended. Giovanni fights with Soranzo, who falls and dies. Soranzo's retainers kill Giovanni, who in dying hopes, 'where'er I go', to see Annabella.

The main lines of force are clear; the opposition of integrity and convention, especially religious teaching, is fairly stated, but the balance is not equal. Our dramatic sympathies are drawn to the positive powers of love experience, or love magic; to youth, to courage, to honour. Belief in spirit life helps where orthodoxy has failed. The general meaning has for us sharp contemporary relevance. Incest is merely the occasion. Elsewhere in literature, in Shelley, in Wagner, it recurs. Sometimes we may suppose that it is being used as a mask for more embarrassing instincts. After all, in the royal houses of ancient Egypt and the Incas of Peru, sister-marriages were honoured. The main opposition we face is that of nature-prompted instincts not in themselves harmful, as against traditional rulings and threats of damnation. Of these there are many: homosexuality is one which, even when firmly ideal and platonic, has for long remained unplaced, because feared, rendering many literary investigations inept.

Meanwhile, the horrors of society, which include murders, ambitions and manifold injustices, rage unchecked: in Ford's surrounding action, and in our society today. Our trust should accord more honour to the authentic light, which is Eliot's 'The one veritable transitory power' of *Ash-Wednesday* (I), wherever and however it appears. Our own 'permissive society' is trying, with all its faults, to do this. Ford is its precursor.

The subject of *Love's Sacrifice* (published 1633) is less disturbing. We have a Duke of Pavia whose young wife, Bianca, is loved by and loves his favourite and friend, Fernando. Fernando insists on keeping his love Platonic. There was at this period a strong cult of 'Platonic' love at the Court of Queen Henrietta Maria, and the drama's valuations would have been easily recognised. The lady is, however less content with platonism than is her lover, and when challenged by her husband becomes so unashamedly and insultingly outspoken that he murders her. When he finds that the lovers have in fact been guiltless, he repents in anguish. At Bianca's funeral both men commit suicide. *Othello* is often recalled. When the Duke's Secretary first arouses his suspicion he is a replica of Iago, sometimes using his very phrases; but the development is characteristically Ford's. It has his own particular idealism and honesty. What, asks Bianca (V. i), are marriage vows and the name of Duchess worth in comparison with real love? *Love's Sacrifice* assists our understanding of *'Tis Pity*; for here we are even more clearly invited to face and honour the *essence* without being distracted by superficialities. That essence may be designed 'platonic': we are to recognise the sovereignty of a fine aspiration, in and as itself, before relating it to external affairs or assuming reprehensible actions.

The Duke was himself in part responsible for what happens:

> Look, Bianca,
> On this good man; in all respects to him
> Be as to me: only the name of husband,
> And reverent observance of our bed,
> Shall differ us in persons, else in soul
> We are all one.
> (I. i)

He is asking for trouble. 'Soul': a spiritual engagement is involved in sharp distinction from the ephemeral rights of marriage. Fernando is, anyway, the Duke's 'divided self' (I. i); that is, his own self only separated by physical existence. Rather similarly Fernando sees himself apart from Bianca as a corpse, saying 'Thus bodies walk unsoul'd', his 'heart' being 'entombed' in Bianca as 'yonder goodly shrine' (I. ii). The love of his 'bleeding heart' is firmly distinguished from 'lust'; it is called 'chaste', being all 'purity' and 'virtue' (II. iii).

The platonic ideal, whether heterosexual or homosexual, is a tightrope course. This it is safest always to recognise in all our discussions; as in the discussion of Shakespeare's Sonnets, for example. Here Bianca more than responds to Fernando's ideal devotion, offering herself freely by night, though he remains firm, refusing to let a 'wanton appetite' profane 'this sacred temple' (II. iv). Divine categories are present.

The darker passions are well dramatised. The Duke's rising wrath is given a compelling rhetoric, and Bianca's answers to her ageing husband's accusations have a scorn and cruelty, together with a shameless admission of her own essential guilt, that makes the Duke's action in murdering her almost reasonable. Whenever the action takes fire, Ford's dramatic powers are impressive, and indeed, despite the difference in style, Shakespearian. Bianca's courage is vivid: she willingly embraces death, asking only that her guiltless lover be spared. The Duke soon realises his error and his repentance follows.

The church scene of the funeral (V. iii) is given a stately ritual with 'solemn' music and a procession, the Duke offering the 'oblations of a mourning heart' to Bianca's 'offended spirit'. When the tomb is opened, Fernando appears from it 'in his winding-sheet'. He denounces the Duke, takes poison, and crying 'I come, Bianca', dies. In this stage ritual, death and love blend in a more than earthly marriage. Fernando's appearance from the tomb corresponds to Giovanni's sense of being himself 'entombed', at his dagger's point, in Annabella's 'heart'.

We have a vivid sense of Bianca's 'spirit'. The Duke had referred to her 'hovering soul' in the murder scene (V. i), and now her 'purity' in death is said to 'hover yet' about her 'blessed bones' (V. iii). The drama's conclusion leaves us feeling that what is denied on earth may yet be justified beyond:

> Let slaves in mind be servile to their fears;
> Our heart is high instarred in brighter spheres.
> (IV. ii)

The 'heart', symbol of both love and courage, is more than physical: it is the earthly counterpart and pointer to the soul's further destiny.

It may be argued that neither of these two dramas is a satisfactory whole; we tend to concentrate on the central story and discount the rest, which has value only in terms of contrast. *The Broken Heart* (published 1633), which surely succeeded them, incurs, as Clifford Leech observes (*John Ford*, 81), no such criticism. The plot has its complications, but everything interweaves and interrelates; it is as much pattern as plot and the pattern is fascinating. Here Ford's human trust attains a noble flowering. We are now to be concerned not only with society, but, even more deeply, with death. Ford likes things Greek; as in Parthenophil's apprenticeship to Athens, Giovanni's reliance on Greek philosophy, and the platonic idealism of *Love's Sacrifice*. *The Broken Heart* is set in Sparta. The action turns on the opposition of a conventionally enforced marriage as against true love. To Ford the heart's affections are far from egocentric; they are characterised by devotion, courage and sacrifice. The 'heart' is that in man which instinctively surmounts, if need be at the cost of death, all self-centredness. It is the bodily correlative of the soul and the soul's courage. In our new play we are aware of its presence suffusing the action with a goodness which

> keeps the soul in tune,
> At whose sweet music all our actions dance.
>
> (II. ii)

That is our new key.

Orgilus' love, Penthea, has been cruelly forced by her brother, the 'death-braving' (I. ii) young commander, Itho-cles, to marry an ageing nobleman. Nevertheless, Ithocles wins our approval: like Shakespeare's Coriolanus, but with a more evident sincerity, he insists that his victory in war is due as much to his soldiers as to himself (I. ii). He soliloquises against ambition as a quick road to disaster and regards the wrong he has done his sister as a 'capital fault' committed by a boy ignorant of 'the secrets of commanding love' (II. ii).

Penthea is meanwhile suffering anguish from the 'divorce betwixt my body and my heart' (II. iii). Her husband Bassanes is a madly jealous man of comic bluster; our comedy here has an exact relevance. But when made to recognise the cruelty and danger of his absurdities, he grows in dignity. Penthea, who should have been 'wife to Orgilus', sees herself as a 'whore' living 'in known adultery' with her official husband (III. ii). Though bitter to her brother, she surmounts her bitterness; and when Ithocles tells her of his love for the Princess, Calantha, her heart is touched, and she forgives (III. ii). It is a drama of self-surmounting.

But what of Orgilus? He has, according to our dramatic tradition, the role of avenger, like Hieronimo or Hamlet. Should he now forgive, as we are urged to forgive in Tourneur's *The Atheist's Tragedy*, leaving revenge to God? That would be too easy a way out: Ford's aim is to transmute, without denying, earthly compulsions. 'Honour', a conception made to attune human rivalries to Christian absolutes, is necessarily involved. Orgilus's tutor, Tecnicus, lectures him on the nature of 'real' as opposed to false 'honour'. Vices can masquerade as honour, and among them may be 'revenge'. Honour is only real if based on 'virtue', 'justice', and *rational* 'valour': above all, 'justice' must be our sovereign concern (III. i).

Orgilus's direction has been uncertain. He has seemed to be forgiving Ithocles. But now her sufferings have driven Penthea mad; how is he to interpret Tecnicus's counsel? His answer comes from Penthea, who in her distracted state points at a significant moment to Ithocles, and Orgilus knows his course:

> She has tutored me,
> Some powerful inspiration checks my laziness.
> (IV. ii)

Her 'madness' has functioned as an 'oracle'. He has now to act; but, so far as may be, in terms of 'real honour'. Penthea dies. Her corpse is shown veiled and seated in a chair. Of two other chairs, Orgilus has one, and offers Ithocles the other, which closes, as a trap. Bitter words are spoken. Orgilus drives home the moral; Ithocles asks no 'compassion', while enjoying the 'statelier resolution' of seeing Orgilus involve himself in a dishonourable – because unequal – murder instead of a duel. Orgilus tells Ithocles of his own intended suicide to follow. They exchange phrases of mutual respect and forgiveness. When the act is accomplished Orgilus calls Ithocles 'fair spring of manhood'. Looking on him and Penthea seated in death, he murmurs, 'Sweet twins, shine stars for ever!' (IV. iv). Every detail is exactly conceived. Orgilus, as we hear later, used a trap instead of honourable combat because he dared not 'engage the goodness of a cause on fortune' (V. ii). He was being guided by his tutor's words on 'real honour' at the cost of conventional honour. The old revenge theme is being, not denied, but elevated to the plane of justice.

As usual, we have a revels scene (V. ii), but with a difference. It is a bridal festivity for the marriage of Orgilus's sister to Ithocles' friend, to which Orgilus, with another transcending of enmity, had generously agreed. There is a dance, during which the Princess Calantha hears news in turn of the King her father's death, Penthea's death, and the murder of Ithocles, her recently accepted lover. Each time she continues the dance, on the third occasion calling for yet brighter music. Even her colour has not changed. She parries criticism by saying that she will not have 'lawful pleasures' interrupted by 'sour censure'. Calantha is conceived as a being of near perfection, and, being that, she is, like Parthenophil in *The Lover's Melancholy*, only on a more realistic level, bisexually conceived as a lady of 'masculine spirit' (V. ii). She is at home with death. She knows that Penthea is the happier for having 'finished a long and painful progress', and as for the others:

> Those that are dead
> Are dead; had they not now died, of necessity
> They must have paid the debt they owed to nature
> One time or other.
> (V. ii)

Calantha is tragedy personified and accepted. Charles Lamb, in a notable appreciation, compared her to Christ.

Calmly she sentences Orgilus, allowing him to choose his way of dying. He elects to let his own blood and bleed to death. Bassanes assists. The action is prolonged, as a means of dramatising, indeed *living*, death; and is endued with glamour. Orgilus dies slowly and 'with unshook virtue'. The heart being Ford's obsession, its blood is necessarily rich, and 'sparkles like a lusty wine'. There is awe, but no sadness. On the contrary, Bassanes, both collaborator and chorus, says:

> This pastime
> Appears majestical; some high-tuned poem
> Hereafter shall deliver to posterity
> The writer's glory and his subject's triumph.
>   (V. ii)

We think of Cassius's words at Caesar's death in Shakespeare's *Julius Caesar*, a play where 'blood' is similarly emphatic and regarded throughout as a lively power:

> How many ages hence
> Shall this, our lofty scene, be acted o'er...
>   (*Julius Caesar*, III. i)

In Ford's version, however, the 'writer' is, presumably, Orgilus himself and the 'subject' his heroic dying. Ford can at a high moment use metaphor powerfully, as when Orgilus, hitherto supported by a staff, weakens:

> So falls the standard
> Of my prerogative in being a creature!
> A mist hangs o'er mine eyes, the sun's bright splendour
> Is clouded in an everlasting shadow;
> Welcome, thou ice, that sitt'st about my heart,
> No heat can ever thaw thee.
>   (V. ii)

The heart, Ford's dramatic deity, is cold. Its marvellous vital fluid, 'life's fountain', is gone. Death appears to be the end: 'everlasting' underlines that, though only in temporal terms. A mystery is certainly being felt. Objectively, to the bystanders, the external results are evident: 'Speech hath left him.' That is simple, if inconclusive. Even more ambiguous is, 'He has shook hands with time', suggesting as it does a courteous and purposeful parting. The 'creature' (i.e. 'created earth-being') has died; what parts is not, at this moment, defined. Elsewhere, as in some of our earlier quotations in this essay, Ford uses the word 'soul'. That 'soul' may have left for some realm beyond, or outside, 'time'. Whatever be the truth, it is 'majestical'.

In our other dramas, there may be, as we have seen, intimations, and at a high moment an assurance, of another life, as when Fernando's 'heart is high instarred in brighter spheres' (*Loves' Sacrifice*, IV. ii). In *The Broken Heart* Penthea goes 'to revel in Elysium' (III. v); peace is to 'usher her into Elysium' (IV. ii); Ithocles is to be 'healthful' in his 'parting from lost mortality' and dies into a 'long-looked-for peace' in 'heaven' (IV. iv). Statements may be darker, though equally firm:

> In vain we labour in this course of life
> To piece our journey out at length, or crave
> Respite of breath: our home is in the grave.
> (II. iii)

These are intimations. Within the whole dramatic action, we can say that negative and positive intermix. A mystery remains:

> Mortality
> Creeps on the dung of earth, and cannot reach
> The riddles which are purposed by the gods.
> (I. iii)

'Dung' recalls *Antony and Cleopatra* (V. ii. 7, often emended to 'dug'; see also I. i. 35), where we have a similar fusion of life and death tilted towards a sense of conquest.

Our last scene is at a temple, with an altar draped in white, and music. Ithocles's body is shown 'in a rich robe'. Then enter 'Calantha in white, crowned, attended by Euphranea, Philema and Christalla, also in white'. Calantha kneels to 'soft music'. She is now Queen, but instead of assuming royal power gives directions for the future. She means to die. She places a ring on Ithocles' finger, wedding him in death. Then she reveals the truth. Within her superb composure has been a suffering not less, but greater, than normality:

> Thus I new-marry him whose wife I am;
> Death shall not separate us. O, my lords,
> I but deceived your eyes with antic gesture,
> When one news straight came huddling on another

> Of death! and death! and death! still I danced forward;
> But it struck home, and here, and in an instant.
> Be such mere women, who with shrieks and outcries
> Can vow a present end to all their sorrows,
> Yet live to court new pleasures, and outlive them:
> They are the silent griefs which cut the heart-strings;
> Let me die smiling.
> (V. iii)

The repetition of 'death' may be allowed to suggest for us mortality in general, and 'danced forward' man's best response, in courage, to its challenge; 'vow a present end' means, presumably, assert that they will die of grief, before recovering and forgetting. Calantha's alternative is a willing and happy acceptance of her own approaching death. Voices from the altar sing a song of her own device repudiating 'the outward senses' and all earthly splendours as, not scorned, but provisional. Though the heart be broken, love is not:

> Love only reigns in depth; though art
> Can find no comfort for a broken heart.
> (V. iii).

Where earthly 'art' is helpless, love enjoys sovereignty. It is as though the heart, through its sacrificial breaking, is as the agent of transmutation, as in Orgilus's gradual outpouring of his blood, from life to death. Calantha accordingly needs no instrument of death: she, directed by her heart, takes to the otherness as a swan ruffling the waters; and, like a swan, dies in music.

What, shall we say, is Ford's 'transvaluation of values'? An insistence on the heart's affections and the heart's courage; and we are expected to believe, as Byron believed, that the heart's affections are, in youth, good.[7] Even the most personal love, even 'sex', is an out-going and an out-giving; a transcending of the self. Whatever may have to be our social rulings and personal denials, to this instinctive drive for unity we must remain, in our own essential selves, true. As Bianca puts it in *Love's Sacrifice*: 'Can there be sin in unity?' (V. i). Perhaps not, though in actual life it may often have to be withheld, or renounced. We may remember St Paul's brilliant

'all things are lawful for me, but not all things are expedient'
(I Corinthians, VI. 12; also X. 23). Drama is not actual life; it
is a way of trying things out; and it points towards, without
stating, solutions. So, following the bold emotional trust of
his earlier young lovers, the actions there only *dramatically*
justified flower, in *The Broken Heart,* into a more rational
survey, criticising society for making 'a ravished wife
widowed by lawless marriage' (IV. ii), but simultaneously
showing the affections of all concerned in generous, heart-
prompted, goodness and courage, even the old revenge
theme being turned to courtesy and sweetness. It is as though
our people were all being attuned to the grace and beauty of
some higher order. Bassanes, at first repellent, becomes
finally an authoritative and noble choric figure. The Prince
Nearchus renounces all claim on Calantha when he knows
that she loves the commoner 'young Ithocles', since he is
aware that the tyrannical thwarting of affections can lead
only to disaster (IV. ii). Reason and the heart become, in this
enlightened society, one.

These values imaginatively established, Ford next directed
them on to a realistic and not too distant subject in his last
play, the much praised *Perkin Warbeck* (published in 1634).
The human reading follows, so far as may be, that of *The
Broken Heart*, with a pretender of royal bearing, a monarch of
instinctive clemency, and an outstandingly loyal wife. In
Ford's hands history appears softened and ennobled.

There are in Ford two marriages to consider: one in life,
one in death. Life and its demands must be honoured.
Calantha refuses to allow her personal grief to disturb the
nuptial dance. All must 'look cheerfully', and to let gloom
interrupt 'lawful pleasures' would be wrong (V. ii). But
earth-life is only the one side. It is necessarily constricted; by
society often, by death always. Man's true home lies beyond.
Following Antony's:

> Heart, once be stronger than thy continent,
> Crack thy frail case

in *Antony and Cleopatra* (IV. xii), Ford's dramas show the
heart breaking its bonds and engaging union with love-in-

death: as in the glory of his lady's heart, called his tomb, on Giovanni's dagger; in Fernando's appearance in his winding-sheet from Bianca's tomb to wed her in death; and in Calantha's ritual marriage to dead Ithocles in *The Broken Heart*. That title is precise: for the heart's breaking is the pivot, or agent, of the mystery being dramatised.

That these refined speculations, transmuting old horrors to something, as Shakespeare's song has it, 'rich and strange', win our respect, will be clear; but can they be called humanly and dramatically successful? True, we shall not look in Ford's people for convincing motivation; they are scarcely 'character' studies; they obey other laws, or another law. They obey the heart's promptings, whether for life or for death. Of dramatic potency there is no lack. Our first two tragedies are vividly dramatic, and *The Broken Heart*, despite its calm and sweet philosophy, has for anyone attuned to its purpose scenes of compelling and peculiar power. Action often does what words could not, as in the stage business of brilliant devising whereby the Princess Calantha indicates her acceptance of Ithocles' hitherto unexpressed devotion (V. i). The revenge, with its three chairs, dominated by the veiled figure of Penthea vociferous in the silence of death, is, in every detail, meaningful and masterly. Orgilus's slow blood-letting, supported by a staff till he falls, rivets attention. In the dance scene Calantha's unexpected calm speaks volumes unknown to rhetoric. In the final rituals of bridal dance and funeral ceremony, music assumes a controlling power. No words can explain the mystery, but it can be dramatised, as Shakespeare dramatises it, with music.

What is Ford's relevance for us today? His modernity on the planes of psychology and sociology has often, from Havelock Ellis onwards, been observed; and today we have our permissive society based similarly on a repudiation of 'old prescription' (*'Tis Pity She's a Whore*, V. iii) and trust in the heart's affections. This may, if we are fortunate, flower into a society, like that which Ford imagines in *The Broken Heart*, of generosity, forgiveness and courtesy. *Perkin Warbeck* serves as an indication. Life's compulsory demands will persist; but what is wanted is their suffusing and inter-penetration, on all levels, by the softer valuations: in war, in the treatment of criminals, in what is perhaps for us the most testing and revealing of all problems, the problem of animal experiments. Sometimes the 'heart', and all it stands for, may be even more important than what is done. It may be the way and manner, rather than the deed, that counts most; as when Orgilus, having decided on implacable revenge, yet performs it with courtesy, almost with love. Today executions sympathetically and gently carried out, as in ancient Greece, perhaps with the help of anaesthetics, might bear stronger witness to social advance than removal of the death penalty. Much is, we know, being improved. Christianity and its derivative in codes of chivalry has laid a basis, now sometimes, but not always, forgotten. Ford's dramatic authorities appear different: while Church tradition is the upholder of moral tyrannies and threats of Hell, he looks rather, in humanist fashion, to ancient Greece; and still more, to those natural springs within the heart which true Christianity has itself, at its best, laboured to encourage.

If our society is to be so directed it must embrace, with all the courage of Ford's young heroes and heroines, new thoughts on death.[8] As John Cowper Powys once put it in *The Art of Happiness* (1935; I, 42–4, 47) we should replace Wordsworth's 'the pleasure which there is in life itself' (*Michael*, 77) by 'The pleasure which there is in life and death'. This Ford's dramas, too, suggest. The heart is broken to make us feel death as, paradoxically, itself the very heart of life. Courage is required. Traditionally, the heart is the seat not only of love but also of courage: the word 'courage' derives from the Latin for 'heart', *cor*. They are twin aspects of self-surmounting. Courage is perhaps always, and certainly at its most purposeful, inspired by some kind of love. Love is, in its essence, infinite. Therefore the heart's affections are necessarily thwarted on earth; the heart as courage presses beyond; it is all one movement, one piston-pulse of human creation. We are not creatures of the earth-plane alone. There is an age-old wisdom which we have forgotten, and need to recapture; we should learn to attune ourselves to Eliot's line in *Ash-Wednesday* (IV): 'While jewelled unicorns draw by the gilded hearse.' Or, as a modern dramatist, Eugène Ionesco, tells us in his *Fragments of a Journal*, death should be 'an occasion for rejoicing' and 'the whole of humanity should be reorganised in this direction.' This does not imply that we should rate life the less. Just as death's advocate Calantha refused to let thoughts of it interrupt a bridal dance, so Ionesco concludes that it is 'because we have staked everything on life that we are incapable of living' (*Fragments of a Journal*, trans. Jean Stewart, London 1968, 143). This may well be a truth for want of which our culture remains parched and our life infertile.

Notes

[1] I give the dramas' dates of publication. Composition may have been a few years earlier.

[2] References follow the Mermaid edition of Ford's dramas (1888), edited by Havelock Ellis.

[3] On the nature of Ford's sub-plots, see Clifford Leech, *John Ford and the Drama of his Time* (London, 1957), 14–16, 51, 81; also Mark Stavig's defence of them, in *John Ford and the Traditional Moral Order* (USA, 1968), 105–9, 122, 142. See also S. Gorley Putt, 'The Modernity of John Ford', *English* (London), XVIII, No. 101; Summer 1969.

[4] Ford's style has been praised by T.S. Eliot in his essay 'John Ford', *Selected Essays 1917–1932* (1932).

[5] In Ford's dramas, wrote Una Ellis-Fermor in *The Jacobean Drama* (London, 1936), 246, we assist at 'the conversion of the seven deadly sins, not at their overthrow.'

[6] Mark Stavig in *John Ford*, writing of *'Tis Pity She's a Whore*, states (notes, 211–12) that Donald K. Anderson Jr, in 'The Heart and the Banquet: imagery in Ford's *'Tis Pity* and *The Broken Heart*' (*Studies in English Literature*, USA, II, 1962, 209–17), notes 'the many references to hearts and to feasting in the play'.

[7] Lady Blessington, *Conversations of Lord Byron* (1834); discussed in my *Lord Byron: Christian Virtues* (1952), 67.

[8] For Ford's early thoughts on death as happy immortality in his prose pamphlet *The Golden Mean* (1613), see Mark Stavig, *John Ford*, 34–5.

Indexes

(by John D. Christie)